The Comfort Women of Singapore in History and Memory

The Comfort Women of Singapore in History and Memory

Kevin Blackburn

NUS PRESS
SINGAPORE

© 2022 Kevin Blackburn

Published by:
NUS Press
National University of Singapore
AS3-01-02, 3 Arts Link
Singapore 117569

Fax: (65) 6774-0652
E-mail: nusbooks@nus.edu.sg
Website: http://nuspress.nus.edu.sg

ISBN 978-981-325-186-1 (paper)

All rights reserved. This book, or parts thereof, may not be reproduced in any form or by any means, electronic or mechanical, including photocopying, recording or any information storage and retrieval system now known or to be invented, without written permission from the Publisher.

National Library Board, Singapore Cataloguing in Publication Data

Name(s): Blackburn, Kevin, 1965- author.
Title: The comfort women of Singapore in history and memory / Kevin Blackburn.
Description: Singapore : NUS Press, [2022]
Identifier(s): ISBN 978-981-325-186-1 (paperback)
Subject(s): LCSH: Comfort women--Singapore--History. | Comfort women--Singapore--Public opinion. | World War, 1939-1945--Women--Singapore. | World War, 1939-1945--Atrocities--Singapore.
Classification: DDC 940.5405082095957--dc23

Cover image: Terrace houses of the Cairnhill Road Comfort Station.

Typeset by: Ogma Solutions Pvt Ltd
Printed by: Integrated Books International

Contents

List of Illustrations   vii
Acknowledgements   ix

Introduction   1
1. Lee Kuan Yew and Masculinist Memories of the Comfort Women   13
2. The Role of the Women of Singapore in the Sex Industry of the Japanese Military   30
3. Inside the Comfort Stations of Singapore   64
4. Korean and Indonesian Comfort Women in Singapore   83
5. The Comfort Women Returning to Live in Postwar Society   109
6. The Silence of the Local Comfort Women of Singapore   135
7. The Comfort Women of Singapore as 'Dark Heritage'   153

Conclusion   177

Bibliography   187
Index   198

List of Illustrations

Maps, Diagram, and Table

Map I.1	Comfort Stations of Malaya	5
Map I.2	Comfort Stations of Singapore (identified by the Women's Active Museum on War and Peace)	9
Map 1.1	Cairnhill Road Comfort Station	15
Map 2.1	Bukit Pasoh Comfort Station in Singapore's Chinatown	59
Map 3.1	Pulau Blakang Mati (Sentosa) Comfort Station	78
Map 4.1	Seletar (Sembawang) Naval Base Comfort Station	90
Map 4.2	Tanjong Katong Road and Katong Comfort Stations	93
Map 4.3	Joo Chiat Road Japanese Red-Light District	95
Diagram 4.1	Diagram of a Common Comfort Station Design	98
Map 7.1	Jalan Jurong Kechil Comfort Station	167
Table 7.1	Operation of the Comfort Station at Jalan Jurong Kechil, Singapore	168

Photographs (between pp. 82 and 83)

Photo 1	Malaysian comfort women from Penang recovered on the Andaman Islands in 1945.
Photo 2	Malaysian comfort women in 1945 on the Andaman Islands. The woman on the right is holding her child from her marriage before she was shipped to the Andaman Islands.
Photo 3	Jalan Jurong Kechil Comfort Station.
Photo 4	Terrace houses of the Cairnhill Road Comfort Station.
Photo 5	Kim Bok-dong (left), the last surviving Korean comfort woman of Singapore, with the comfort woman statue outside the Japanese Embassy in Seoul.
Photo 6	Ho Kwai Min in 1940. She worked in the prewar Singapore sex industry and successfully resisted being forced into the comfort women system.

Acknowledgements

The research project on the comfort women of Singapore in history and memory would not have been possible without the gracious help of many people from different organisations and countries. I am indebted to the National Institute of Education, Nanyang Technological University, for providing the initial funds for the research project. Of great assistance were the librarians, oral historians, and archivists at the Oral History Centre, National Archives of Singapore, and National Library of Singapore, in particular Mark Wong. The National University of Singapore librarians were also of considerable assistance, in particular, Tim Yap Fuan, and the librarians in charge of the Japanese and Chinese collections. Sean Lee and Pauline Ang at the National Institute of Education's library at Nanyang Technological University gave valuable support.

The staff of the Imperial War Museum in London were very obliging. The National Archives of Malaysia staff were likewise very accommodating. The staff of the Women's Active Museum on War and Peace in Tokyo were gracious in their assistance, in particular, Fumiko Yamashita. The collections of Japan's National Diet Library, National Archives of Japan, the online Japan Center for Asian Historical Records, and the National Institute for Defense Studies are also rich sources of historical material managed by equally dedicated and gracious staff, as are the National Archives and Record Administration in the United States and the Australian War Memorial. I would also like to acknowledge the extraordinary value of the research materials and oral history testimonies collected by the Korean Council for the Women Drafted for Military Sexual Slavery by Japan and its affiliated research organisations.

I wish to express my appreciation and thanks to many of my colleagues who, either paid or unpaid, were able to provide research and linguistic assistance. Tan Swee Ngin at the National Institute of Education has been self-sacrificing in assisting me with her knowledge of Chinese dialects and Malay. My graduate students Pauline Fun Kar Whye and Wong Sook Wei also gave invaluable assistance with Chinese dialects and Malay. Edith Kaneshiro has been a very good Japanese-language research assistant over the last eight years. Ryoko Nakano, of Kanazawa University in Japan, has given her time graciously and freely. Karl Hack has always been a good friend with good advice. Frederik Tobias Rettig has been very helpful with German-language material. Roger Nixon has diligently provided research assistance from London for decades, as has Glenda Lynch at the Australian War Memorial for over a decade. Jeff Leng has been an excellent mapmaker for almost two decades.

Acknowledgements

I have been assisted by Lee Sang-dong and Lee Sin-choel of Sungkyunkwan University, Seoul, and their colleagues from other South Korean universities who in 2017 gathered historical materials on the comfort women for a South Korean government project. In Tokyo, Yosuke Watanabe has been very helpful in providing his research advice. The former Singapore journalist Phan Ming Yen has been generous with his time in sharing his research work from the 1990s. Intellectually, I am particularly indebted to Hayashi Hirofumi, of Kanto Gakuin University in Japan, whose work from the 1990s on the comfort women in Malaysia and Singapore was invaluable to the research in the book. He has always been willing to share his research findings since the early 2000s when I first met him at the National Archives of Singapore and later invited him to a conference on the Japanese Occupation for the 60th anniversary of the end of the Second World War in the Asia-Pacific. Last, but not least, I would like to express my sincere thanks to Peter Schoppert, Director of NUS Press, for his invaluable support and encouragement.

Introduction

When the Korean writer and activist Kim Il-myon went through the memoirs and diaries of Japanese veterans in his early study of the comfort women in 1976, he discovered that Singapore was perceived by many as an island for their sexual pleasure with brothels of subjugated women from different ethnicities providing sex.[1] Singapore was a major centre of comfort stations for ordinary Japanese soldiers and *ryotei*, or restaurants providing sexual services for officers and administrators. Koreans, Japanese, Chinese, Taiwanese, Europeans, and Indonesians, as well as local Singapore women worked in the Japanese military's sex industry in Singapore. This is confirmed by the work of Hayashi Hirofumi, a Japanese historian and an authority on the comfort women in Malaysia and Singapore. He observes, too, that the diaries and memoirs of Japanese veterans regularly mention the presence of local Chinese, Malay, Indian, and Eurasian women at the comfort stations.[2] Yet, in the 1990s, when former comfort women in other Asian societies spoke out about their memories after long silences, Singapore women did not. This book is an effort to explain this silence and other contradictions in this transnational history and memory of the different women who were sexually enslaved in Singapore by the Japanese military. It is not only a history of their traumatic experiences in Singapore, but an exploration of how the trauma has been remembered after the war.

At the start of this investigation, matters of terminology need to be discussed. The term 'comfort women', or in Japanese *ianfu*, was a euphemism used by the Japanese military for women whom it sexually enslaved. 'Comfort stations', or *ianjo*, were places of sexual enslavement. These terms were awful euphemisms for even more terrible realities. However, the terms have been used so widely and there are no adequate replacements for them. In order to indicate the deceptive nature of the terms, they are often placed in quotation marks in

---

[1] See Chapter 10, 'Nanpo sensen no ian-sho' [Comfort Stations of the Southern Front], in Kim Il-myon, *Tenno Guntai to Chosenjin Ianfu* [The Emperor's Armed Forces and the Korean Comfort Women] (Tokyo: Sanichi Shobo, 1992), originally published in 1976, pp. 190–4.
[2] See his comments in *The Straits Times*, 19 August 1995, but also his academic work, such as 'Japanese comfort women in Southeast Asia', *Japan Forum* 10, no. 2 (1998): 214. His Japanese-language studies, which are more detailed, are mentioned below.

the scholarship on the comfort women, but in many book-length discussions, quotation marks are often removed for reasons of readability. This book follows the practice of omitting quotation marks for readability, while still recognising that they were terrible euphemisms for sexual slavery.

The 'Disappearing' Local Comfort Women of Singapore

The lives and memories of the comfort women were shaped not just by Japanese militarism but also the patriarchal societies to which they returned after the end of the war. Many scholars researching the comfort women have documented how Korean society forced long silences of shame and guilt on the comfort women as 'fallen' women.[3] These women were ostracised and faced abuse and discrimination when they returned to the same Korean society that they had been part of before they became comfort women.[4] Finally in December 1991, this transnational history first became an international controversy when legal action against the Japanese government was taken by Korean comfort women, who, as they reached old age, increasingly banded together in solidarity. Pyong Gap Min and Eika Tai are two of many scholars of the comfort women who emphasise how crucial the support from emerging South Korean and Japanese feminist movements focusing on women's human rights was to the activism of the comfort women in the 1990s.[5]

While most of the comfort women were Korean, many were not, as the Japanese military also sexually enslaved women from the countries they conquered. Historians and activists Hayashi Hirofumi, Nakahara Michiko, and Yoshimi Yoshiaki have described how widespread publicity of this 1991 legal action resulted in Southeast Asian comfort women, principally in Indonesia, Malaysia, and the Philippines, becoming vocal in recording their experiences

---

[3] See, for example, C. Sarah Soh, *The Comfort Women: Sexual Violence and Postcolonial Memory in Korea and Japan* (Chicago: University of Chicago Press, 2008), pp. 236–7.
[4] An example of this work is Maki Kimura, *Unfolding the 'Comfort Women' Debates: Modernity, Violence, Women's Voices* (London: Routledge, 2016), pp. 193–215.
[5] Pyong Gap Min, *Korean "Comfort Women": Military Brothels, Brutality, and the Redress Movement* (New Brunswick: Rutgers University Press, 2021), pp. 19–85; and Eika Tai, *Comfort Women Activism: Critical Voices from the Perpetrator State* (Hong Kong: University of Hong Kong Press, 2021). See also Soh, *The Comfort Women*, p. 57; Kimura, *Unfolding the 'Comfort Women' Debates*, pp. 193–215.

and seeking apologies and compensation after what appeared as long silences.[6] These women, like their Korean sisters, were supported in coming forward by women's movements, governments, and non-governmental organisations in their own countries.

Surprisingly, no local comfort women of Singapore emerged from these long silences, although Singapore was a centre for comfort stations. This reticence prompts the question: Why were voices of the local comfort women in Singapore missing or absent? While the women themselves were silent, there has been representation of them and their plight in popular culture over the years as this question was explored. Most recently, Singapore writer Jing-Jing Lee, using actual oral history accounts in the National Archives of Singapore of the abduction of Singapore women by Japanese military, sought to investigate the question in her 2019 debut novel, *How We Disappeared*.

Lee poignantly told the fictional story of Singapore comfort woman Wang Di, who at the age of 75 struggled to earn a living by collecting cardboard, while coming to terms with the death of her husband, whom she never told about her background. The character Wang Di was, at the age of 17, forcibly taken by Japanese soldiers from her family in a Singapore village with a number of other teenage girls to a local comfort station where she was kept prisoner in a cubicle and forced to provide sex to queues of 40 Japanese soldiers a day. Lee also painted a stark picture of when the war was over and they returned to their families and local neighbourhoods only to face disapproval and rejection for being 'fallen' women. Their response was to keep quiet about their experiences, so they gradually faded from collective memory of the war. Wang Di's past after decades of silence still haunts her well into her old age.[7] Reviewers of *How We Disappeared* have commented that Lee's questions about how the local comfort women of Singapore 'disappeared' need to be answered beyond the realm of historical fiction by investigating the role comfort women played in history and memory in Singapore.[8]

---

[6] Nakahara Michiko, 'Comfort Women in Malaysia', *Critical Asian Studies* 33, no. 4 (2001): 581–9; Yoshimi Yoshiaki, *Comfort Women: Sexual Slavery in the Japanese Military During World War II*, trans. Suzanne O'Brien (New York: Columbia University Press, 2000), originally published in 1995 in Japanese as *Jugun Ianfu*, pp. 196–7; and Hayashi, 'Japanese comfort women in Southeast Asia', pp. 211–9.
[7] Jing-Jing Lee, *How We Disappeared* (London: One World, 2019), pp. 274–5.
[8] Clarissa Oon, 'Shameful histories', *Mekong Review*, Issue 5, April 2019, https://mekongreview.com/shameful-histories/.

Malaysian Comfort Women

Before exploring the Singapore case, it is worth briefly chronicling the history and memory of the comfort women of Malaysia as a close comparison. The history of the comfort women in Malaysia and Singapore is often researched together by scholars such as Hayashi Hirofumi because the countries do have a shared past. What is the experience of Singapore's nearest neighbour given that the two countries do share this common past? Have Malaysian comfort women 'disappeared' too?

In the early 1990s, Hayashi, while researching in the archives of the Japanese Self-Defense Agency's National Institute for Defense Studies, chronicled in detail the known comfort stations in both Japanese-occupied Malaya, or what is now called Peninsular Malaysia, and Singapore, where comfort women from different ethnic backgrounds were sexually enslaved.[9] Hayashi's Japanese language studies are still the standard references for studying the comfort women in Malaysia and Singapore.[10] During his years of fieldwork in Malaysia and Singapore from the mid-1980s onwards, Hayashi recorded the exact locations of many comfort stations, even photographing many of the buildings that had housed the women during the Japanese Occupation. He discovered that comfort stations were dotted all over Peninsular Malaysia in surprising locations. They were not just concentrated in the cities of Kuala Lumpur, George Town, and Ipoh, but were located in many regional towns. Even smaller rural towns had comfort stations. Some locations had more than one comfort station—Kuala Lumpur had 16 known comfort stations.

In 1993, Hayashi concluded that, despite documenting so many comfort stations in Peninsular Malaysia, 'what I know is still only a small part of the full picture'.[11] He indicated how endemic in the Japanese military was the practice of setting up comfort stations with Koreans and local women for the ordinary soldiers, and *ryotei* or restaurants with Japanese women, but also local women if there were not enough Japanese women. These women were used

---

[9] See Yoshimi Yoshiaki and Hayashi Hirofumi, eds, *Nihongun Ianfu: Kyodo Kenkyu* [Japanese Military Comfort Women: Joint Research] (Tokyo: Otsuki Shoten, 1995).
[10] Hayashi Hirofumi, 'Shingaporu no Nihongun Ianjo' [Comfort Stations of the Japanese Army in Singapore], *Senso Sekinin Kenkyu* [Studies in War Responsibility] 4 (1994): 34–43; and Hayashi Hirofumi, 'Mare hanto no Nihongun Ianjo' [Comfort Stations of the Japanese Army in the Malay Peninsula], *Sekai* [The World] (March 1993): 272–9. Hayashi later updated his work on the comfort women of Singapore in his book *Shingaporu Kakyo Shukusei: Nihongun wa Shingaporu de nani o shitanoka* [The Purge of the Singapore Chinese: What the Japanese Military Did in Singapore] (Tokyo: Kobunken, 2007), pp. 178–84.
[11] Hayashi, 'Mare hanto no Nihongun Ianjo', p. 279.

Map I.1 Comfort Stations of Malaya

to provide sexual services for officers and administrators. Hayashi illustrated his observation with a quote from the Japanese language memoirs of Mamoru Shinozaki, who was briefly Education Officer in the Japanese administration of Singapore until August 1942, after which he became Welfare Officer. Shinozaki compared Japanese imperialism to that of the Western colonial powers:

> When the British get a colony, they build a road. The French build a church. The Spanish bring in a church and take out the gold and silver. The Japanese bring in a restaurant and a woman.[12]

The presence of so many comfort stations in Malaya had implications for local women. Hayashi estimates that by mid-1942 there were about 1,000 comfort women in Malaya, many of whom were local women, particularly in the comfort stations located in rural areas. Chinese, Malay, Indian, and Eurasian women were recruited from the local population and sexually enslaved.[13] It is often noted that large numbers of women were forcibly recruited from the Chinese community in particular.[14] Archival records offer evidence for these observations. One revealing and often-cited document comes from the archives of Japan's National Institute for Defense Studies. This document details the regulations for comfort stations and restaurants with prostitutes issued by the Japanese administration of Malaya. Article 7 states that it was preferred that local women and non-Japanese women should be recruited into the comfort stations.[15] The comfort stations were for the ordinary soldiers. At the *ryotei*, Japanese women were preferred as prostitutes or 'low-grade' geisha for officers and administrators. In the National Archives of Malaysia, the report of the Selangor and Kuala Lumpur Branch of the Kuomintang to the British Military Administration at the end of the war in September 1945 also reveals large numbers of local Chinese women in comfort stations in Malaya:

---

[12] Hayashi, 'Shingaporu no Nihongun Ianjo', p. 41; and again in Hayashi, *Shingaporu Kakyo Shukusei*, p. 180. See the original in Mamoru Shinozaki, *Shingaporu Senryo Hiroku: Senso to Sono Ningenzo* [A Secret Memoir of the Occupation of Singapore: The War and the Human Image] (Tokyo: Hara Shobo, 1976), p. 82. The criticism does not appear in the much shorter English-language version of his memoirs, *Syonan: My Story: The Japanese Occupation of Singapore* (Singapore: Asia Pacific Press, 1975).

[13] Hayashi, 'Japanese comfort women in Southeast Asia', p. 214.

[14] See, for example, George Hicks, *The Comfort Women: Sex Slaves of the Japanese Imperial Forces* (Sydney: Allen & Unwin, 1995), pp. 89–93.

[15] Hayashi, 'Japanese comfort women in Southeast Asia', p. 214; and see Shimizu Hiroshi and Hirakawa Hitoshi, *Japan and Singapore in the World Economy: Japan's Economic Advance into Singapore* (London: Routledge, 1999), p. 140.

> Young Chinese girls and women were drawn from respectable families by force, and together with a large number of prostitutes, were shipped to such places as Java and other occupied territories to fill the Military Comfort Houses. To meet the requirements of these Comfort Houses, it was estimated that a few thousands of young Chinese women of respectable families were kidnapped from their respective homes.[16]

The forcible sexual enslavement in comfort stations was vividly described by Malaysian women themselves in the early 1990s when they sought acknowledgement, compensation, and apologies, following in the footsteps of the Korean comfort women. The comfort women of Malaysia were encouraged to come forward publicly by representatives of the youth wing of the ruling party of Malaysia, the United Malays National Organisation, and its coalition partner, the Malaysian Chinese Association, who took up their cause. Historian and activist Nakahara Michiko's oral history interviews with both Chinese and Malay comfort women during this time reveal that the Malaysian women came forward publicly because they believed it was their 'first and last chance to seek justice'.[17] At the time of her fieldwork in Malaysia, Nakahara was part of the feminist movement in South Korea and Japan that supported the comfort women's cause as part of a broader focus on women's human rights. She had been involved in setting up the Asian Tribunal of Women's Human Rights in March 1994 at Waseda University in Tokyo at which many comfort women gave their testimony.

Nakahara's oral history interviews deal not only with being forcibly recruited by the Japanese military as described in the archival documents, but also with the legacy and memory of that experience. She observed from her interviews with Malaysian comfort women: 'The pain of the girls and women who were victims of sexual violence was exacerbated by their rejection when they returned to their own communities' as the 'women were forced to suffer in shame and silence'. She learned from her interviewees that the comfort women of Malaysia 'were spat on by their own village people and were despised as a disgrace to the family. The communities they returned to looked at them as responsible for their own tragedies.'[18] Nakahara also observed that some families of the Malaysian comfort women did not like them speaking to her about their

---

[16] Treatment of People in Malaya During the Japanese Military Occupation, Memorandum compiled by the General Affairs Section of the KMT, Selangor Branch, Kuala Lumpur, September 1945, in Chinese Affairs Review of Occupation, file ADM/8/1, British Military Administration (National Archives of Malaysia).

[17] Nakahara, 'Comfort Women in Malaysia', p. 585.

[18] Nakahara, 'Comfort Women in Malaysia', p. 589.

experience, rendering further contact with them impossible.[19] Nonetheless, due to the activities of Nakahara and the Malaysian political parties, as well as non-governmental organisations of the 1990s, Malaysian comfort women did not 'disappear' as appears to have happened to their Singapore counterparts.[20]

The Comfort Stations and Comfort Women of Singapore in History and Memory

Singapore, like Peninsular Malaysia, had comfort stations, with some even located on its neighbouring smaller southern islands. In Singapore, Hayashi has so far identified ten known comfort stations but admits that it is likely that there were considerably more. He had initially identified seven in the 1990s. These were the terrace houses along Cairnhill Road; the shophouses along Tanjong Katong Road; the Chin Kang Huay Kuan Chinese clan association premises at 27 Bukit Pasoh Road in Chinatown; the shophouses along Jalan Jurong Kechil at Bukit Timah; the Seletar (Sembawang) naval base; a comfort station on Pulau Blakang Mati (now Sentosa); and another island comfort station on Pulau Bukom.[21]

Given the proliferation of the Japanese military's sex industry in Singapore during the war, uncovering new comfort stations, brothels, and *ryotei* has been an ongoing project. By December 2019, three more comfort stations were identified by Hayashi using Japanese-language sources in a project to map comfort stations across the Asia-Pacific for the Women's Active Museum on War and Peace (WAM) in Tokyo, dedicated to the study of the comfort women.[22] These additional comfort stations were: another in the Katong area, one in Kallang, and another for the Japanese navy on St John's Island. Knowing the locations of the comfort stations can be one starting point for a closer examination of the comfort women system in Singapore and the women who were enslaved in it.

---

[19] Nakahara, 'Comfort Women in Malaysia', p. 585.
[20] For further comparison between the experiences of the comfort women of Malaysia and Singapore, see Kevin Blackburn, 'The Comfort Women of Malaysia and Singapore as Transnational History and Memory', *Women's History Review* (forthcoming).
[21] Hayashi, *Shingaporu Kakyo Shukusei: Nihongun wa Shingaporu de nani o shitanoka*, pp. 178–84.
[22] Website of the Women's Active Museum on War and Peace (WAM): https://wam-peace.org/ianjo/area/area-sg/.

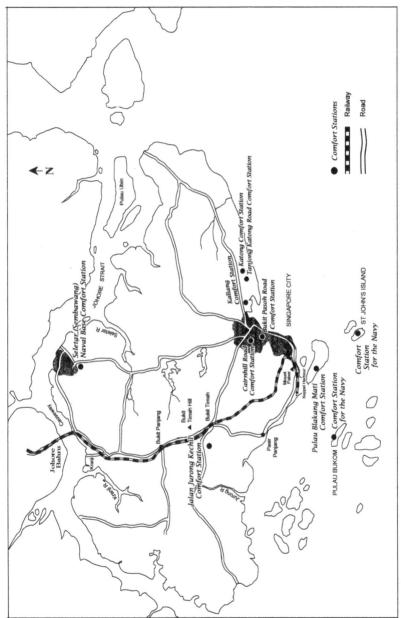

Map I.2 Comfort Stations of Singapore (identified by the Women's Active Museum on War and Peace)

Summing up, this investigation thus uncovers to the extent possible the histories and memories of these forgotten comfort stations and the stories of the many varied groups of women who became comfort women in Japanese-occupied Singapore during the Second World War. It offers explanations for why local Singapore women have not come forward with their testimonies as other comfort women have done so since the 1990s. At the same time, the book explores the presence of the comfort women in Singapore collective memory and popular culture, which has developed significantly after the comfort women became an international issue in the 1990s.

The investigation aims to add Singapore to the scholarship on the comfort women of Asia by making a detailed study from which comparisons and contrasts can be drawn in this transnational history. Much of the literature on the comfort women concerns Korean comfort women, with a growing scholarship on the comfort women from China, Japan, and Indonesia. There is also work on Hong Kong, Taiwan, the Philippines, and some on Malaysia, but little has been done on Singapore.[23]

The flow of the investigation is outlined in the sequence of the chapters of the book. Chapter 1 begins the book by assessing reactions in Singapore to the international controversy over comfort women after December 1991. Lee Kuan Yew's influential February 1992 statement on the comfort women of Singapore is crucial to understanding the reactions in Singapore and how the comfort women are remembered in Singapore to this day. Before the international controversy erupted, Lee said he did not realise the comfort women he saw in Singapore during the war were Korean, as he believed they were Japanese prostitutes. In February 1992, when discussing his memory of the Cairnhill Road comfort station, Lee said that he believed the Korean women had 'saved the chastity' of Singapore women, implying that few Singapore women were involved in the sex industry of the Japanese military. Did Lee's statement contribute to the silence of the Singapore women who were comfort women? None spoke up about their experiences.

---

[23] See, for example, Nakahara, 'Comfort Women in Malaysia', pp. 581–9; Qiu Peipei, with Su Zhiliang and Chen Lifei, *Chinese Comfort Women: Testimonies from Imperial Japan's Sex Slaves* (Oxford: Oxford University Press, 2014); Kimura, *Unfolding the 'Comfort Women' Debates*, pp. 193–215; Kawata Fumiko, *Indoneshia no 'Ianfu'* [The Comfort Women of Indonesia] (Tokyo: Akashi Shoten, 1997); Maria Rosa Henson, *Comfort Woman: A Filipina's Story of Prostitution and Slavery under the Japanese* (Lanham, Maryland: Rowman & Littlefield, 1999); and Suzuki Shogo, 'The Competition to Attain Justice for Past Wrongs: The "Comfort Women" Issue in Taiwan', *Pacific Affairs* 84, no. 2 (2011): 223–44.

Chapter 2 further assesses Lee's statement by examining the involvement of Singapore women in the sex industry of the Japanese military, not only as comfort women at comfort stations, but also working in the *ryotei* that supplied sexual services. The chapter focuses on the early period of the Japanese Occupation in 1942 and explores the extent to which Singapore women were coerced into providing sexual services for the Japanese military. The role of local Singapore women vis-à-vis that of Japanese women in the military's sex industry is also examined. Chapter 3 moves onto the later years of the Japanese Occupation and studies the established patterns of sexual enslavement of women in Singapore by using testimony and archival records to describe what daily life was like inside the comfort stations of Singapore for the women working in them. Chapter 4 then examines in detail the Korean and Indonesian comfort women, of whom significant numbers were sexually enslaved in Singapore, and reveals how they had been trafficked to Singapore. The chapter traces how Indonesian women began to be trafficked into Singapore from 1943 onwards while numbers of Korean women were being trafficked into Singapore continually after 1943, although not in the large numbers of 1942 when many of the comfort stations were first set up.

The lives of the comfort women immediately after the war are analysed in Chapter 5, which traces how in 1945 at the end of the war many of the comfort women of Singapore preferred not to return to their homes and communities to face humiliation and abuse for being 'fallen' women. Instead, they remained as hostesses and prostitutes. Colonial authorities rounded up many of these women from the streets and put them into a home for the 'rehabilitation' of prostitutes. This began the silencing of these women after the war. Local women who had been involved in the Japanese military's sex industry chose to keep silent about their experiences so they could integrate back into society. Chapter 6 then continues with this theme and examines the reasons why the local comfort women of Singapore maintained their silence in the 1990s despite Singapore journalists asking them to tell their stories.

Chapter 7 assesses how in Singapore from the 1990s the experiences of the comfort women have been commemorated and represented in popular culture as 'dark heritage'. It traces how some of the comfort stations of Singapore have become sites of 'dark heritage' for Japanese and Korean tourists through the efforts of historians or their owners. Singapore's heritage authorities have been reluctant to mark this heritage because of the 'history wars' between Japan and South Korea over the comfort women. The chapter sums up the difficulties for the Singapore state in dealing with the comfort women as transnational history. At the same time, we see how since the 1990s both foreign and local comfort women have been increasingly portrayed in Singapore plays, television dramas, and movies.

Finally, the conclusion of the book addresses how the Singapore experience adds to the Asian-wide debate over the comfort women in history and memory. It assesses how the history of the comfort women in Singapore contributes to the main arguments and areas of dispute over the comfort women that have been frequently raised since the 1990s. In early 2021, these debates came to the fore again with the claim by Mark Ramseyer, Mitsubishi Professor of Japanese Legal Studies, Harvard University, that the comfort women were not sex slaves, as the existing scholarship suggests, but paid prostitutes on contracts.[24] In Japan the widely circulating right-wing conservative newspaper *Sankei Shimbun* was quick to use Ramseyer's claim to deny the existence of the comfort women. Scholars have since presented a large amount of evidence to dispute Ramseyer's assertions.[25] But the claim has been a perennial one among the right-wing nationalists in Japan, who have great difficulty accepting the existence of the comfort women, as they see the stories of these women as a threat to their sense of national pride in Japan. What does the experience of the comfort women in Singapore add to these controversies?

---

[24] See his controversial article, 'Contracting for Sex in the Pacific War', *International Review of Law and Economics* 65 (March 2021), 105971, doi:10.1016/j.irle.2020.105971.
[25] Concerned Scholars, 'Responses by Concerned Scholars to the Problematic Scholarship of J. Mark Ramseyer', https://sites.google.com/view/concernedhistorians/home?fbclid=.

1
Lee Kuan Yew and Masculinist Memories of the Comfort Women

C. Sarah Soh suggests in her research work on the Korean comfort women that there existed soon after the war a masculinist hegemony over memories of the comfort women that kept the surviving Korean comfort women silent for fear of being seen as 'sexually defiled women'.[1] In these masculinist memories, women were subordinated and objectified as either 'pure' and 'chaste', or 'fallen' and 'defiled'. As Yonson Ahn contends, such perspectives are hard to escape, being culturally embedded and drawn from Confucian ideals of a woman's virtue being based on her chastity until she devotes herself to one man and becomes a wife and a mother.[2] Soh elaborated that in Korea, the comfort women 'simply did not merit encompassment in the postwar or postcolonial nationalist discourse on the social, cultural, and political category of "woman", which embodies feminine morality rooted in sexual purity and maternity'.[3] She argues that 'in Korea, it was the feminist humanitarian perspective that helped break the long silence about the "comfort women" issue' in the 1990s.[4]

In Singapore, has there been a similar masculinist hegemony, stemming from male-dominated patriarchy, that has influenced collective memories of the comfort women? In order to answer this question, the chapter examines the public expression of memories of Cairnhill Road, the most well known of the

---

[1] C. Sarah Soh, *The Comfort Women: Sexual Violence and Postcolonial Memory in Korea and Japan* (Chicago: University of Chicago Press, 2008), p. 225.
[2] Yonson Ahn, *Whose Comfort?: Body, Sexuality and Identities of Korean "Comfort Women" and Japanese Soldiers during WWII* (Singapore: World Scientific, 2020), pp. 65–74, 107–10.
[3] Soh, *The Comfort Women*, p. 225.
[4] Chunghee Sarah Soh, 'Prostitutes versus Sex Slaves: The Politics of Representing the "Comfort Women"', in *Legacies of the Comfort Women of World War II*, ed. Margaret D. Stetz and Bonnie B.C. Oh (New York: M.E. Sharpe, 2001), p. 84.

comfort stations of Singapore. Singapore's founding prime minister Lee Kuan Yew shared his memories of the comfort women of Cairnhill Road in a speech to a Japanese audience in 1992. To what extent did Lee's very public memories represent the kind of male hegemony explained above? How influential were they over the later public representation of memories of the comfort women in Singapore?

Lee Kuan Yew's 1992 Statement on the Comfort Women of Cairnhill Road

The comfort station at Cairnhill Road in the city area of Singapore was among the first to be set up in Singapore. Mamoru Shinozaki, the Japanese Welfare Officer for Singapore during the Japanese Occupation, describes how once the city of Singapore was secured at the end of February 1942, the military confiscated the terrace houses of the wealthy Peranakan Chinese on Cairnhill Road and turned them into a comfort station run by a male brothel manager from Korea and a well-known Taiwanese woman with a Japanese name, Kimiko Yamaguchi. She managed the women.[5]

Tan Sock Kern, a schoolteacher, in an oral history interview in October 1993, recalled that her home at 57 and 59 Cairnhill Road was taken over by the Japanese military. Number 59 became a restaurant while number 57 became an administration building for the comfort station that served the ordinary Japanese soldiers. At the same time, she witnessed the school where she taught at just down the road, Singapore Chinese Girls' School, turned into a *ryotei* that offered high-ranking military administration officials sexual services.[6] Tan found through a friend another house elsewhere in Singapore to live in during the Japanese Occupation. The comfort women were kept in the terrace houses on the other side of the street from Tan's confiscated terrace houses. The Cairnhill Road area was barricaded off with barbed wire, and only the Japanese military was allowed to enter the comfort station.

---

[5] Mamoru Shinozaki, *Shingaporu Senryo Hiroku: Senso to Sono Ningenzo* [A Secret Memoir of the Occupation of Singapore: The War and the Human Image] (Tokyo: Hara Shobo, 1977), p. 83.

[6] Tan Sock Kern, interviewed by Yeo Geok Lee, 20 October 1993, accession number 001427, reel 14, pp. 214–5 (National Archives of Singapore); Ooi Yu-lin, *Pieces of Jade and Gold: An Anecdotal History of the Singapore Chinese Girls' School, 1899–1999* (Singapore: Singapore Chinese Girls' School, 1999), p. 29; and Mamoru Shinozaki, *My Wartime Experiences in Singapore: Institute of Southeast Asian Studies, Singapore Oral History Programme Series No. 3 August 1973* (Singapore: Institute of Southeast Asian Studies, 1973), p. 56.

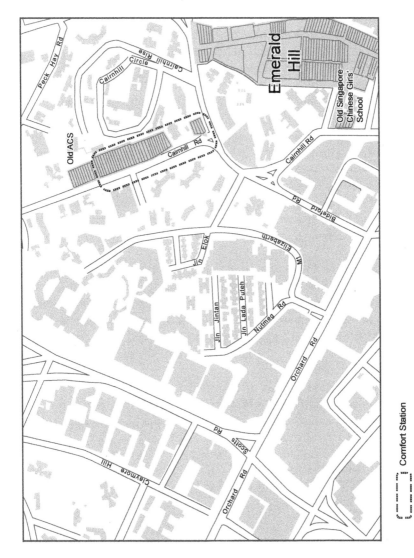

Map. 1.1 Cairnhill Road Comfort Station

The Cairnhill Road comfort station, according to most first-hand accounts, appears to have been staffed almost wholly by Koreans. However, the presence of Malay women at the comfort station is indicated by at least one first-hand account of the comfort station in 1942. In his memoirs, Naoi Masatake of the Japanese independent automobile 42nd battalion writes that when he visited the Cairnhill Road comfort station during what appears to be the early months of the Japanese Occupation, he noticed that while 'there were many Korean prostitutes, there were also some Malays', as well as 'Japanese prostitutes for luxury'.[7] He mentions that 'the sound of a guitar flowed from a Malay pretending to play a shamisen'.[8] He evokes tropical images of Japanese soldiers standing among coconut and palm trees, taking soothing baths and waiting for their turn to disappear into the rooms of the comfort women in the double-storey terrace houses. Imagery aside, Naoi's account is evidence that local women were used at that comfort station. However, this is just one account of one visit; most accounts only mention Koreans. The playing of music by the Malay women and the festive atmosphere may indicate that it was a special occasion when there would be music and dance to entertain the Japanese soldiers.

The presence of Malay women at the Cairnhill Road comfort station so early in the occupation is one important piece of evidence indicating that local Singapore women were being forcibly recruited into comfort stations, although they were not as numerous as the Koreans and Japanese. Japanese soldiers in February 1942 were already going into both Chinese and Malay kampongs, or villages, and abducting young women for comfort stations, as Chapter 2 will explore in greater detail.

The Cairnhill Road comfort station was the most well known in Singapore during the Japanese Occupation because it was just off the main thoroughfare of Orchard Road, and the most famous witness of the Cairnhill Road comfort station in Singapore's public discourse was Lee Kuan Yew, who recounted his memories when the comfort women issue became very public in December 1991, after several former Korean comfort women had sued the Japanese

---

[7] Cited by Hayashi Hirofumi, 'Shingaporu no Nihongun Ianjo' [Comfort Stations of the Japanese Army in Singapore], *Senso Sekinin Kenkyu* [Studies in War Responsibility] 4 (1994): 37. See also Hayashi Hirofumi, *Shingaporu Kakyo Shukusei: Nihongun wa Shingaporu de nani o shitanoka* [The Purge of the Singapore Chinese: What the Japanese Military Did in Singapore] (Tokyo: Kobunken, 2007), p. 179.

[8] Naoi Masatake, *Sen Tamashi: Shingaporu Koryaku-sen Parao-jima Boei-sen* [Battle Spirit: The Fall of Singapore, The Defensive Battle of Palau Island] (Tokyo: Tosen Publishing, 1973), p. 112.

government for compensation and an apology. In a keynote speech at the Kansai Zaikai seminar for Japanese business leaders in Kyoto on 13 February 1992, Lee told the audience:

> I saw long queues of Japanese soldiers lining up for their turn at Cairnhill Road, an upper middle class district, within four weeks of the capture of Singapore in February 1942. I thought then that this saved the chastity of many Singaporean girls. But I did not know that they were not voluntary prostitutes but Korean schoolgirls and young women abducted and conscripted into this service.[9]

Later, in his 1998 memoirs, Lee returned to the topic of the comfort women and elaborated on his 1992 recollection. He reiterated his belief that the Japanese military's use of comfort stations in Singapore had helped 'save the chastity' of Singapore women by preventing rapes:

> I thought then [1942] that the Japanese army had a practical and realistic approach to such problems, totally different from that of the British army. I remembered the prostitutes along Waterloo Street soliciting British soldiers stationed at Fort Canning. The Japanese high command recognised the sexual needs of the men and provided for them. As a consequence, rape was not frequent. In the first two weeks of the conquest, the people of Singapore had feared that the Japanese army would go on a wild spree. Although rape did occur, it was mostly in the rural areas, and there was nothing like what had happened in Nanking in 1937. I thought these comfort houses were the explanation.[10]

Lee then listed the nationalities of the women who were comfort women, and Singapore women were conspicuously absent: 'I did not then know that the Japanese government had kidnapped and coerced Korean, Chinese and Filipino women to cater to the needs of the Japanese troops at the war front in China and Southeast Asia. They also made some Dutch women serve Japanese officers.'[11] Thus, Lee believed that Singapore women did not become comfort women during the Japanese Occupation of Singapore. Or at any rate, he was not willing to admit the possibility.

In his 1992 statement on the comfort women, Lee recommended that Japan should acknowledge that it had enslaved the comfort women and apologise to

---

[9] *The Straits Times*, 14 February 1992.
[10] Lee Kuan Yew, *The Singapore Story: Memoirs of Lee Kuan Yew* (Singapore: Singapore Press Holdings, 1998), p. 59.
[11] Lee, *The Singapore Story*, p. 59.

them. He argued, 'For Japan to deny for so many years that (the comfort women syndicate) was organised by the army was a mistake.' He added, 'Unfortunately, unlike the Germans, the Japanese have not been open and frank about the atrocities and horrors committed in World War II. By avoiding talk about it, the victims suspect and fear that Japan does not think these acts were wrong, and that there is no genuine Japanese change of heart.'[12]

Lee's remarks about the Korean comfort women of Cairnhill Road were given extensive and prominent coverage in Singapore's Chinese, Malay, and English press.[13] His comfort women statement made the front page of the Malay *Berita Harian*, while the Chinese and English newspapers ran considerable reporting of his speech in their 'Top of the News' sections as major stories. In Japan, only *Asahi Shimbun* carried Lee's statement on the comfort women as a major story. It appeared on page two with the caption: 'Former Singapore Prime Minister criticises Japan's attitude towards the comfort women and calls for frank discussions'.[14] Lee's comments urging Japan to acknowledge the injustices done to the comfort women were very compatible with *Asahi Shimbun*'s existing campaign on redress for the comfort women. *Yomiuri Shimbun*, Japan's largest circulating daily, also carried the story in its morning edition, but not prominently. Japan's more conservative and right-wing newspapers were reluctant to admit the existence of the comfort women, or endorse any apology. They buried the story in very brief accounts for their evening editions.[15] The Japanese Ministry of Foreign Affairs, when asked about Lee's comments by *The Straits Times* correspondent in Japan, Kwan Weng Kin, also wanted to bury the story. A spokesperson told Kwan in an apparent attempt to explain away the criticism: 'We have seen the newspaper reports but not the full text of the speech. Anyway, Mr Lee's remarks were delivered in his private capacity at a business seminar and they are not new.'[16]

However, it was in Singapore that Lee's comments had their most significant impact and consequences. His 1992 statement would have given the impression that there would not be a huge amount of government support for local comfort women coming forward. In conjunction with the ensuing media coverage, it not only minimised the role of local Singapore women in the comfort women system but also suggested to any women who might have

---

[12] *The Straits Times*, 14 February 1992.
[13] *Lianhe Zaobao*, 14 February 1992; *Berita Harian*, 14 February 1992; and *The Straits Times*, 14 February 1992.
[14] *Lianhe Zaobao*, 3 March 1992.
[15] *The Straits Times*, 15 February 1992.
[16] *The Straits Times*, 15 February 1992.

considered speaking out that they could not expect sympathy and support from the media. Lee's comments reflected a section of public opinion in Singapore that remembered the comfort women of Singapore—at least up until 1992—as being mainly Japanese prostitutes, rather than as Korean women who were sexually enslaved. Apparently, he could not tell the difference between Japanese women and Korean women, and he was not alone in being unable to do so. He also explicitly stated his belief that the women of Singapore were spared from rape because the Japanese military had brought Korean women to Singapore. These statements suggested that Singapore women were not comfort women or involved in the Japanese military's sex industry set-up in Singapore. In Lee's terms, Singapore women kept their 'chastity' during the war; they were not 'fallen' women like the Korean women. His statement provoked no controversy inside or outside Singapore.

Such statements clearly draw on the sort of patriarchal ideas that Soh and Ahn saw at work in Korea, for example, the comment that the Korean comfort women were 'saving the chastity of many Singaporean girls'. They also reflected assumptions that had been present in the wartime Japanese military. Senior officers in the Japanese military viewed it as a necessity that Japanese soldiers be served by women at the comfort stations. These soldiers were each given a ticket that gave them at most 30 minutes for sex, but in reality it could be as little as 5 minutes. The assumption in the Japanese military was that without comfort stations, its soldiers would otherwise go on violent sprees raping local women, which would bring 'dishonour' to the Japanese military. Yoshimi Yoshiaki has noted that the brutal nature of the Japanese military training did not encourage good human relationships with women.[17]

C. Sarah Soh argues that the Japanese soldiers saw the comfort women as little more than the 'receptacles of their sexual energy', which was 'released through recreational sex'.[18] These soldiers were guilty of 'regarding the non-Japanese women as sex objects and in exercising violence against them to release their tension'.[19] They often referred to the comfort stations as a 'public toilet' or *kyodo benjo*, where they relieved themselves sexually. They would use the

---

[17] Yoshimi Yoshiaki, 'Historical Understandings of the "Military Comfort Women" Issue', in *War Victimization and Japan: International Public Hearing Report*, ed. Executive Committee, International Public Hearing Concerning Postwar Compensation of Japan (Tokyo: Toho Shuppan, 1993), pp. 81–93.
[18] Soh, 'Prostitutes versus Sex Slaves: The Politics of Representing the "Comfort Women"', p. 77.
[19] Soh, 'Prostitutes versus Sex Slaves: The Politics of Representing the "Comfort Women"', p. 78.

colloquial term *pi* to describe such short-term encounters. Soh argues that this notion of dehumanising sexual 'public toilets' for men to relieve themselves sexually is historically embedded in Japanese male sexual culture and refers to it as 'masculinist sexism'.[20]

Lee's memories of the role of the comfort stations of Singapore prompt the question: have the comfort women of Singapore been remembered through masculinist perspectives? When Lee made his comments in 1992, his recollections evoked similar memories by Singaporean males of his generation. Goh Sin Tub stated: 'I agree with the Senior Minister. As far as I know, there were no complaints of women in the Emerald Hill and Cairnhill Road areas being molested or raped by the Japanese. There were quite a number of beautiful women there, too. I believe the women were spared because the "comfort girls" were available.'[21] Goh had been a teenager living in the area during the Japanese Occupation, and after the war became a prominent civil servant and businessman who wrote short stories and novels.

Within days another male witness to the Japanese Occupation wrote to *The Straits Times* to affirm what Lee and Goh had said about the Korean comfort women 'saving the chastity' of Singapore women. Chan Swee Kung wrote in his letter to the editor: 'Comfort girls alone did not save women's chastity.' He argued that it was also due to the strict discipline of the Japanese military police, the *kempeitai*: 'It was not the comfort girls' presence alone, however, that reduced the danger of a rampaging soldiery on our local maidenhood. It was also the fear of drastic punishment at the hands of the dreaded kempeitai, or military police.'[22]

While affirming the 'purity' of 'our local maidenhood', Chan later wrote scathingly of the local women who provided sexual services for the Japanese military, suggesting that only local prostitutes sexually consorted with the Japanese military: 'There might have been imported sexual slaves but local prostitutes did not have any qualms about servicing Japanese soldier clients in the early Occupation days.'[23] He recollected what he had witnessed in one red-light district of Chinatown near where he lived: 'Soon after the British surrender of Singapore, they resumed business promptly and the neighbourhood of Tanjong Pagar, which boasted call girls of the select kind, was disturbed nightly by the boisterous entertainment of their Japanese officer clientele, who even

---

[20] Soh, *The Comfort Women*, pp. 39–41.
[21] *The Straits Times*, 15 February 1992.
[22] *The Straits Times*, 19 February 1992.
[23] *The Straits Times*, 3 September 1993.

took pains to familiarise the girls with martial songs.'[24] Chan recalled 'a two-storey residential unit at the corner of Tras Street and Enggor Street, across the road from the present Amara Hotel' that 'was frequented by Japanese military personnel — both enlisted men and officers, distinguished by their side adornments of bayonet or samurai sword — who were greeted by women of Chinese, Taiwanese, Korean or maybe even Japanese origin, judging from their physical features. Without much ado, the men were then led further into the house for the obvious purpose.'[25]

Goh Sin Tub, like Chan, also expressed his male-centric opinions about the comfort women of Singapore based upon his limited observations of the red-light district near his home at Emerald Hill. In 1989, Goh had written a fictional book about six Singapore Chinese young women who worked as waitresses at the Cairnhill Road comfort station under a Japanese female brothel keeper. The title of his book, *The Nan-Mei-Su Girls of Emerald Hill*,[26] was taken from the name he said the Japanese used for the Cairnhill Road comfort station, 'gathering of Southern beauties'.[27] Literary critic Ronald D. Klein has commented that because of his Japanese-language schooling during the Japanese Occupation, Goh admired the Japanese considerably and romanticised the lives of these young Chinese Singapore women in his book. They were depicted as girls who had romances with Japanese soldiers and who were looked after by the Japanese brothel keeper, who was portrayed as a caring motherly figure.[28] When commenting on Lee Kuan Yew's 1992 memories, Goh also described the Singapore waitresses at the Cairnhill Road comfort station in a similarly romanticised way:

> More than a dozen of them lived in a special hostel set up for them in Emerald Hill Road. They were young, probably teenagers, and wore slim-cut white dresses with red belts and light make-up.
> I used to talk to them quite a bit, and some of them confided in me. A few of them were in love with Japanese soldiers.[29]

---

[24] *The Straits Times*, 3 September 1993.
[25] *The Straits Times*, 3 September 1993.
[26] Goh Sin Tub, *The Nan-Mei-Su Girls of Emerald Hill* (Singapore: Heinemann Asia, 1989).
[27] *The Straits Times*, 15 February 1992.
[28] Ronald E. Klein, *The Other Empire: Literary Views of Japan from the Philippines, Singapore, and Malaysia* (Diliman, Quezon City: University of the Philippines, 2008), pp. 184–6, 209–10.
[29] *The Straits Times*, 15 February 1992.

What is most damning in Goh's description of the waitresses is that they wore the white 'nurse's uniform' with a red belt that some comfort women had to wear in the comfort stations in Singapore and other places occupied by the Japanese. He added that he 'does not know if any were raped or molested by Japanese soldiers in the brothel'.[30] Thus, he would not have known for sure if the Singapore Chinese waitresses were pressured into offering sexual services at the comfort station. As will be discussed in the next chapter, it was common for the Japanese military to employ Singapore women in such waitressing jobs with the aim of eventually pressuring them into the sex industry that they set up around the *ryotei*. These women, although not directly providing sexual services, were often the objects of sexual advances from members of the Japanese military. Surprisingly, Goh's novel *The Nan-Mei-Su Girls of Emerald Hill*, with its romanticised view has not evoked any criticism in Singapore. The Cairnhill Road comfort station was not perceived in memories of the Japanese Occupation as a place where Singapore women were sexually enslaved.[31]

Masculinist Memories of the Comfort Women of Cairnhill Road

It was not just Lee Kuan Yew, Goh Sin Tub, and Chan Swee Kung who expressed these male-centric views of the Cairnhill Road comfort station. Other male memories of the comfort stations of Singapore have been noticeably masculinist and coloured with acceptance of notions of male sexual entitlement—that men because of their gender are owed recreational sexual pleasure by women. These memories of the Japanese Occupation were first systematically revealed in the 1980s by the work of the Oral History Department set up in Singapore's Ministry of Culture. The Department became the Oral History Centre in 1992 and part of the National Archives of Singapore. Among its first projects on Singapore national history was one that involved interviews with people who had lived through the Japanese Occupation. This oral history project was called the *Japanese Occupation in Singapore 1942–1945*. Interviewing began in June 1981 and was completed in December 1985. It produced an impressive 655 recorded hours of interviews with 175 persons.[32] In subsequent years, more

---

[30] *The Straits Times*, 15 February 1992.
[31] See the reviews of Goh Sin Tub's *The Nan-Mei-Su Girls of Emerald Hill* in *The New Paper*, 23 November 1989; *The Business Times*, 11 December 1989; *The Straits Times*, 10 May 1989; and also *The Business Times*, 14 March 1988.
[32] Oral History Department, *Syonan: Singapore under the Japanese: A Catalogue of Oral History Interviews* (Singapore: Oral History Department, 1986).

interviews were added to the project, which was subsumed under the National Archives of Singapore. The sheer number of interviews makes the collection a valuable source for collective memory of the Japanese Occupation of Singapore.

Interviewees recalling the comfort stations are mostly male, as female interviewees rarely mention them, and if they do, these women do not go into as much detail as the men. Tan Sock Kern, whose house at Cairnhill Road was taken over by the Japanese military to be a comfort station and whose place of work as a schoolteacher was turned into a *ryotei*, never described their operations. In contrast, many male interviewees go into detail in their descriptions, and tend to see comfort stations as they were seen by Lee Kuan Yew—necessary for the release of sexual tension by men in the Japanese military.

The Cairnhill Road comfort station, in particular, seems to have been remembered as an object of male curiosity and amusement. The absence of noticeable numbers of Singapore women at the comfort station and the perception that it was staffed by Japanese prostitutes partly explains these memories. In the interviews, there is an implicit acceptance of masculinist ideas that the women in the comfort stations were simply objects or tools for men's sexual gratification. Lee Kip Lin, an architect who was a teenager at the time, recalled in a June 1984 interview the actions of the Japanese military in Singapore: 'The other great thing they did was opening what we used to describe as comfort houses, which were just brothels. They brought in Japanese prostitutes from Japan. And most of them were housed in the terrace houses in Cairnhill Road between the Anglo-Chinese School and Cairnhill Circle.' He recalled his amusement at the scenes of the comfort station: 'Eventually they had a barrier, and a gate and they would not allow people through. And only the Japanese soldiers could go…. If you stand around the corner of Cairnhill Road without actually entering the area, you could see the houses from some distance where it was rather amusing to see the Japanese soldiers queuing to get in. They had a queue of about 50 people at each house waiting to get in. And it's like a cinema queue, very strange.'[33]

What C. Sarah Soh in her studies of the comfort women has called 'masculinist sexism' permeated male memories of the comfort women of Singapore. She asserts that this is a 'masculinist perspective of the troops, which was derived from their patriarchal sexist culture' that 'regarded the "comfort women" as sex objects to be purchased for men's recreational activity'.[34] As male

---

[33] Lee Kip Lin, interviewed by Low Lay Leng, 4 June 1984, accession number 000016, reel 8, p. 96 (National Archives of Singapore).
[34] Soh, 'Prostitutes versus Sex Slaves, p. 83.

Singapore observers gazed from a distance at the comfort women of Singapore, they too saw little that was wrong with what they were witnessing, and indeed found comfort stations and comfort women necessities and objects of sexual amusement rather than sexual exploitation.

Chee Keng Soon, a civil servant, in an October 1996 interview gave his account of the Cairnhill Road comfort station that was next to his school, Anglo-Chinese School (ACS). His memories were very male-centred. The comfort station and its women were remembered as sources of amusement for him and his classmates at the boys' school:

> The back courtyard [of the comfort station] has a balcony which is almost on level with the [school] canteen, slightly lower. Once a week, all the women would come up, completely naked, to have a sun bath and [this] created panic for the principal, Mr Camphors. He had the teachers and prefects to shoo everybody away to the other side of the school.[35]

In his 'boy's own' account of the 'rollicking good fun' of his school days of studying next to a brothel or comfort station, Chee seemed unaware or unable to recognise that there was any sexual exploitation or enslavement of the women. He continued in this vein:

> Little boys, 10–15 years old, [would] go and collect the used condoms. Washed it, put it into bamboo tubes, powdered it, then rolled it back and sold it back. Some of our boys, I suppose, picked up some, [then] started to blow and created havoc with our Mr Camphors, [who] got excited during the early morning exercise. He tried to explain: 'You mustn't do that. You see, inside is the dirt of the man, outside is the dirt of the woman.' [laughs][36]

Chee admitted that his memories had been influenced by his mistaken understanding that the women were Japanese prostitutes rather than Korean comfort women. He only became aware that they could have been Korean after the comfort women became an international issue in 1991:

> I had at that time assumed they were Japanese girls because they were speaking [Japanese]. After reading [about] the event recently I say, could

---

[35] Chee Keng Soon, interviewed by Tan Beng Luan, 7 October 1996, accession number 001776, reel 1, p. 10 (National Archives of Singapore).
[36] Chee Keng Soon, 7 October 1996, p. 10.

be Koreans among them? Because the Koreans could speak Japanese fluently, they could be, I don't know.[37]

Chee's comment about his having assumed that the women of the Cairnhill Road comfort station were Japanese mirrors the view of Lee Kuan Yew. The comfort women seem to have been regarded in popular memory as mainly Japanese prostitutes.

The Consequences of Lee Kuan Yew's 1992 Comfort Women Statement

What was the impact of Lee Kuan Yew's comments that the Korean comfort women 'saved the chastity' of Singapore women, with its implication that Singapore women were not involved in a significant way in the sex industry established by the Japanese military? His comments set the tone for the public debate. It is worth exploring whether these comments hampered investigations into the stories of local comfort women and perhaps discouraged local Singapore comfort women from coming forward to speak out as they did in other countries during 1992.

Within days of Lee's statement, when marking the 50th anniversary of the fall of Singapore to the Japanese military on 15 February 1942, the local press reiterated Lee's assumption that it was mostly Korean women rather than Singapore women who were involved in the sex industry set up by the Japanese military in Singapore.[38] The newspaper that tried the hardest to run stories of local Singapore comfort women was the sensationalist Chinese *Lianhe Wanbao*, an evening paper that fed its readership a regular diet of sex and murder stories. *Lianhe Wanbao* started out with the statement that the date marked the day families began to hide away their girls from the Japanese so they would not become comfort women.[39] The story with the headline 'Young Women from Singapore Sent to Comfort Station' was translated into a slightly different English version and also run on the same day by *The New Paper*, *Lianhe Wanbao*'s sensationalist English-language equivalent.[40]

Lianhe Wanbao's 50th-anniversary story started with the declaration: 'The Japanese unleashed their mayhem in places they conquered and when they chanced upon any girls, they would capture these girls and ravage them.' Under

---

[37] Chee Keng Soon, 7 October 1996, p. 10.
[38] *Lianhe Zaobao*, 14 February 1992.
[39] *Lianhe Wanbao*, 15 February 1992.
[40] *The New Paper*, 15 February 1992.

the subheading 'Abduction of pretty girls along the streets', the *Lianhe Wanbao* story used the testimony of male interviewee Teo Soon Koon, aged 75, to describe the experiences of the comfort women of Singapore. Since 1935, when he came to Singapore from China, Teo had been a member of the Chin Kang Huay Kuan Chinese clan association, whose premises at 27 Bukit Pasoh Road in Chinatown were turned into a comfort station. The story suggested that the women at that comfort station were Korean or Taiwanese. Teo recalled: 'Sometimes we saw girls walking in and out of there. They looked to be in their twenties and wore kimonos.'[41] 'Although reports mentioned that the comfort women were girls from Korea and Taiwan', Teo, according to *Lianhe Wanbao*, 'reckoned that there were local girls among them. He had seen many pretty girls along the streets being taken away by the Japanese.'[42] The newspapers' discussion of Cairnhill Road also highlighted that the comfort women were Koreans. Goh Sin Tub's testimony was used to affirm this: 'The local girls used to work as waitresses at the comfort houses. I used to see them walking up Emerald Hill. I don't remember seeing any prostitutes.'[43] Thus began a trend in the Singapore press of the local comfort women keeping their silence while witnesses of their plight gave their testimony.

This memory of the Cairnhill Road comfort women being mostly Koreans, or Koreans who were mistaken to be Japanese, had consequences for the debate over the comfort women in Singapore. In 1992, as a result of the international controversy over the Korean women going to Japan to sue for compensation, the comfort women of the countries occupied by Japan during the war, such as China, Taiwan, the Philippines, Indonesia, and Malaysia, started to give their testimonies and also demand compensation. Their governments scrambled to investigate and take up the cases of these comfort women in their dealings with Japan. In Singapore, this did not happen, partly because of Lee Kuan Yew's statement that the 'chastity' of many Singapore girls had been 'saved' by the Korean comfort women. If Singapore women remained 'chaste' during the Japanese Occupation, this implied that there were no local Singapore comfort women forced into sexual slavery and that any local women in the Japanese military's sex industry were existing prostitutes who willingly consorted with the Japanese military. Indeed, this view was a common early postwar assumption and will be explored in considerable detail in Chapter 5. Local

---

[41] *The New Paper*, 15 February 1992.
[42] *Lianhe Wanbao*, 15 February 1992.
[43] *Lianhe Wanbao*, 15 February 1992.

comfort women would have been very reluctant to come forward given these types of assumptions about them.

In Singapore, television coverage started in March 1992, when a local current affairs documentary on the Chinese channel *Jiaodian* [Focus] dealt with not just the Korean comfort women, but women who were forced to serve as comfort women in the other occupied areas. This programme on Singapore's most popular television channel set the tone for media reporting of the comfort women in Singapore, with extensive coverage of comfort women from other Asian countries, but no mention of Singapore women being among them.[44]

Throughout 1992, the Singapore Chinese press in particular chronicled in detail comfort women speaking out, and demanding apologies and compensation in other Asian countries. The Chinese press in Singapore has had a long history of extensively investigating and reporting on Japanese wartime atrocities compared to its English, Malay, and Tamil counterparts, as the Chinese community during the war was singled out for brutal treatment for helping China in its resistance to Japan's invasion. Memories of this treatment by the Japanese have lingered in Chinese public memories of the Japanese Occupation.[45] The Chinese press also reported extensively on how the governments of other Asian countries investigated the claims of the comfort women and raised them in their foreign relations with Japan.

In February and March 1992, Singapore's highbrow morning Chinese newspaper, *Lianhe Zaobao,* in co-ordination with its much less highbrow evening sister newspaper, *Lianhe Wanbao,* reported in detail on Taiwan's parliamentary debate on investigations of Taiwanese comfort women and the Taiwanese government's rebuke of Japan for failing to deal with their grievances.[46] In February 1992, the Chinese press in Singapore was quick to report on how the government of China took up the cause of Chinese comfort women and discussed apologies and compensation for them.[47] And in July 1992, there was extensive coverage of the Fidel Ramos administration in the Philippines investigating the claims of Philippine comfort women. There were further stories on Ramos making representations on their behalf to the Japanese government in September 1992.[48] In July 1992, the Chinese press of Singapore

---

[44] *Lianhe Zaobao,* 14 March 1992.
[45] See Kevin Blackburn and Karl Hack, *War Memory and the Making of Modern Malaysia and Singapore* (Singapore: NUS Press, 2012).
[46] *Lianhe Zaobao,* 9 and 22 February 1992; *Lianhe Wanbao,* 13 March 1992; and *Lianhe Zaobao,* 8 July 1992.
[47] *Lianhe Zaobao,* 29 February 1992.
[48] *Lianhe Zaobao,* 10 July and 23 September 1992.

gave coverage to the claims of Indonesian comfort women that were being voiced in the Indonesian press.[49]

By August 1992, the Chinese press of Singapore was reporting on comfort women in Malaysia.[50] In the same month, the Japanese government initially denied that local Malaysian women had worked as comfort women.[51] But within a few days, the Singapore press was reporting on the findings of Hayashi Hirofumi's research indicating the widespread forcible recruitment of local Malaysian women for comfort stations across Peninsular Malaysia.[52] By October 1992, it was widely reported that members of the ruling coalition parties of Malaysia were encouraging their local comfort women to come forward and make their claims for compensation and demands for apologies.[53]

The voices of the comfort women across Asia in 1992 were described as 'the roar of Asian women' [*yazhou funu de housheng*] by Xie Yong Guang, veteran Hong Kong journalist and editor, in his early 1993 book on the comfort women, *Rijun Weian Fu Neimu* [Inside the Comfort Women Issue]. Xie asked why had local Singapore comfort women not been part of this 'roar' in 1992 and why so little was known about them?[54] Behind the scenes, Singapore journalists were asking these questions and investigating this issue. But unlike their counterparts in other Asian countries, local women did not feel empowered to come forward. In a short story on 27 July 1992, *Bendi Weian Fu* [Local Comfort Women], *Lianhe Zaobao* went through what few historical records of comfort women in Singapore it could find to come up with some scanty details. The journalist writing the story went back to when the comfort women of Singapore had last been discussed in the press just after the end of the Japanese Occupation in the 1940s. He uncovered details about the comfort women from a popular 1950 book about Japanese atrocities *Xue Hai* [Sea of Blood], which was published by the Chinese press.[55] He described how there were comfort women of various races working for the Japanese military in Singapore. There were also 'low-grade' Japanese geisha who provided sexual services as well as some types of cultural entertainment, and women from China.

---

[49] *Lianhe Zaobao*, 10 July 1992.
[50] *Lianhe Zaobao*, 8 August 1992.
[51] *The Straits Times*, 18 August 1992.
[52] *Lianhe Zaobao*, 8 and 19 August 1992. See also *The Straits Times*, 15 August 1992.
[53] Nakahara Michiko, 'Comfort Women in Malaysia', *Critical Asian Studies* 33, no. 4 (2001): 581–9; and *The Straits Times*, 29 October 1992.
[54] Xie Yong Guang, *Rijun Weian Fu Neimu* [Inside the Comfort Women Issue] (Hong Kong: Mingpao Publishing, 1993), p. 200.
[55] Xie Song Shan, *Xue Hai* [Sea of Blood] (Singapore: Nanyang Baoshe, 1950).

The *Lianhe Zaobao* journalist in his July 1992 story also drew upon Singapore Chinese war veteran Colonel Chuang Hui-Tsuan's collection of many Chinese eyewitnesses' recollections of the Japanese Occupation, which were published in 1984.[56] In his story, the journalist used an account by Hong Jin Tang from Chuang's collection of stories to describe how, soon after Singapore fell, there were advertisements for women between the ages of 17 to 28 to work at $150/month in restaurants as waitresses and hostesses, with the suggestion that women who had worked as prostitutes would be very suitable. Applicants were asked to apply to Raffles Hotel, which had been taken over by the Japanese military. However, as the journalist reported, according to Hong, there were no applicants, so the Japanese military simply rounded up about 100 local women and distributed them to various Japanese units.[57]

The *Lianhe Zaobao* story was the full extent of its investigations into the local comfort women of Singapore in 1992. Questions undoubtedly remained, but the impression given by the Singapore media was that there had not been significant numbers of local comfort women, or at least significantly fewer than in other Asian countries. Perhaps more importantly, in 1992, the impression was also given that there was no one arguing for local comfort women to come forward to demand justice and compensation, and no one offering to support them.

In summary, in 1992, the news of the Korean women demanding compensation encouraged other Asian women to also 'roar', but there was a noticeable silence about the local Singapore comfort women. It seems likely that Lee Kuan Yew's statement at the beginning of 1992 suggested to potential witnesses that there would not be a sympathetic government to support them in speaking out, unlike in other countries. Neither would the media coverage have encouraged the women to come forward. Memories of the experiences of the comfort women of Singapore appeared dominated by a male hegemony. Lee Kuan Yew's very public statement about the Korean women at Cairnhill Road 'saving the chastity' of Singapore women was simply an expression of these memories. The 1992 public discussion of the comfort women in the Singapore press leads to the question that is explored in the next chapter: What was the role of local Singapore women in the comfort stations and *ryotei* set up by the Japanese military in Singapore?

---

[56] The account was specifically Hong Jin Tang, 'Ri Kou Yu Ge Minzu' [The Japanese Army and the Ethnic Groups], in *Malayan Chinese Resistance to Japan 1937–1945—Selected Source Materials*, ed. Shu Yun-Ts'iao and Chua Ser-Koon, comp. Chuang Hui-Tsuan (Singapore: Cultural and Historical Publishing House, 1984), p. 462.

[57] *Lianhe Zaobao*, 27 July 1992.

2
The Role of the Women of Singapore in the Sex Industry of the Japanese Military

In 1992, the masculinist memories of Lee Kuan Yew, Goh Sin Tub, and Chan Swee Kung not only suggested that very few women from Singapore were raped by Japanese soldiers, but also that local Singapore women were not involved in the sex industry set up by the Japanese military. Their memories imply that local Singapore women remained 'chaste' while Korean women were the 'fallen' women providing sexual services for the Japanese military. Both suggestions were wrong. This chapter sets out to answer the question that was being asked by journalists in Singapore in 1992 as the comfort women of other Asian countries came forward to give their testimony in what Hong Kong journalist Xie Yong Guang at the time called 'the roar of Asian women'.[1] This question can be summed up simply as: What was the role of local Singapore women in the sex industry of the Japanese military? This chapter explores this question mainly in the context of 1942 as the Japanese military went about setting up its comfort women system of sexual slavery in Singapore. In 1942, local Singapore women can be defined as Chinese, Malay, Indian, and Eurasian women who were residing in Singapore, many of whom were originally immigrants. The immigrant women possessed transnational identities. They quickly fitted into life in the already well-established ethnic communities of Singapore and had

---

[1] Xie Yong Guang, *Rijun Weian Fu Neimu* [Inside the Comfort Women Issue] (Hong Kong: Mingpao Publishing, 1993), p. 200.

become 'localised'. But at the same time, they were strongly attached to their cultural 'homelands' from where they or their families had emigrated.[2]

The Rape and Sexual Enslavement of Singapore Women in 1942

Yoshimi Yoshiaki has made the point that the setting up of comfort stations did not stop rapes by Japanese soldiers. The soldiers of the Japanese 25th Army that first occupied Singapore, according to Japanese army documents collected by Yoshimi, had a reputation for raping women in the territories they conquered.[3] Indeed, this would be a likely outcome from a military system that needed comfort stations to channel the sexual violence of its soldiers. For Singapore women, being raped by Japanese soldiers could lead to their abduction and being taken away to comfort stations, as soldiers were rounding up women for the local comfort stations the Japanese military was establishing in 1942, and rapes occurred during this process. Indeed, as Hayashi Hirofumi concludes in his assessment of the abduction and rape of local women across Southeast Asia by the Japanese military: 'In my view, whether or not they were authorized as comfort women, any woman detained by the military for a certain period and forced to have sexual intercourse with soldiers should be considered a military comfort woman.'[4] What occurred in Singapore was similar to what happened in Peninsular Malaysia and other places where the Japanese military had been engaged in conquering. As Hayashi says: 'There are numerous cases of Japanese soldiers forcing their way into people's houses, carrying off young women through the use of violence, gang-raping them and forcing them to become comfort women. Such cases have been reported in areas such as mainland China, the Philippines and Malaya.'[5]

---

[2] See Fujio Hara, *Malayan Chinese and China: Conversion in Identity Consciousness, 1945–1947* (Singapore: Singapore University Press, 2003); Kernial Singh Sandhu, *Indians in Malaya: Some Aspects of their Immigration and Settlement (1786–1957)* (Cambridge: Cambridge University Press, 1996); and Anthony Milner, *The Malays* (Oxford: Wiley-Blackwell, 2011).
[3] Yoshimi Yoshiaki, *Comfort Women: Sexual Slavery in the Japanese Military during World War II*, trans. Suzanne O'Brien (New York: Columbia University Press, 2000), originally published in 1995 in Japanese as *Jugun Ianfu*, pp. 78–9.
[4] Hayashi Hirofumi, 'Japanese comfort women in Southeast Asia', *Japan Forum* 10, no. 2 (1998): 214.
[5] Hayashi, 'Japanese comfort women in Southeast Asia', p. 214.

In 1992, 50 years after the fall of Singapore, the fear of rape and sexual enslavement was a memory that remained embedded in the minds of many Singapore women who lived through the Japanese Occupation. They remembered the early months of 1942 when rape was common as the conquering Japanese army settled into its occupation of Singapore. In the later years of the Japanese Occupation, as the military functioned more as a garrison army with its established comfort stations, rape was far less common, although the women were still fearful. These memories were evident at the time of Lee Kuan Yew's statement on the comfort women. This fear of rape also found its expression in the media in the form of a television documentary. In February 1992, *Between Empires* became the first Singapore television documentary to graphically depict the atrocities of the Japanese Occupation. It aired on the local TV channels for English-language viewers (15 and 16 February) and Chinese-language viewers (11 and 18 February). This two-part docu-drama was made in order to commemorate the fall of Singapore. The mixture of oral testimony of war victims and dramatisation of their experiences helped achieve an unprecedented large audience for a documentary.[6] This popularity encouraged the channels to release it as a video for sale to the public to cater for the demand.[7] This too was unprecedented.

Between Empires did not show Singapore women as comfort women, or even include any comfort women at all in its long list of Japanese atrocities. Production had ended before the comfort women became an international issue in December 1991 and well before questions started to be asked about the existence of local comfort women in 1992. But the documentary did show the fear of rape among Singapore women. There was a re-enactment of the oral testimony of Tan Ah Seng describing how soon after Singapore fell, the Japanese soldiers came calling for girls for their sexual pleasure. Tan Ah Seng was interviewed on camera. She recalled:

> I was at my mother's house and we dared not open the door. The girls would have to be hidden. Every day and night we would hear the Japanese knocking on doors shouting: 'Girls, girls!' My sisters and I were so scared that we hid ourselves under the bed. When the Japanese couldn't find any girls they went to the other households. I heard the girls there screaming. The mother cried the whole night, cursing the Japanese. Next day we were told that her daughter was raped.[8]

---

[6] *The Straits Times*, 10, 12, and 22 February 1992.
[7] *Between Empires*, VHS (Singapore: Singapore Broadcasting Corporation, 1992).
[8] *Between Empires*.

Another interview with Tan Peck Siok described some of the measures families took to stop their girls from being raped by the Japanese:

> At that time, my mother asked me to cut my hair short and I dressed like a boy. She was worried that being a girl and having long hair I might be dragged off by the Japanese.[9]

In the oral history of the Japanese Occupation of Singapore, there are many first-hand witness accounts of women being raped or taken away to be sexually enslaved by Japanese soldiers in early 1942. Often the testimony is from a close friend, relative, or neighbour. When women retell the stories of seeing or hearing women close to them raped or taken away, they are sometimes distraught. Understandably, none of the women who were raped or taken away and sexually enslaved would want to relive the trauma in an interview. The reliving of the trauma is often difficult for the witnesses who were close to the women raped or sexually enslaved. Loh Poh Ying, who was 17 years old when the Japanese Occupation started, recounted in an interview of March 2001 how her next-door neighbour and close friend Ah Hua, only one year younger than herself, was raped by Japanese soldiers during the early days of the occupation. In the interview, she raged against what the 'Japanese demons' had done to Ah Hua, describing how this 'beastly act' had caused the suicide of Ah Hua, who was only 16 years old at that time. At the end of remembering the trauma, Loh, aged 77, lamented, 'If Ah Hua was still alive, she would have been a grandmother now, enjoying a blissful life with her children and grandchildren.'[10]

Most women raped or taken away appear to have been Chinese, but Malay women also reported similar traumatic experiences associated with the coming of Japanese soldiers to their villages in Singapore and the subsequent abduction of women for rape and sexual enslavement. When the soldiers arrived at Malay villages, they also displayed a preference for unmarried young females. Salimah bte Ehksan recollected in October 2002 her vivid memories of early 1942 when she was a 22-year-old housewife and saw Japanese soldiers enter her Malay village in the eastern part of Singapore. 'The Japanese came to ask who had a husband and who didn't. Those who were married were actually safe; those who weren't would just point to any male and say that's her *abang* (husband).' However, Salimah continues: 'Those who owned up to not being married were

---

[9] *Between Empires*.
[10] Loh Poh Ying, interviewed by Chua Hong Lin, Lynette, March 2001 (National Institute of Education, Nanyang Technological University, Oral History Collection).

taken away and raped. There was a girl that I know of (in the kampong), she got raped. Yeah, she was taken away and raped.'[11]

Women remembered that they did not act uniformly towards the threat of rape even within the same household. Patricia Oh Choo Neo alias Mrs Chia Kin Teng, in an interview done in May 1995, described how Japanese soldiers entered her home at Kampong Lorong Engku Aman, opposite Haig Road, on the tenth day after the fall of Singapore. She, aged 16, was taken to a room by a Japanese soldier who threatened her with a knife to her throat and was about to rape her. Oh remembered that she showed no fear and knelt down before the soldier and prayed to God, imagining that she was an early Christian thrown to the lions. Puzzled, the soldier took her to the kitchen, and when he let go of her, she again knelt in prayer. Taking advantage of the soldier being startled by her behaviour, Oh quickly unlatched the door and ran away. However, her 14-year-old cousin who, according to Oh, was 'submissive, no protest', which she said the Japanese soldiers preferred, was raped in another room of the house that night.[12]

Rape could be followed by the Japanese soldiers taking a woman away, sometimes for a short period of sexual enslavement, sometimes never to return again. Tan Hoe Song, who was 14 when the Japanese Occupation started in 1942, describes how the Japanese soldiers came 'barging into our house' and the house next door at Jalan Besar. While she successfully hid, next door a 13-year-old girl was brutally gang raped by several soldiers in front of her father. According to Tan, whose family was very close to the family of the girl, she was taken away by the Japanese to serve as a comfort woman, never to return.[13] Koh Kim Hiang, interviewed in October 2004, also recalled that when she was a teenager living in the Hougang area in 1942, the Japanese came looking for girls. She and the other girls of the village successfully hid in the air raid shelters or their houses, but one 18-year-old girl was found, 'violated', then taken away not to be seen again.[14]

---

[11] Salimah bte Ehksan, interviewed by Angeline Chia, October 2002 (National Institute of Education, Nanyang Technological University, Oral History Collection).

[12] Oh Patricia Choo Neo alias Mrs Chia Kin Teng, interviewed by Bonny Tan, 17 May 1995, accession number 001631, reel 3, p. 56 (National Archives of Singapore).

[13] Tan Hoe Song, interviewed by Wang Shiyun, Jaslyn, March 2004 (National Institute of Education, Nanyang Technological University, Oral History Collection).

[14] Koh Kim Hiang, interviewed by Oh Kok Choon, October 2004 (National Institute of Education, Nanyang Technological University, Oral History Collection).

Seeing other women being abducted to be sexually enslaved by the Japanese military was also vividly etched into the memories of Singapore women from the Japanese Occupation. 'Luo Mei' and 'Granny Loke', two women who had been friends since they lived in the same village in the Lim Chu Kang area, recounted in March 2001 what happened. 'Luo Mei' said: 'When the Japanese came, the girls in my village would flee. We would escape to all the possible places we could think of, including the temple. But the Japanese beasts would even search the temple and drag the girls away by force.... They did not care if it was a sacred place.... They were taken away to be singsong girls, dance hostesses and "comfort women".' 'Granny Loke' added, 'They would not spare you just because you are married, they did not care, just as long as you are not too old and nice looking. My neighbour's daughter-in-law was dragged away by them leaving behind a toddler and she never returned.'[15]

Yang Fan, in an interview conducted in September 2002, remembered in tears the time when she was aged 16 in 1942 and first saw Japanese soldiers come into her mainly Malay village. She recalled: 'There were already rumours of girls being taken away to work as comfort women. When one particular soldier came near me, I did not dare to look up. I was trembling inside, praying hard that they would not discover that I was a girl. My skin colour was rather fair and I certainly did not look like a man. Fortunately, I managed to escape till he left with his other soldiers and nothing happened to my father or anybody else in my family.' However, other women in the village were not as lucky or 'blessed'. 'I remember seeing the Japanese soldiers taking away some Chinese young girls. But, most girls who were taken away were Malays. I was blessed but I knew that disguising as a man was not a long-term solution. What would happen to those girls was that they would become comfort women and be forced into sexual activities with the Japanese soldiers.'[16] The solution that her parents came up with was an arranged marriage with a rubber tapper who was 15 years her senior.

In early 1942, the Japanese soldiers particularly took the women for brief periods of sexual enslavement. Ang Guan Hiang, who was aged 22 when she worked in the village near the eighth mile point of Bukit Timah Road, recounted in an interview in October 2006: 'My towkay's [boss] youngest daughter was taken away by Japanese soldiers. She returned home after a week. She told me

---

[15] 'Luo Mei' and 'Granny Loke', interviewed by Foo Yean Fung, March 2001 (National Institute of Education, Nanyang Technological University, Oral History Collection).
[16] Yang Fan, interviewed by Lee Li Choo, Kelly, September 2002 (National Institute of Education, Nanyang Technological University, Oral History Collection).

that she was tied to a bench and was gang raped by soldiers.' Ang was close to the victim and said that the experience left the woman 'deeply psychologically scarred'.[17] Also in a village along Bukit Timah Road, Lim Ah Hua, who was 16 years old in 1942, told in October 2002 how she dressed as a boy when Japanese soldiers came looking for women just after the fall of Singapore. She described the fate of her sister:

> They turned towards my sister and took her away. My sister was screaming for me but I was too afraid to go to her aid for I feared that I also would be caught and my identity exposed to them. My sister was raped and only a week later, she returned home looking dazed. They [Japanese soldiers] also asked my brother-in-law to get for them 4 or 5 women. They told him that if he didn't bring them, they would chop off his head. My brother-in-law left but didn't return....
>
> Interviewer: How did you and your sister feel about the incident?
> My sister was always crying at night but I was not really affected.[18]

Most women slowly recovered their lives after rape and sexual enslavement. 'Madam Sze' was 12 years old when the Japanese soldiers entered her village at Lim Chu Kang and raped her stepsister: 'All the women ran away but she was too slow and was caught by one "Japanese Ghost" [colloquial derogatory Chinese name for the Japanese soldiers]... They took her away.' 'Madam Sze' continued: 'After that my father arranged for her to be married to a man older than her, a widower much older than her. They had two children, and the two children have families now.'[19] Her stepsister died of cancer of the womb, but while alive her stepsister would regularly confide in 'Madam Sze' about her experience of brief enslavement by the Japanese military and sought solace from those discussions.

While the Japanese soldiers sought out young women themselves, they also asked village men to procure young women for them or to lead them to the young women. Ng Chin Heng, a student, in his September 1981 interview, was astonished at the 'Japanese soldiers' desire for women and girls' in the

---

[17] Ang Guan Hiang, interviewed by Tan Si Hua, October 2006 (National Institute of Education, Nanyang Technological University, Oral History Collection).
[18] Lim Ah Hua, interviewed by Saminathan Moghan, October 2002 (National Institute of Education, Nanyang Technological University, Oral History Collection).
[19] 'Madam Sze', interviewed by Neo Jia Hwee, October 2004 (National Institute of Education, Nanyang Technological University, Oral History Collection).

months after the fall of Singapore.[20] Lee Beng Kway, also a student living in a village at the Clementi area, in his October 1984 interview described how in the early days of the occupation, he was asked by two Japanese soldiers to lead them to his village's girls, who had gone into hiding. He deceived them and as punishment, he was slashed but managed to escape.[21] Tan Guan Chuan, a government servant, in March 1984, recollected that in 1942 Japanese soldiers in the Hougang area entered houses in the daytime, then came back at night looking for girls they had seen in order to rape them. He recalled girls running into the nearby bushes and crying for help when these raids occurred at night.[22] Lim Ming Joon, a photo studio shop owner also living in the Hougang area, in the sixth milestone village (now the area at the major junction of Simon Road and Tampines Road with Upper Serangoon Road), confirmed this in his September 1983 interview. He vividly remembered his horror at how the Japanese soldiers went searching for girls in the area. The Japanese soldiers asked him for young women but he pretended not to understand, even when they wrote down on a piece of paper the character for *ji*, or prostitute. He told them he had 'no eggs' as the Chinese pronunciation for prostitute and chicken sounds the same.[23] Lim Seng alias Lim Tow Tuan, a photo studio shop assistant, who also lived in the Hougang area, remembered in his January 1984 interview that in his own community at Hougang, the Japanese soldiers found the village's girls and raped them.[24]

Masculinist perspectives in male memories of the rape of Singapore women are perceptible in oral history interviews on the Japanese Occupation. While these male perspectives may be common, even hegemonic, it is important to bear in mind that not all men have strongly uniform masculinist views on rape in war. However, as Yonson Ahn describes in her work on the comfort women, there certainly exists a dominant masculinist view based on 'an essentialist understanding of male sexuality as something uncontrollable', in which the sexual assault of women in war and other such actions of male

---

[20] Ng Chin Heng, interviewed by Chua Ser Koon, 1 September 1981, accession number 000096, reel 2 (National Archives of Singapore).
[21] Lee Beng Kway, interviewed by Tan Beng Luan, 8 and 15 October 1984, accession number 000484, reels 2 and 3 (National Archives of Singapore).
[22] Tan Guan Chuan, interviewed by Low Lay Leng, 21 March 1984, accession number 000414, reel 2, p. 29 (National Archives of Singapore).
[23] Lim Ming Joon, interviewed by Tan Beng Luan, 30 September 1983, accession number 000333, reel 2 (National Archives of Singapore).
[24] Lim Seng alias Lim Tow Tuan, interviewed by Tan Beng Luan, 5 January 1984, accession number 000089, reel 3 (National Archives of Singapore).

soldiers are seen as 'inevitable and unavoidable'.[25] Charlie Cheah Fook Ying, a government servant, in December 1983, remembered that in the building where he lived at Tiong Bahru in 1942, Japanese soldiers broke into flats that housed young female cabaret dancers and raped them. He recalled his reaction when one of the women described what had happened and how afterwards she darkened her face with charcoal and wore very drab clothes. Cheah's response may reflect his feelings of powerlessness in the situation, but he does so in language that implicitly adopts the masculinist view that rape in war was to be accepted. 'I said, "Well it can't be helped, that's all."' To another cabaret girl who had also been raped that night, his friend's sister, he said, '"Well, it is just one of those things."'[26]

Having a comfort station in the neighbourhood meant that women had even greater reason to be fearful. In contrast to what Goh Sin Tub had said about how the presence of the Cairnhill Road comfort station ensured the safety of women in the nearby Emerald Hill area and prevented them from being sexually molested, in his February 1982 interview, Heng Chiang Ki, a student, remembered that things were not so simple. He recalled Japanese soldiers regularly walking along Cairnhill Road on the way to the comfort station. Some would become disoriented and would knock on his neighbours' doors asking for 'kunjang'. The neighbours would tell the Japanese, 'No kunjang', and 'later on they would just go off', he said.[27] At Heng's home in Emerald Hill Road, his mother and sister feared being sexually assaulted by Japanese soldiers passing by in the street so they kept to the back of the house to avoid Japanese soldiers, 'because if you started dressing nicely and walking about, there, you are attracting their attention. Then they just start coming into your house.'[28] Heng's testimony suggests that because residents took many precautions, there were indeed no rapes of the women in the houses of the Emerald Hill area. He remembers: 'Other places, I heard a lot of stories about Japanese soldiers getting into the houses, looking for girls. And some escaped, some got raped and all

---

[25] Yonson Ahn, *Whose Comfort?: Body, Sexuality and Identities of Korean "Comfort Women" and Japanese Soldiers during WWII*, p. 67.

[26] Cheah, Charlie Fook Ying, interviewed by Low Lay Leng, 30 December 1983, accession number 000385, reel 3, pp. 18–9 (National Archives of Singapore). See a critique of this position in Nicola Henry, *War and Rape: Law, Memory and Justice* (London: Routledge, 2011), and the chapter on war and rape in the classic Susan Brownmiller, *Against Our Will: Men, Women, and Rape* (New York: Simon and Schuster, 1975).

[27] Heng Chiang Ki, interviewed by Chua Ser Koon, 2 February 1982, accession number 000152, reel 2, p. 23 (National Archives of Singapore).

[28] Heng Chiang Ki, 2 February 1982, reel 3, pp. 23–4.

that stuff. You can do nothing about it.'[29] Heng's testimony, as well as Cheah's, express what feminist historian Yonson Ahn says is a masculinist acceptance that male sexual assault against women during war was seen as 'uncontrollable', 'inevitable and unavoidable'. But it also suggests perhaps a helplessness in a situation that was beyond their control.

Making Singapore Girls Comfort Women

Japanese soldiers were not just interested in one-off rapes and the haphazard taking away of young women. The abduction of young women for rape or sexual enslavement in early 1942, although appearing chaotic, seems to have fulfilled the military intention of satisfying the sexual appetites of the soldiers of the 25th Army at a time when comfort stations were only just being established. It is no surprise that some of these women who were raped and enslaved were being forced into these early comfort stations, as Hayashi has pointed out had also happened in China and across Southeast Asia. Only on 4 July 1942 did the General Headquarters of the 25th Army issue a directive that prevented its soldiers from going to private brothels and effectively mandated that they visit comfort stations instead, as a considerable number had been established by then and more were being set up.[30] This frantic rush to establish comfort stations up and down Peninsular Malaysia in early 1942 is occasionally mentioned in the war diaries of the units of the Japanese 5th Division, which are held in the archives of the Japanese Self-Defense Agency's National Institute for Defense Studies. Oral history testimonies of Japanese veterans from the Malayan Campaign gathered by Hayashi Hirofumi also suggest how they hastened to create local comfort stations and recruit local women. These Japanese sources confirm the accounts of Singapore women as the Japanese 25th Army conquered Malaya and Singapore.[31]

Singapore women in their oral history testimonies often remark that the number of Japanese soldiers coming to look for women started to decline after the middle of 1942. The change in behaviour of the troops was noticed. Ong Soo Mui, who was a young girl living at Kim Chuan Road in 1942, remembered in an interview from October 2006 that 'their raping and looting happened

---

[29] Heng Chiang Ki, 2 February 1982, reel 3, p. 24.
[30] Yoshimi Yoshiaki, *Comfort Women: Sexual Slavery in the Japanese Military during World War II*, p. 75; and see the directive in Yoshimi Yoshiaki, ed., *Jugun Ianfu Shiryoshu* [Collection of Comfort Women Materials] (Tokyo: Otsuki Shoten, 1992), pp. 353–4.
[31] See the published documents from the archives in Yoshimi, ed., *Jugun Ianfu Shiryoshu*, pp. 349–61; and Hayashi, 'Mare hanto no Nihongun Ianjo', pp. 272–9.

only for the initial few months. After that, they were not allowed to do so.'[32] Goh Yu Yap, a 15-year-old girl who stayed around the Boat Quay area near the Singapore River, also recalled in an October 2004 interview that 'the Japanese soldiers simply catch girls and made them prostitutes at the chaotic period just after the battle. But after that, I am not very sure.'[33]

The apparent acceptance by the military authorities of Japanese soldiers committing rape and enslaving Singapore women in the early months after the fall of Singapore in 1942 seems to confirm the work of Yuki Tanaka. He contends that although rape was an offence in the Japanese military code, the senior officers rarely took it seriously and were reluctant to prosecute soldiers for rape. In the code it was seen as secondary to looting as a crime, with some officers even viewing it as assisting in building up aggression in troops. Tanaka points to the ridiculously small number of soldiers who were convicted of rape in the Japanese military. In 1939, 15 men were convicted of looting, rape, and manslaughter; 4 soldiers in 1940; and 2 in 1941. Tanaka suggests that for the Japanese military, the best solution to the problem of its men's sexual lust was to provide comfort women and that 'the provision of comfort women was the most appropriate means of providing their men with some leisure'.[34]

Rape and the rounding up of women in the early days of the Japanese Occupation served the Japanese military's intention to both immediately allow its soldiers sexual gratification and in the longer term set up comfort stations as a permanent and ordered solution. This was apparent to members of the Chinese business community who had dealings with the Japanese military. Lim Soo Gan, a merchant, in his April 1982 interview, recalled the Japanese military's frenzy for women in early 1942. His testimony is worth repeating at length as Lim seems through his contacts in the business community to have had considerable knowledge of what was occurring. Lim's view does not fit into the masculinist hegemony over the perceptions of women, rape, and the comfort women during the Japanese Occupation. His actions suggest that conditions were not 'uncontrollable', and through the actions of men such as himself, the sexual assault of women need not be 'unavoidable'. His testimony demonstrates that male responses varied. He describes how at first he assisted

---

[32] Ong Soo Mui, interviewed by Tan Weiqi, Christer, October 2006 (National Institute of Education, Nanyang Technological University, Oral History Collection).
[33] Goh Yu Yap, interviewed by Margaret Teo Kar Sze, October 2004 (National Institute of Education, Nanyang Technological University, Oral History Collection).
[34] Yuki Tanaka, *Japan's Comfort Women: Sexual Slavery and Prostitution during World War II and the US Occupation* (London: Routledge, 2002), p. 29.

in rescuing female members of his own family who were taken away for sexual enslavement as they were unmarried young women:

> Everyone was afraid, especially the women. Girls who were 16 or 17 years old were married off or the Japanese might take them away. I met a relative whose daughter-in-law and daughter were taken away for a few days. My relative told me they went to look, and were told by the Japanese soldiers that they wanted to see their marriage certificates. My relative asked if I could forge some for them. I managed to get my clerk to forge some by copying an old marriage certificate. My relative showed the certificates to the Japanese and was told they could take the girls back the next day.[35]

In his testimony, Lim paints an apocalyptic picture of Singapore in early 1942 as he describes what he saw on the streets and starts to realise the scale of what was happening and how systematic the forcible procurement of young women for sex was:

> The Japanese would round up girls when they see them on the streets. Sometimes they would stop the vehicles and gather the girls. The girls wouldn't know why they were rounded up. Some thought they were going to be offered jobs. If the girls were factory workers in factories producing Japanese goods, they would be spared.
>
> Once, my friend told me the Japanese took away more than 30 girls. I asked how the girls were. My friend did not dare to say too much and we knew that the girls were in trouble. My friend asked if I could help forge any more marriage certificates. I chided my friend for telling so many people what I had done, as I was worried that this would spread and I would be in trouble. My friend told me that I was saving the lives of the girls.[36]

Lim voices his shock when he was told the kind of numbers that the Japanese military were requesting from his business friends in the cabaret and hostess industries for the comfort stations:

> During the first one to four months, the Japanese approached this man who used to work in the night club to look for girls. They asked if he could help supply 200 girls on a monthly basis. The man said he couldn't as the night club had closed down and the girls had all moved

---

[35] Lim Soo Gan, interviewed by Chua Ser Koon, 15 April 1982, accession number 000085, reel 18 (National Archives of Singapore).
[36] Lim Soo Gan, 15 April 1982, reel 18.

away. Actually, usually it was the girls who dressed up shabbily that were taken away, not those dressed decently walking along the streets.

Interviewer: Where were the girls taken to?

Lim: I believe they were taken to the comfort stations. After a year or so, the Japanese sent another group of women to Singapore, I believe all Japanese. Some of these women were sent to entertain Chinese businessmen like us. I told them that was unnecessary. Why would we need these women to entertain us? We only wanted to do business....[37]

The Japanese military actively sought out collaborators and procurers in order to obtain such numbers of young women for their comfort women system in Singapore. Not surprisingly many of these procurers came from the existing prewar sex industry. Susannah Tan, a medical doctor from Kandang Kerbau Hospital, described how these procurers operated under the Japanese military administration when she found herself in February 1942 reporting with many Chinese families to a Japanese screening centre on a field near Jalan Besar. After three days, the women and children were told to go home, as the Japanese military was only looking for anti-Japanese adult males as part of its *Sook Ching* [cleansing] operations to purge the anti-Japanese Chinese. While the women and children were still at the screening centre, she noticed 'some Japanese came along accompanied by some unsavoury characters—pimps, madams and *souteneurs*', whom she recognised as they used to bring prostitutes to her for medical treatment. She recalled that 'these people went around picking out all the known prostitutes, cabaret girls and other ladies of the night. Then they turned their attention to the young girls, especially those in their teens; the pretty ones were taken away and the plain ones left behind.' She and her doctor brother-in-law He Wen-Lit concluded, 'they were recruited for the Japanese "comfort houses" or brothels as prostitutes to begin a life of shame, misery and disgrace.'[38]

The Japanese military, according to teacher N.I. Low and his co-author H.M. Cheng, writing just after the war, was engaged in early 1942 in a process in which they 'rounded up all the sing-song girls, dance hostesses, prostitutes' to fill the comfort stations.[39] The Japanese military used numerous local collaborators to obtain these women. In the known red-light districts of Chinatown, women

---

[37] Lim Soo Gan, 15 April 1982, reel 18.
[38] He Wen-Lit, *Syonan Interlude* (Singapore: Mandarin, 1991), p. 88.
[39] N.I. Low and H.M. Cheng, *This Singapore (Our City of Dreadful Night)* (Singapore: City Book Store, 1947), p. 13.

were particularly fearful of the local procurers. In an interview done in October 2004, 'Mr Chin', a young teenage boy in 1942, described how in these 'city areas, there were traitors who brought the Japanese soldiers to find women. Daughters and wives living in Chinatown were spotted by these traitors who led the soldiers to rape them. It was really traumatic.'[40] Hayashi Hirofumi and Japanese researchers Shimizu Hiroshi and Hirakawa Hitoshi describe how Japanese prostitutes who had lived in prewar Malaya and Singapore, known as the *karayuki-san*, were also used by the Japanese military to procure women from the sex industry and to set up comfort stations. When prostitution was banned in 1930, these women had continued to work as prostitutes in Japanese *ryotei* that surreptitiously offered sexual services to a Japanese clientele. With their knowledge of the sex industry, they proved to be invaluable collaborators in procuring young women for the comfort women system.[41]

Even in the Japanese-controlled newspapers of Singapore, there is clear evidence that the Japanese military was using all available means for recruiting local women to work in its own sex industry. Hayashi Hirofumi describes how the Japanese military tried recruiting women using advertisements in the Chinese press during March 1942 for restaurant 'hostesses'. On 5 March 1942, there was an advertisement in the middle column of the third page of the Singapore Chinese-language newspaper, *Syonan Jit Poh* [Syonan Daily News, also known as *Syonan Nippo*], entitled: 'Request for War Service Women'. *Syonan Jit Poh* was a Chinese newspaper taken over and published by the Japanese Army Propaganda Unit after 21 February 1942 to keep the Chinese community informed of the military's orders while other Chinese newspapers were closed down. This advertisement stated:

> We want to recruit 100 'serving women' from across the different ethnic groups. Ideally, women should be between 17 to about 28 years old. The women who are recruited will receive a monthly remuneration not less than 150 dollars (one day of rest each month). At the time of enlistment, the women recruited will receive three dollars, and any person recruiting them will receive two dollars. The place of application will be at the Raffles Hotel, Beach Road. It is ideal for the women to

---

[40] 'Mr Chin', interviewed by Micki Hoe Mei Fong, October 2004 (National Institute of Education, Nanyang Technological University, Oral History Collection).
[41] Hayashi, 'Japanese comfort women in Southeast Asia', pp. 212–3; and Shimizu Hiroshi and Hirakawa Hitoshi, *Japan and Singapore in the World Economy: Japan's Economic Advance into Singapore* (London: Routledge, 1999), p. 141.

have had experience as prostitutes [referred to as the 'dark arts' or 'arts of the night'].[42]

The same language was used in advertisements published in the *Syonan Jit Poh* on 6, 7, and 8 March 1942. On 6 and 7 March, the advertisement was printed at the bottom of the second page. On 8 March, it was printed at the bottom of the first page. Hayashi makes the point that the use of the term 'serving women' indicates that the Japanese army wanted the women to serve as 'comfort women', as comfort women were seen as women serving in the military.[43] He makes the point that similarly worded advertisements were used in both Japan and Korea to trick women into becoming comfort women.[44] While there was no mention in the advertisements of the organisation that had placed them, the place to apply to was listed as Raffles Hotel, which was occupied by the Japanese military, with commissioned officers using the hotel for military business. Also, the advertisements were in sections of the newspaper that contained proclamations and notifications from the Japanese military. These factors would indicate that the Japanese military itself was involved in recruiting local comfort women.

These were not the only advertisements recruiting comfort women. On 18 April, in the *Syonan Jit Poh*, Hamada Jitaro of the comfort station known as the Asahi Club at Tanjong Katong Road published an advertisement under his name to recruit 'serving women, aged 18 to 25, persons with healthy bodies'.[45] According to the advertisement, unmarried women of any ethnicity were preferred, and it was mentioned that dozens of overseas Chinese women working as 'serving women'. It stated that 'applicants will be interviewed at the main clubhouse' and that 'travel expenses will be paid at the main clubhouse'.[46]

Were these advertisements effective in tricking Singapore women to join the military's sex industry that the Japanese were setting up soon after their conquest of Singapore? The Chinese and Japanese sources differ on this point. According to Hong Jin Tang, a Chinese writer who lived through the Japanese Occupation, there were few or no applicants to these types of advertisements, and the Japanese military had to resort to ordering their soldiers to gather about

---

[42] Hayashi Hirofumi, 'Shingaporu no Nihongun Ianjo' [Comfort Stations of the Japanese Army in Singapore], *Senso Sekinin Kenkyu* [Studies in War Responsibility], Vol. 4, 1994, p. 34.
[43] Hayashi, 'Shingaporu no Nihongun Ianjo', p. 34.
[44] Hayashi, 'Shingaporu no Nihongun Ianjo', p. 35.
[45] Hayashi, 'Shingaporu no Nihongun Ianjo', p. 35.
[46] Hayashi, 'Shingaporu no Nihongun Ianjo', p. 35.

100 women, including rounding up prostitutes and abducting ordinary girls from their homes. Hong writes that even the well-to-do were not spared.[47]

In contrast, according to a Japanese military source, at one early comfort station set up by the headquarters of the Japanese Imperial Guards division on 27 February 1942, there was no need to abduct women, as the response from Singapore prostitutes was so enthusiastic that it surprised the clerk handling recruitment. According to Fusayama Takao of the Signal Corps of the Imperial Guards division, the quota was easily met—and exceeded—by Singapore prostitutes. They were interested in replacing their British army partners with Japanese officers as their new source of income. When the women arrived by truck to the army brothel, Fusayama described how, 'as the truck was circling to enter, they waved their hands and wielded their charms from the top of the truck to the newly arrived Japanese soldiers'.[48]

The life of 'serving women', or comfort women, in the Japanese military was different from the life of a prostitute, as these women soon found out. Before the war, many of the prostitutes had each provided sexual services to one British army partner a day. When placed in a comfort house and forced to have sex with long lines of Japanese soldiers, after sex with four to five men, these women started to object. Yoshimi Yoshiaki and Hayashi Hirofumi quote the memoirs of Fusayama as a source for how these women were tricked into sexual slavery. At the comfort station, the soldier in charge tried to put a stop to it after the women objected, but the soldiers in line rioted. So he tied 'the women's arms and legs to their beds' and they were forced to have sex with the lines of Japanese soldiers.[49]

Where did the local Singapore comfort women go? In Singapore, Kallang was one comfort station with many of these local women. Hayashi Hirofumi has identified this comfort station from examining the memoirs of Japanese veteran Fukumizu Rikimatsu, and locates it behind the Japanese military barracks at the Kallang airfield. According to Fukumizu, this Kallang comfort station had local Singapore Chinese, Indian, and Eurasian comfort women as

---

[47] Hong Jin Tang, 'Ri Kou Yu Ge Minzu' [The Japanese Army and the Ethnic Groups], in *Malayan Chinese Resistance to Japan 1937–1945—Selected Source Materials*, ed. Shu Yun-Ts'iao and Chua Ser-Koon, comp. Chuang Hui-Tsuan (Singapore: Cultural and Historical Publishing House, 1984), p. 462.

[48] Fusayama Takao, *Nankai no Akebono* [South Seas Dawn] (Tokyo: Sobunsha, 1983), p. 150. See also the reproduction of the account in Yoshimi, *Comfort Women*, p. 124; and Hata Ikuhiko, *Comfort Women and Sex in the Battle Zone*, trans. Jason Michael Jordan (Lantham, Maryland: Rowman & Littlefield, 2018), p. 278.

[49] Yoshimi, *Comfort Women*, p. 124, and Fusayama, *Nankai no Akebono*, p. 151.

well as Indonesians serving Japanese soldiers stationed at the airbase. It was a local house remodelled to look like a geisha house, in a manner similar to that of many *ryotei* in Singapore.⁵⁰

Comfort stations with local women were set up near military bases or in existing red-light districts. Kiong Beng Swee, in an interview in October 2006, recounted that when he worked as an office boy for the Japanese at the Seletar military base, every day on his way to and from work, he would go pass a comfort station near the base that was housed in a row of shophouses along Jalan Kayu. He recollected: 'That place ah...all the Japanese soldiers would go there at night ah...at night...drink and then have a good f*** here and there...free, you know... no need to pay what. So these comfort women were a lot of Singaporeans.... They were all.... They were all taken by force and forced to entertain the Japanese soldiers.'⁵¹ Local Singapore women were also sent to red-light districts in Chinatown that had been appropriated by the Japanese military for comfort stations. Sundarajulu Lakshmana Perumal, a harbour labour contractor for the Japanese, in a May 1982 interview, mentioned that nearby where he worked in Tanjong Pagar and along Cantonment Road the Japanese military had set up comfort stations with 'local girls taken from local families'.⁵²

Small numbers of local Singapore comfort women were also spread out in comfort stations across Singapore with women from Korea, Japan, Taiwan, Indonesia, and other places. In Chapter 1, Japanese veteran Naoi Masatake mentioned seeing a few Singapore Malay comfort women at the Cairnhill Road comfort station. In the same chapter, the Chin Kang Huay Kuan Chinese clan association at 27 Bukit Pasoh Road is thought by Teo Soon Koon to have also housed some local Singapore women as comfort women.

It is worth looking at additional evidence for local Singapore comfort women working at the Bukit Pasoh Road comfort station. Ho Teck Fan came to Singapore from China as a teenager in 1937 to join his brothers working at On Cheong Goldsmiths in Chinatown. In an interview conducted in March 2006, Ho describes some local Singapore Chinese women being present at the comfort station along Bukit Pasoh Road, where there were predominantly Taiwanese and Japanese comfort women. Ho remembers the comfort station as it was in Chinatown near where he worked and lived: 'The Japanese soldiers had

---

⁵⁰ See entry for Kallang at the website of the Women's Active Museum on War and Peace (WAM): https://wam-peace.org/ianjo/area/area-sg/.
⁵¹ Kiong Beng Swee, interviewed by Iskander bin Zainalludin, October 2006 (National Institute of Education, Nanyang Technological University, Oral History Collection).
⁵² Sundarajulu Lakshmana Perumal, interviewed by Lim How Seng, 17 May 1982, accession number 000173, reel 5, p. 63 (National Archives of Singapore).

military prostitutes. They brought Japanese military prostitutes here. Once they were here, they also rounded up local women to serve as military prostitutes. The location was at Bukit Pasoh. The place was for soldiers to enjoy. When there were insufficient Japanese military prostitutes, they would force local women to serve as military prostitutes. You can't escape once you are in there.'[53]

Singapore women who were forcibly recruited as comfort women were also sent out of Singapore to Java, Malaysia, and Thailand. Writing soon after the war, teacher N.I. Low and his co-author H.M. Cheng describe knowing of 15 young women from Singapore who were sent to Java and who only returned after the war had ended.[54] Malay and Chinese women from Singapore would also be sent to Peninsular Malaysia. Jumaiyah bte Masbin, who was a girl in 1942, remembers in an October 1991 interview that she was living in a Malay village at Woodlands when the Japanese soldiers 'first arrived', and 'in households where they had many girls, they'd take the girls by force....' Then 'they'd bring them to Malaysia...yes to Malaysia, those girls. When parents of daughters realised girls were being taken by force, they'd keep their daughters at home; everyone was scared and worried. The Japanese had no compunction about taking what they wanted.... I saw such things.'[55]

Singapore women were sent further afield into Peninsular Malaysia than just across the Causeway from Woodlands into Johore. There is a documented account of 20 Cantonese prostitutes, or sing-song girls, being forcibly recruited and sent to Taiping, Perak. Sing-song girls were 'high-class' prostitutes who were able to entertain wealthy Chinese businessmen by singing songs, playing music, and engaging in sophisticated conversation, as well as providing sex. These Cantonese prostitutes sent to Taiping were among 50 rounded up by the Japanese military in Chinatown to serve in comfort stations outside of Singapore. Of this group, 30 women went to comfort stations in Thailand. Before the war, all 50 of them had been trafficked into prostitution when their families sold them at a young age to procurers for brothels in Canton. They were trained as sing-song girls and sent to work in the prostitution industry in Singapore. They described themselves as having been abducted by the Japanese military from the Cantonese prostitution areas of Chinatown in Singapore and sent to work as comfort women outside of Singapore. They told their story to Leow Shuan Fong, who during the war supplied cigarettes

---

[53] Ho Teck Fan, interviewed by Lim Lai Hwa, 22 March 2006, accession number A003042, reel 9 (National Archives of Singapore).
[54] Low and Cheng, *This Singapore (Our City of Dreadful Night)*, p. 13.
[55] Jumaiyah bte Masbin, interviewed by Mohd Yussoff Ahmad, 23 October 1991, accession number 001316, reel 7 (National Archives of Singapore).

and other goods to the two comfort stations in Taiping and got to know the comfort women well. He later gave an account of what they told him in a long feature-length interview for the Malaysian *Shin Min Jit Poh* newspaper on 1 October 1992, which was later reprinted in the local history of Taiping under the Japanese Occupation.[56]

The lives of the 20 Singapore Cantonese women who were sent to Taiping give a good indication of the role of local Singapore comfort women in the sex industry of the Japanese military. In Taiping, there were two comfort stations. One was along Railway Station Road, in two Malay houses. There were eight comfort women there from Taiwan who could speak Japanese and were managed by two Chinese brothers with the surname of Lim. This comfort station was for the officers. The other comfort station was located in the Old Club, which later became part of Taiping Municipal Hall. It was here that the 20 Cantonese women from Singapore worked, serving long lines of ordinary soldiers. At 11am the women would start sexually serving soldiers who were brought in by trucks. This continued until 10pm. The men came continually in trucks of four or five men each. The women received a military ticket from each man, which he had bought for $2. After serving ten men, a woman was given a break and another woman would take over while she rested.

In Singapore, when they worked as prostitutes, the women usually had a rest when they were menstruating as men regarded them as unclean, but for these Japanese men, menstruating women only increased their sex drive as they believed that the women had a higher sex drive during menstruation. Therefore, the women had no rest even when they were menstruating. The experiences of the Singapore Cantonese comfort women as indicated to Leow suggests that they suffered more than their Taiwanese counterparts who were just serving the officers in the other comfort station of Taiping. However, the women said that both comfort stations were tightly guarded and that there was no way any women could escape.[57] Thus, to further gauge the role of Singapore women in the sex industry of the Japanese military, it is worth examining in greater detail the comfort stations meant for officers, which were also known as *ryotei*.

---

[56] Lee Eng Kew, *Riben Shou: Taiping Ri Ju San Nian Ba Ge Yue* [In Japanese Hands: The Japanese Occupation at Taiping for Three Years and Eight Months] (Petaling Jaya, Selangor, Malaysia: SIRD, 2006), pp. 50–2.

[57] Lee, *Riben Shou*, pp. 50–2.

The *Ryotei* Providing Sexual Services for the Japanese Military

Along with the comfort stations, there were *ryotei* with mainly Japanese women providing sexual services to officers and high-ranking civilian administrators. Singapore Chinese Girls' School, near Cairnhill Road was not the only school to be turned into a *ryotei*. The most well known of the *ryotei* was the converted Nan Hwa Girls' School on Sophia Road. The story of this *ryotei* illustrates how within the Japanese administration there were differences of opinion about providing these places. The account of this *ryotei* and others in Singapore by Mamoru Shinozaki makes clear the differences between the various institutions of the Japanese sex industry in Singapore, and his own critical view of them. He was initially Education Officer in the Japanese administration of Singapore, then in August 1942 became Chief Welfare Officer.

Shinozaki in a 1973 oral history interview with staff from Singapore's Institute of Southeast Asian Studies describes how the *ryotei* differed from comfort stations. These *ryotei* often employed 'low-grade' geisha from the ranks of the many geisha in Japan in the 1930s whose services resembled more the activities of prostitutes than that of cultural entertainers. In many Japanese prefectures, a number of women held 'dual permits' as both geishas and prostitutes under Japan's system of licensed prostitution.[58] In 1930s militarist Japan, the 'low-grade' geisha of Japanese cities were not the traditional higher-end, glamorous women of well-established geisha houses, where they entertained their male guests using the arts of erudite conversation and culturally sophisticated musical and dancing performances. In the lower-end geisha houses of many cities, the evening did not stop at polite conversation and a quick song and dance; it was expected to end with sex.[59]

Shinozaki was clear about how the *ryotei* and comfort stations differed in Singapore:

> These restaurants were more like *geisha* houses, offering very delicious food like the Japanese inns in Japan. Only the high officials and the managerial class of big companies could go there. The ordinary soldiers went to the 'comfort' houses which were meant to prevent the rape of

---

[58] Hata, *Comfort Women and Sex in the Battle Zone*, p. 26.
[59] See William Johnston, *Geisha, Harlot, Strangler, Star: A Woman, Sex, and Morality in Modern Japan* (New York: Columbia University Press, 2005), pp. 40, 60–3; and Sayo Masuda, *Autobiography of a Geisha*, trans. G.G. Rowley (New York: Columbia University Press, 2003), pp. 6–7.

innocent girls. Mostly Korean girls were to be found there. They were run by Korean and Formosan Japanese citizens.[60]

Shinozaki, who felt very sympathetic towards the plight of the local population, described his dislike of the *ryotei*, even though they were meant for high-ranking officials like himself:

> Such restaurants or inns greatly astonished the local people who were living under such hard conditions, and were so poor. But the Japanese side were spending so freely, living luxuriously, eating and drinking a lot. I always felt so shameful over it. I never went therefore to such restaurants or geisha-houses during the Occupation. That was my resistance. (Laughter)[61]

The *ryotei* that occupied Nan Hwa Girls' School was called Tsuruya and was modelled on a famed crab-dish restaurant in Omori, Tokyo. About 80 Japanese women wearing kimonos were employed by Tsuruya.[62] It occupied all three storeys of the school, with tatami mats on each of the floors. Shinozaki, as Education Officer in the first few months of the Japanese Occupation, described how he sought to close down this *ryotei* and return its use to a school after discovering the embarrassment that it was causing:

> They had brought geisha girls over from Japan and there were complaints from the people nearby because it was very noisy every night. Also it was broadcasted from New Delhi that the Japanese military were using girls' schools as geisha-houses. I was very ashamed.[63]

Shinozaki approached the manager of Tsuruya, whom he described as a former gangster from Japan with a long scar on his face. The manager told Shinozaki that 'he could not give up the building because so much money had been spent on it and he had come with the support of an Army staff officer.'[64]

---

[60] Mamoru Shinozaki, *My Wartime Experiences in Singapore: Institute of Southeast Asian Studies, Singapore Oral History Programme Series No. 3 August 1973* (Singapore: Institute of Southeast Asian Studies, 1973), p. 56.

[61] Shinozaki, *My Wartime Experiences in Singapore*, p. 56.

[62] Shimizu and Hirakawa, *Japan and Singapore in the World Economy*, p. 143; and see for more details Shingaporu Shiseikai [Singapore Municipal Association], *Shonan Tokubetsu-shi Shi: Senji-chu no Shingaporu* [Syonan Special Municipality History: Singapore During the War] (Tokyo: Nihon Shingaporu Kyokai [The Japan-Singapore Association], 1986), pp. 202–4.

[63] Shinozaki, *My Wartime Experiences in Singapore*, p. 51.

[64] Shinozaki, *My Wartime Experiences in Singapore*, p. 51.

Shinozaki then asked for help from the Mayor of Singapore Odate Shigeo, who approached Field Marshall Terauchi Hisaichi at the Staff General Office, and thereafter Tsuruya closed.

Shinozaki and Mayor Odate were crucial too in shutting down another *ryotei* that was also an embarrassment to them. This *ryotei* was known as the Yamato Butai (*butai* being the name for military unit). It was located at the premises of the Singapore Cricket Club, just opposite the mayor's municipal offices at the City Hall building. Yamato Butai was established by Takase Toru, the deputy of Wataru Watanabe, Chief of the Military Administration Department. According to Shinozaki:

> Takase, the close friend and advisor of Col. Watanabe, was closely connected with a big restauranteur and hotel owner in Izu, a holiday resort outside Tokyo. Now that he was so powerful, he wanted to bring this hotel proprietor into Singapore. This hotel proprietor collected many young girls in Japan on the pretext that he was opening some business in Syonan and needed typists and clerks and brought them here. But once here they were used as hostesses, service girls. Some of the girls were very disappointed, some cried but it could not be helped.[65]

He affirmed that 'officially they were called typists and clerks. But they were much more, most of them.'[66]

Shinozaki recalled that once established, the *ryotei* occupying the Singapore Cricket Club 'became very noisy'.[67] 'Every afternoon,' he recounted, the sounds of 'drunken officers' and 'the noisy laughter of these girls could be heard in the mayor's office in City Hall a couple of hundred of metres away.'[68] He remembered: 'We were very uncomfortable. The local staff were looking and laughing. We were so ashamed. Mayor Odate was very angry.'[69] Once again, Shinozaki and Odate resorted to letting Field Marshall Terauchi know. This time they did so by inviting him around to a game of *go* when the *ryotei* restaurant was at its noisiest. Shinozaki described Terauchi's outrage, and how 'shortly afterwards the *Yamato Butai* was closed. Those girls who were genuine

---

[65] Shinozaki, *My Wartime Experiences in Singapore*, p. 51.
[66] Mamoru Shinozaki, *Syonan: My Story: The Japanese Occupation of Singapore* (Singapore: Asia Pacific Press, 1975), p. 51.
[67] Shinozaki, *My Wartime Experiences in Singapore*, p. 51.
[68] Shinozaki, *Syonan: My Story*, p. 51.
[69] Shinozaki, *My Wartime Experiences in Singapore*, p. 51.

typists were allowed to remain; they became office workers. The rest returned to Japan.'[70]

While the *ryotei* occupying Nan Hwa Girls' School and the Singapore Cricket Club were closed down because they were public embarrassments, the rest of the many *ryotei* in Singapore remained very much open. Perhaps the most luxurious of the *ryotei* that operated in Singapore was Chikamatsu, by the beach and near the comfort station at Tanjong Katong Road. Chikamatsu was run by Imai Koshizu, who had previously managed a *ryotei* of the same name at Harbin in Japanese-occupied Manchuria. Imai, herself, according to those who knew her well, was 'not content with the narrow life' that women were allowed in Japan.[71] Supported by the army, she arrived in Singapore in August 1942, around the same time that Shinozaki and Odate were shutting down the *ryotei* at Nan Hwa Girls' School and the Singapore Cricket Club.[72] Kamata Hisako, who was a typist at the municipal offices of Shinozaki and Odate, recalls that she and her office were aware that Imai arrived with 90 geisha—50 from Tokyo, 30 from Osaka and 10 from Nagoya.[73] The most well known of these geisha was Nakagawa Hana, who came with her own hair stylist and dressmaker. After the war, Nakagawa returned to Tokyo to live in one of the old red-light districts from the Edo period, Yoshiwara. There, Nakagawa managed the Maruhana *ryotei* at Asakusa. Kamata described Singapore's Chikamatsu as being fitted with expensive floor coverings and decorations from Japan, with 800 tatami mats from Hiroshima, costing 7,000 yen, and other furniture imported from Japan. For a banquet, Imai charged 50 yen per high-ranking military personnel and 75 yen per senior Japanese civilian.

Most of Imai's clientele were military officers, including several generals. Among them was the Japanese Southern Army's Chief of Staff, Lieutenant General Kuroda Shigenori. He was well known for his womanising and frequented Chikamatsu many times. However, Imai was said to have given Kuroda 'the cold shoulder' at times when his sexual demands became too much.[74] The commissioned officers came from Peninsular Malaysia, Java,

---

[70] Shinozaki, *Syonan: My Story*, p. 51.
[71] Kamata Hisako, 'Chikamatsu no Okami: Imai Koshizu' [Chikamatsu's Proprietress: Imai Koshizu], *Minamijujisei* [Southern Cross] (Singapore: Japanese Association of Singapore, 1978), the magazine of the Japanese Association of Singapore compiled into a single volume in 1978 by the Japanese Association of Singapore, p. 552.
[72] Shingaporu Shiseikai, *Shonan tokubetsu-shi shi*, pp. 202–4, 297–8.
[73] Kamata, 'Chikamatsu no Okami: Imai Koshizu', p. 552. See the discussion in Shimizu and Hirakawa, *Japan and Singapore in the World Economy*, p. 143.
[74] Kamata, 'Chikamatsu no Okami', pp. 552–4.

Sumatra, and Burma. Entering Chikamatsu, they said, 'reminded them of Japan's aroma and scent'.[75] When queried about whether there was too much extravagance and opulence at the *ryotei* by Mayor Odate, and whether it was worth the expense during wartime, Imai replied: 'No, sir, because of these decorations, the soldiers returning from Burma and Sumatra are happy and they say it feels like they are returning to Japan.'[76]

The Role of Singapore Women in the *Ryotei* Offering Sex

There was a variety of *ryotei*, not just those like Imai's Chikamatsu establishment at Katong, which was only meant for high-ranking officers and the senior civilian administrators. Historians of the Japan-Singapore relationship, Shimizu Hiroshi and Hirakawa Hitoshi sum up the varied nature of the *ryotei*. Many of the more humble establishments did not employ 'low-grade' geisha, or even Japanese women, but women from other places, including Singapore. Shimizu and Hirakawa quote from the recollections of Sukemura Iwao, who was working in the city council as an engineer:

> From the early period of occupation, there was a wide variety of Japanese *ryotei* and the like, ranging from high-class *ryotei* to cafes and their owners and employees came from Japan, Manchuria, Taiwan, and Korea. There was no shortage of these places.[77]

The range of women that the Japanese military used to provide sexual services out of the *ryotei*, brothels, and hotels was extensive. Colonel Takami Toyotaro, of the Field Artillery Regiment of the 53rd Division in Burma, recorded the variety of women made available to him for his sexual pleasure in his diary on 16 April 1942 when he stayed at a large Singapore hotel confiscated by the Japanese military from the British. He wrote that he arrived in the morning and 'a captured English girl' came to his room to bathe him, and she 'satisfied my bodily needs from being a half month at sea'. Later in the evening, a 'French prostitute came to my room with drinks and stayed the night'.[78]

---

[75] Kamata, 'Chikamatsu no Okami', p. 553.
[76] Yamata, 'Chikamatsu no Okami', p. 553.
[77] Shimizu and Hirakawa, *Japan and Singapore in the World Economy*, p. 143.
[78] Kim Il-Myon, *Tenno no Guntai to Chosenjin Ianfu* [The Emperor's Armed Forces and the Korean Comfort Women] (Tokyo: Sanichi Shobo, 1992), originally published in 1976, p. 190. See also the translation in George Hicks, *The Comfort Women: Sex Slaves of the Japanese Imperial Forces* (Sydney: Allen & Unwin, 1995), p. 90.

Local Singapore Chinese women and women recruited directly from China were also employed in the *ryotei*. They were compelled to offer sexual services as prostitutes for the Japanese officers. The life of the Chinese women working with 'low-grade' Japanese geisha in these restaurants cum brothels for officers and senior civilian administrators was vividly described by Chinese journalist Xie Song Shan in his 1950 book of his memories of the Japanese Occupation, published by Nanyang Press, called *Xue Hai* [Sea of Blood].[79] Xie condemned one former lawyer, who after quitting law operated, not far from Cairnhill Road, a restaurant cum brothel for the Japanese military. He was known as 'Ojisan' or 'uncle'.[80]

'Ojisan' moved south with the Japanese army to set up a restaurant cum brothel in Singapore. He employed mainly women from 'good Chinese families' from China and 'low-grade' Japanese geisha from Japan. Xie recalled that when 'Ojisan' was asked by a dressmaker who made clothes for his prostitutes why he engaged in such 'bad business' of prostituting women for the Japanese military, he replied that 'there is no such thing as bad business, just business, and wartime was all about making easy money in business.'[81] One of the most pitiful women was a Cantonese singer and actress from Guangzhou whom he had tricked into coming to his Singapore brothel and working with the geisha to entertain customers and offer them sex. She was upset and angry when she found out that she had been cheated by him.[82]

Despite the risks, local Singapore women were also drawn into the Japanese military's *ryotei*, as living conditions began to deteriorate for the local population, but not for the Japanese. A number of women who were slipping into poverty were willing to hope that the false promises of earning a high wage working as a 'waitress' or a 'hostess' for the Japanese may be true. Many of these lower-class *ryotei* were eager to employ local women as demand from the Japanese military for sexual services far exceeded the supply of available women. James Francis Warren in his study of prostitution in colonial Singapore argues that before the war, many restaurants were fronts for brothels and their operators acted as procurers of women for prostitution.[83] Under the Japanese military this method of procurement of women for prostitution became more common. Chen Su Lan, a leader of the Chinese

---

[79] Xie Song Shan, *Xue Hai* [Sea of Blood] (Singapore: Nanyang Baoshe, 1950).
[80] Xie, *Xue Hai*, p. 68.
[81] Xie, *Xue Hai*, p. 68.
[82] Xie, *Xue Hai*, p. 68.
[83] James Francis Warren, *Ah Ku and Karayuki-san: Prostitution in Singapore 1870–1940*, 2nd edition (Singapore: Singapore University Press, 2003), p. 176.

community, when speaking in the Singapore Advisory Council of the British Military Administration in November 1945, painted a stark picture of what happened to these women:

> During the Jap occupation, the Japanese did not want men-waiters. They only wanted young, attractive, educated women. You could see in the Syonan Times or Syonan Shinbun any day advertisements for young, attractive, educated women. As a result many went to serve their Japanese masters as waitresses and service girls and clerks in their offices. And what has happened to these girls everybody knows. The demoralisation of Singapore womanhood is so bad that it will take years for Singapore women to regain their modesty, not to mention virtue.[84]

Hundreds of Singapore women were unable to prevent themselves from being drawn into providing sexual services for the Japanese in Singapore. Often they had little control over their conditions and terms of work. Recruitment into the Japanese military's sex industry sometimes followed the practices that had been used before the war to recruit women into prostitution—when agents or procurers bought unwanted daughters from poor families and sold them into a life of prostitution. These practices of human trafficking were well documented by historian James Francis Warren.[85]

D.R. Horne, the Assistant Secretary of the early postwar Social Welfare Department in Singapore, outlined his analysis of why a significant number of Singapore women became prostitutes during the Japanese Occupation. Horne, whose department was in charge of postwar underage prostitutes detained by the police, observed 'how the Occupation pressed very severely on the women of Singapore' as 'family life was disrupted by the cessation of overseas commerce, by the massacre of fathers, husbands and by the swift inflation of the currency'. He noted that 'the removal of the family protector found many women and girls ill-fitted to withstand the exceptionally adverse economic conditions'. Thus, Horne concluded:

> Many such women were driven by force of circumstances into accepting employment in the dubious cafes and restaurants which sprang up to meet the needs of the occupying forces and their close associates in the Black Market. This type of employment nearly always compelled

---

[84] Chen Su Lan, *British Military Administration, Malaya, Advisory Council, Singapore Report of Proceedings*, 14 November 1945, p. 19 in Singapore Advisory Council, File Number BMA (H) HQ CH 36-45, Microfilm Number NA 869 (National Archives of Singapore).
[85] Warren, *Ah Ku and Karayuki-san: Prostitution in Singapore 1870–1940*, pp. 77–81.

such women and girls to accept a life of prostitution as an alternative to starvation.

Others were employed by the Japanese under such conditions that made it inevitable that they should become the mistresses of their employers.

The ever increasing intensity of hunger and need caused a sharp revival of the practice of seeking female children to procuresses or their agents. All circumstances seemed to combine to degrade the female population of the city.[86]

Other postwar social commentators also described how young local women were sold into prostitution during the Japanese Occupation. Ken Jalleh similarly highlighted the role of local procurers, who he said were often unscrupulous Chinese marriage brokers engaged in delivering unwanted daughters of poor families into the sex industry that served the Japanese military.[87] This was an existing prewar pattern. Prewar British colonial reports on prostitution in Singapore had emphasised how many women were involved in prostitution because of what Horne and other social commentators called female 'procuresses'. In Singapore, it was common that the procurers, operators, and managers in prostitution were all females rather than males.[88]

The Japanese military's profitable demand for sexual services encouraged local Chinese businessmen to prostitute local Chinese women to the Japanese military. Xie, in his 1950 recollections, recalled that while it was initially Japanese entrepreneurs who came to Singapore to open up *ryotei* that were in effect brothels, soon Chinese businessmen were collaborating with members of the Japanese military to open such restaurants cum brothels just for the patronage of the Japanese military. According to Xie, their Chinese managers recruited beautiful local Singapore Chinese women to be waitresses and hostesses, and pressured them to offer sexual services. Only the Japanese were admitted to these restaurants and there were banners outside indicating that the local people were not allowed entry. Some of these restaurants catered to specific Japanese military units and were located near their barracks.[89] Lim Ming

---

[86] *Singapore Free Press*, 25 March 1947.
[87] *The Straits Times*, 18 September 1949.
[88] Prostitution in Singapore, 1939, CO 273 659/50657 and Prostitution in Singapore, 1941, CO 273 667/50657 (The National Archives, Kew). See the comments of Chen Su Lan made while attending the British Military Administration's Advisory Council in the file The Women and Girls' Protection Ordinance: Amendments to:-, File Number BMA (H) HQ S. DIV. BMA 60-46, Microfilm Number MSA 025 (National Archives of Singapore).
[89] Xie, *Xue Hai*, p. 65.

Joon, a photo studio shop owner, in his September 1983 oral history interview recalled that Chinese businessmen had opened similar restaurants meant only for the Japanese along North Bridge Road where he worked.[90] Japanese veteran Harami Keiji, in his memoirs, described visiting one of these restaurants in a Singapore shophouse, which operated as a local coffee shop. It was staffed by local Chinese waitresses dressed in uniforms of red tops and blue skirts. After he sat down, one waitress asked him in broken Japanese to go upstairs and took him by the hand. He paid 10 cigarettes to have sex on a double bed in a dimly lit room.[91]

Ho Kwai Min and the Sex Industry of the Japanese Military in Singapore

Despite the power of the Japanese military's sex industry, Singapore women working in it should not be seen just as passive victims of this system. Where they could, many of these women sought out opportunities to exercise control over their conditions of employment. Admittedly, these opportunities were limited. The life during the Japanese Occupation of prewar Singapore Cantonese 'high-class' prostitute in Chinatown, Ho Kwai Min, as recounted in her interview with the Singapore Oral History Centre in December 1992, reveals much about how women resisted control and sought to have greater autonomy in the sex industry of the Japanese military. Yet it also illustrates the physical violence used by the male figures controlling the Japanese military's sex industry in Singapore, including Chinese businessmen as well as Japanese military figures.

Ho Kwai Min was born in 1922 to a poor family in the countryside of Shunde district in Guangdong. At the age of six, she was sold by her family to a teacher, a spinster living with her brother's family. This family disliked Ho and constantly bullied her. Ho's adoptive family moved to Guangzhou, and when she was 14, they fled to Hong Kong to escape the Japanese invasion of China. At 18, she left Hong Kong for Singapore, when her adoptive mother received 150 Hong Kong dollars in exchange for a three-year contract obliging Ho Kwai Min to work as a prostitute in Singapore. In her December 1992 interview with the Oral History Centre, Ho was adamant that she chose to

---

[90] Lim Ming Joon, interviewed by Tan Beng Luan, 30 September 1983, accession number 000333, reel 4 (National Archives of Singapore).
[91] See the documentation for Singapore in the Women's Active Museum on War and Peace (WAM), which is on its map of comfort stations in the Asia-Pacific: https://wam-peace.org/ianjo/area/area-sg/.

work in the prostitution industry of Singapore; she was not forced to do so. Yet she conceded that with hindsight, she would not have made this choice, as she said life could be very difficult indeed. In Singapore, she lived and worked at 10 Teck Lim Road, which was in the Chinatown red-light area known as the 'Blue Triangle'.[92] But she also worked out of the Air View Hotel, at 10 Peck Seah Street, off Maxwell Road, which was also in Singapore's Chinatown.

Ho was a 'high-class' prostitute serving wealthy Chinese businessmen. She did not play musical instruments, such as the Chinese *pipa*, but she could sing and engage in entertaining conversation with wealthy customers in the 'Blue Triangle'. When Ho visited her clients, she was accompanied by a female chaperone, who was the adoptive daughter of her female boss, whom Ho called 'auntie'. She displayed genuine affection towards 'auntie' when she visited her at Keong Saik Road, also in the 'Blue Triangle'.[93] Ho was able to acquire property working in her job, as she saved her money rather than spent it, and became the owner of two properties on Bukit Pasoh Road. She contrasted her attitude to her sister prostitutes' attitudes of spending freely and wasting their earnings.

Ho was popular among her many Chinese businessmen clients. Soon after the fall of Singapore, she was recommended to Japanese officers by Chinese businessmen and pimps, who were unknown to her. Ho was regularly asked by the Japanese officers whom she served to join the military's sex industry, but she refused. During the Japanese Occupation, Ho remained working out of Teck Lim Road and the Air View Hotel with her female chaperone, but she was still required to serve clients in the Japanese military. When she refused to

---

[92] For a full description of the 'Blue Triangle', see Eddie Chan Fook Pong, *Chinatown Unspoken: The Untold Story of War, Vice and Glory in One of Singapore's Most Notorious Districts* (Singapore: Candid Creation Publishing, 2020), pp. 83–98.

[93] Ho Kwai Min, interviewed by Tan Beng Luan, 24 December 1992, accession number 001393, reel 1 (National Archives of Singapore). See also her interview about her life in the Chinese press, *Lianhe Zaobao*, 8 April 2012. The press account is based on the interview from the National Archives of Singapore. For the lives of the Cantonese prostitutes and women known as the *pipa tsai*, see Koh Choo Chin, 'Implementing Government Policy for the Protection of Women and Girls in Singapore 1948–66: Recollections of a Social Worker', in *Women and Chinese Patriarchy: Submission, Servitude and Escape*, ed. Maria Jaschok and Suzanne Miers (Hong Kong: Hong Kong University Press, 1994), p. 132; and Fu Peilin, 'Yi gu "pipa zai" yue xiao yan yi ai renjian juan bisheng jixu 29 wan yuan gei san jigou' [The late "Pi Pa Girl", Yue Xiao Yan, donating her life savings of $290,000 to three organisations], Channel 8 online news, 4 May 2021, https://www.8world.com/news/singapore/article/tuesday-report-streets-of-memory-s2-e1-keong-saik-road-1466601.

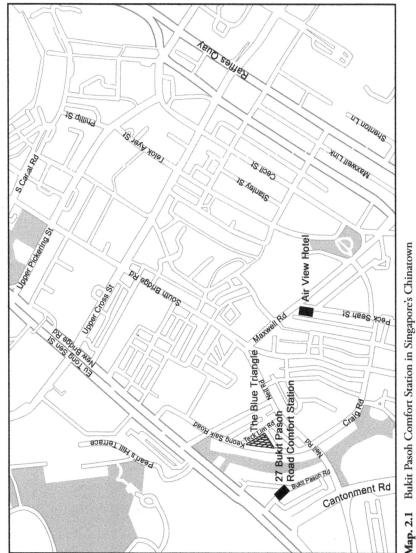

Map. 2.1 Bukit Pasoh Comfort Station in Singapore's Chinatown

go beyond just entertaining with conversation and song, the Japanese officers slapped and beat her for refusing to have sex with them.[94]

Ho only nominally retained her autonomy because she would be repeatedly summoned by the Japanese officers to serve them. She could not openly say no. Also, like other women serving the Japanese military, Ho endured physical violence from the Japanese officers. She was hit and slapped at their places of residence in Singapore, which included private bungalows. Her female chaperone always accompanied her to their residences to help keep her safe, even though she too could be subjected to physical violence. On one occasion, when Ho was avoiding customers from the Japanese military and did not go to one Japanese officer's house, the officer took her chaperone and held her hostage. After that incident, Ho started to make herself look ugly and dirty for that one Japanese officer who demanded sex with her.

One day, two Japanese soldiers and a local Chinese man recruiting comfort women came to see Ho and 'auntie'. The Chinese man, or *hanjian* [Chinese traitor] as Ho called him, demanded that Ho and another 'high-class' prostitute serve in the comfort stations. She refused. She knew enough about what working in the Japanese military's sex industry was like. Ho's residence and workplace at Teck Lim Road was near the comfort station at the Chin Kang Huay Kuan Chinese clan association, 27 Bukit Pasoh Road in Chinatown. She had no intention of losing her nominal autonomy by being a comfort woman. The 'Chinese traitor' told Ho that in order to get out of being forcibly recruited, Ho would have to find two other women to take their place. Ho and 'auntie' then persuaded two very 'low-class' prostitutes, or *zhu-ma* [literally pig-horse], to take Ho and her co-worker's places. They were employed by Ho's 'auntie' and happened to be at her place when the 'Chinese traitor' arrived. Ho referred to these women as engaging in the 'lowly service' of 'cannon shooting', or masturbating men, at the New World amusement park. The 'Chinese traitor' insisted that he would only accept this exchange if Ho and the other 'high-class' prostitute had sex with him. They accepted. Both Ho and her colleague went into hiding for a while and later returned to work. Ho learned that the two *zhuma* later escaped from a comfort station at a military camp in Malaya during an explosion. They eventually returned to Singapore.

Ho was asked by her interviewer Tan Beng Luan during her December 1992 interview with the Oral History Centre whether there were any differences

---

[94] Ho Kwai Min, interviewed by Tan Beng Luan, 24 December 1992, accession number 001393, reel 4 (National Archives of Singapore). See also her interview about her life in the Chinese press, *Lianhe Zaobao*, 8 April 2012.

between her Chinese customers and Japanese military officers. She replied that there was no difference, except maybe that the Japanese were *yindang*, or sexually lewd.[95] Ho was not alone in making this observation. Comfort women serving the Japanese military made similar comments. Bae Tok Gan told interviewer Dai Sil Kim-Gibson about serving the officers in China: 'The soldiers didn't have much time but it was the different for the officers. They did all kinds of things. I can't bring myself to talk about them.' Bae added, 'Those officers they made such weird requests! You want me to talk about them? Yuck, how can I?'[96]

Ho's most frightening encounter during the Japanese Occupation was not with the Japanese officers, but with a man who was part of the influx of Taiwanese who had come with the Japanese after the fall of Singapore to serve the Japanese military. This Taiwanese man may have been forcibly recruiting prostitutes for the Japanese military's sex industry. He followed Ho home after a night of entertaining at the Air View Hotel, broke into her room and demanded to have sex with her. He beat Ho and pulled her plaited hair, then tied her plaited hair with that of her chaperone. The Taiwanese threw them down three flights of stairs. Outside, he hired two rickshaws to take them back with him, as only two people could ride in one rickshaw. However, the rickshaw pullers were sympathetic to Ho and her chaperone and decided to help them. After moving through the streets of Chinatown, the rickshaw that took Ho and her chaperone got separated from the rickshaw of the Taiwanese man. Ho stated that the injury she received from being thrown down the stairs and hitting her head left her with pain for many years afterwards. She continued working as a prostitute for 'auntie' for two years after the war and freelanced for another three years until she married her husband, a regular customer, who had courted her for five years. Her earnings helped save his canteen business as she was able to clear his debts. She had no children from her marriage. Ever conscious of her autonomy, Ho said she stopped working because as women in the sex industry got older, they had less choice and were treated worse than younger women.[97]

The remarkable interview with Ho Kwai Min from December 1992 is unique as it is the only testimony that was ever given in 1992, or thereafter, by a Singapore woman involved in the sex industry surrounding the Japanese military of Singapore. Her interview with Tan Beng Luan was part of the Oral History Centre's early 1990s *Women Through the Years* oral history project,

---

[95] Ho Kwai Min, interview 24 December 1992, reel 4.
[96] Dai Sil Kim-Gibson, *Silence Broken: Korean Comfort Women* (Parkersburg, Iowa: Mid Prairie Books, 1999), p. 68.
[97] Ho Kwai Min, interviewed 24 December 1992, reel 4.

not the *Japanese Occupation in Singapore 1942–1945* project of the 1980s. However, Tan had been one of the principal interviewers for the *Japanese Occupation* project. The *Women Through the Years* project was pioneered by feminist activist and sociologist Lai Ah Eng, who had researched the lives of Chinese prostitutes in colonial Malaya and Singapore.[98] Lai's and Tan's role was similar to that of their feminist counterparts in South Korea and Japan, who were able to obtain testimony from women who had first-hand experience and knowledge of the Japanese military's sex industry. They focused on the human rights of women, and how women from different social classes sought autonomy in their lives.

The interview with Ho Kwai Min raises questions among oral historians in Singapore about whether she can be considered as having worked inside the Japanese military's sex industry.[99] Ho was nominally working outside of the sex industry set up by the Japanese military and by her own volition and actions was able to stay formally outside of it, in full knowledge of the violence and coercion inside it. Yet she experienced that same violence and could not openly refuse to serve Japanese officers.

Ho's oral history interview and the oral history testimonies of trauma given by many other women in Singapore during the war presented in this chapter raise interesting questions about the nature and limitations of historical sources and evidence. Hayashi Hirofumi has made the point that the archival documents on the comfort women system tell us much about how it was set up and organised by the Japanese military, but they tell us very little about the women themselves—who they were and what their lives were like.[100] Oral history is best suited for obtaining these stories using the voices of 'history from below'. The testimony given by many women in this chapter is about how their sister, stepsister, cousin, close next-door neighbour, or childhood friend were traumatised at the hands of the Japanese military setting up its sex industry in Singapore in 1942. It is about what they experienced and saw themselves. Many relived their trauma by retelling it, and sometimes gave their testimony in tears. In the case of Ho Kwai Min, it is about the trauma she experienced when the

---

[98] Lai Ah Eng, *Peasants, Proletarians, and Prostitutes: A Preliminary Investigation into the Work of Chinese Women in Colonial Malaya* (Singapore: Institute of Southeast Asian Studies, 1986). See her account of the project in Lai Ah Eng, 'The Women I Met', in *The Makers and Keepers of Singapore History*, ed. Loh Kah Seng and Liew Kai Khiun (Singapore: Ethos, 2010), pp. 221–31.

[99] Mark Wong, Director of the Oral History Centre, National Archives of Singapore, discussion and correspondence, September–November 2019.

[100] See Hayashi Hirofumi's comments in *The Straits Times*, 19 August 1995.

Japanese military attempted to sexually enslave her. The smaller number of male testimonies are also first-hand accounts of what they witnessed. Oral history as a historical source is special because it connects the past as memory with the present, specifically the time when the interview is done. Nonetheless, like all forms of historical evidence, it can also be corroborated and validated to form conclusions about what happened in the past. What are these conclusions?

In conclusion, the role of Singapore women in the sex industry of the Japanese military in 1942 tends to suggest that there was not just one way of becoming entrapped in the military's procurement of women for sex. There were women who had been forcibly abducted and then enslaved, as there were women who were tricked and trafficked by local agents and procurers from their own community. The experiences of women in Singapore under the Japanese military's rule also confirm that there was a variety of experiences for women in the sex industry. There were the comfort stations at which women served long lines of ordinary Japanese soldiers. There were also the *ryotei* restaurants at which 'low-grade' geisha and Japanese women served the officers of the military and high-ranking civilian administrators. There were yet other restaurants cum brothels that employed many local women. The next chapter explores what it was like inside these places in Singapore for the women working in them.

3
Inside the Comfort Stations of Singapore

What was it like inside the comfort stations for the women who worked in them for the Japanese military? This chapter moves on from the establishment of the comfort stations in Singapore during 1942 and examines how they functioned and how the women coped with the working conditions from 1943 to 1945 when the comfort stations proliferated and flourished in Singapore. The chapter explores the testimonies, memories, and written records of individuals who entered the comfort stations in Singapore and had an intimate acquaintance with what it was like inside. These range from the comfort women themselves, the comfort station managers, Japanese male visitors, to Singapore male visitors who accompanied the Japanese they worked for in the military.

Tan Kek Tiam Remembers His Visit to the Cairnhill Road Comfort Station

Viewing the comfort stations from a distance did not seem to unnerve many local Singaporeans. But seeing what happened inside a comfort station could be an unsettling experience for the local people, as is evident in the memories of Tan Kek Tiam. His recollections were recorded in an oral history interview done in August 1993. Tan was working for the Japanese municipal government when his Japanese friend, who was a businessman in uniform, took him to the Cairnhill Road comfort station. When his Japanese friend discussed business matters upstairs, Tan was left to wait downstairs and observed the women 'all panting and sweating' in rows on mats on the floor, 'looking tired' and 'distressed'. He said, 'I don't think they liked that, the way they were treated.' They were 'all lying on the floor, soldiers coming and going', he recalled, adding, 'as a young man I felt sorry, too. How can they make these women lie in a row?' He recollected, 'I felt pity for them.'[1] He said that he saw no local women, only women from Korea, Japan, or Taiwan.

During the interview, Tan's voice began to quiver, and he sounded unnerved and upset from remembering what actually happened in the Cairnhill Road comfort station. He had no idea at that time that they were Korean women who may have been forcibly recruited by the Japanese military. Tan said that he tried to accept what he saw as prostitution that was part of Japanese military life. However, he sounded as if he had never been able to come to terms with what he saw inside the Cairnhill Road comfort station. He sometimes tried to affirm the masculinist stereotypes, but became aware that such words sounded hollow: 'When you travel with soldiers, you are bound to accept your profession, you know what is coming on. I didn't know they were forced.'[2] Given the sense of unease in his voice, it is unlikely that Tan would have previously talked about his experience at all. While most male Singaporeans remembering the Cairnhill Road comfort station had the luxury of seeing the operation of the comfort station from the outside, Tan experienced the shock of seeing it from the inside, even if only briefly, as his Japanese friend came downstairs after a few minutes and they left.

Memories of the Korean Women Working in the Comfort Stations of Singapore

The Korean comfort women's own memories of the Cairnhill Road comfort station and other comfort stations in Singapore were as bleak as that of Tan's, and corroborate much of what he saw inside the comfort station. Kim Sang-hi gave a vivid account in April 1993 to an International Commission of Jurists in Seoul investigating the human rights abuses of the comfort women. Kim had been kidnapped by Japanese soldiers at the age of 16 when she ignored her father's advice not to go out of the house in the Korean city of Taegu. After being repeatedly raped when she first arrived at a comfort station in China, she remembered: 'Thereafter, everyday from ten to thirty soldiers used to visit me and force sex upon me.' She tried to commit suicide by drinking poison. In the spring of 1943, she was sent with ten other women to the comfort stations in Singapore:

---

[1] Tan Kek Tiam, interviewed by Daniel Chew, 25 August 1993, accession number 001055, reel 4 (National Archives of Singapore).
[2] Tan Kek Tiam, 25 August 1993, reel 4.

I was in Singapore until the end of the war. There was no way to escape from any of these places. In each of these places we were required to service thirty to forty soldiers a day for each girl. In Singapore the comfort house was a wooden house and in other places we lived in brick houses. Towards the end of the war I developed cancer of the womb and my uterus had to be removed.[3]

Tan Kek Tiam's and Kim Sang-hi's testimonies on how dire conditions were at the comfort stations of Singapore are confirmed by the experiences of other Koreans who worked in them. Kim Bok-dong was the last surviving Korean comfort woman to have worked in Singapore when she died at the age of 92 on 28 January 2019. At the age of 14, her family was tricked into letting Kim leave with the Japanese authorities to ostensibly work in a factory. In fact she was sent to a comfort station in China. She recollected her life in Singapore in the final few months of the war but also at comfort stations in Guangdong, Hong Kong, Malaysia, and Indonesia. She described how bad the weekends in the comfort stations were for her: 'On Saturday, I would start from noon to 6pm. They stood in queues. If there is a delay the guy next in line starts banging the door.... Just one after the other. I did it so many times, I lost count. By 5pm I couldn't even get up. I couldn't walk properly. My entire lower body was in pain.' She elaborated: 'At the end of the day the medics would come to treat the areas of our bodies that needed it. They injected us with shots, and told us to take medicine.' Kim described the unrelenting nature of the experience: 'On Sundays, I had to have sex from 8am to 5pm. That was Sundays. That is how it went on.' She poignantly added that 'because we did what we were told we weren't beaten.'[4]

Other Korean comfort women, who also worked in Singapore, have described similar experiences to interviewers from the 2005–06 *Can You Hear Us?* oral history project. This South Korean project was the work of the Commission on Verification and Support for the Victims of Forced Mobilization under Japanese Colonialism in Korea. 'Doo', as the interviewer called her to protect her identity, could not recall the exact location of the comfort station she worked at, but said it was an 'enormous' single-storey 'Western-style house' in a rural area, far from the town. The Japanese called the comfort station 'Sinmazi'. She served the army, not the navy. Soldiers would walk in groups of five or six to the comfort station from presumably a nearby army barracks. The comfort women

---

[3] Ustinia Dolgopol and Snehal Paranjape, *Comfort Women: An Unfinished Ordeal: Report of a Mission* (Geneva: International Commission of Jurists, 1994), pp. 101–2.
[4] Kim Bok-dong gave her last interview on the YouTube channel *Asian Boss* in October 2018: https://www.youtube.com/watch?v=qsT97ax_Xb0.

had sex with soldiers in small cubicle-like rooms. There was not much room in the cubicle except for a bed, on which they also slept. Next to the bed they kept their belongings. The rooms were in two rows on both sides of a large corridor. Each room had a number on it. The soldiers would go to the desk manned by a comfort station operator, whom 'Doo' called her 'master', pay money, collect a ticket, then proceed to whichever woman they wanted. The 'master' kept track of how many soldiers each comfort women served. 'Doo' recalls never seeing any of the money.[5] 'Coo', another comfort woman working in Singapore interviewed for the *Can You Hear Us?* project in 2005, also recalled that almost every item—clothes, trips, food, make-up—were all added to the debt that she was supposed to pay off to her manager. 'Coo' said: 'I wasn't paid at all because I owed so much. He [her manager] said I have nothing to get minus my debt.... They say all our debts will be reduced.'[6]

In Korea, 'Doo' had been told that she would be doing laundry, cleaning, and nursing work for the Japanese military. When she was forced to provide sex for the soldiers in Singapore, 'Doo' resisted. 'I cried out in pain. I swore loudly, I cried demanding to be sent back to Korea. I refused to eat.' She recalls her 'master', who recruited her in Korea, scolding her, 'Haven't you come here to make money? Then why don't you take in the men?'[7]

Drug addiction occurred among the comfort women in Singapore as a way to ease the physical and mental strain that the women felt. 'Doo' recollects: 'I had to take in soldiers all day. But I couldn't take in more than three or four because I hated them and it was painful. They gave us some ointment. It gave me immediate relief.' 'Doo' describes her 'master' and the doctors, at her regular check-ups, giving the Korean comfort women 'shots' or injections when they caught diseases or felt unwell. However, there were Korean comfort women who would go elsewhere to get 'shots' because they had become addicted to what appears to have been opium. 'Doo' says:

> There were certain girls who would get shots outside. They stole other girls' clothes and sold them for money. They needed money to buy shots, that's why. If we asked them why they needed the shot, if because of diseases, they just say 'We've got no diseases.' So we watched and followed them secretly. They would go to the town center and enter into

---

[5] Ji-hyeon Yoon, ed., *Can You Hear Us? The Untold Narratives of Comfort Women: Oral Narrations of Japanese Military Comfort Women* (Seoul: In-hwan Park, Kindle Edition, 2014), pp. 161–3.
[6] Yoon, *Can You Hear Us?*, p. 150.
[7] Yoon, *Can You Hear Us?*, p. 165.

a certain house. It wasn't a hospital but a private house. They would get shots there. They would enter the house half dead but when they emerge from the house they were totally different from before, alive and ecstatic. They were happy and in rapture, beyond measure. The shot must make people experience heaven. They no longer minded serving men.[8]

'Coo' in her interview also referred to drug use at her comfort station, which was 'a concrete house' where the women slept on the floor. In 2005, she recalled: 'One of the girls committed suicide because they were sick and tired of servicing soldiers. They cremated her body. I heard she died of [a] drug overdose.'[9]

The Korean comfort women were required to make sure that soldiers wore condoms. They also cleaned themselves after sex with each soldier to prevent pregnancies and the spread of venereal disease. 'Coo', when asked about pregnancies, said: 'No, you couldn't get pregnant. I heard about an incident though. They say that the baby died. We could hardly get pregnant because we had to wash ourselves down with disinfectant right after intercourse…. We did that each and every time we served soldiers. We washed down there in the outdoor lavatory, not to get pregnant.'[10] A more effective method was insisting that the Japanese soldiers wear the condoms that were stored in a box in the cubicle, which was filled up every morning by the comfort station manager. 'Coo' describes how the soldiers did not need to bring condoms 'because we had a whole case of condoms in the room. Every one of them had to use it. Otherwise, they would be kicked out. Actually, I kicked one of them with my foot out of my room.'[11]

Oral history interviews with Korean comfort women who worked in Singapore indicate that while pregnancies were not common, they did occur. 'Doo' described what usually happened: 'Some customers would not wear condoms. So we were told to make sure every one put on a condom before the action. Even with such caution, some girls still got pregnant. They had to be brought to the hospital for an abortion.'[12] 'Doo', when asked whether any of the comfort women she worked with in Singapore got pregnant and had the baby, told a sad story about one comfort woman. She gave birth to a baby and 'because she had to earn money', she 'put the baby under the care of the woman who sold vegetables', paying her 'a certain amount each month. She used to go

---

[8] Yoon, *Can You Hear Us?*, p. 165.
[9] Yoon, *Can You Hear Us?*, p. 147.
[10] Yoon, *Can You Hear Us?*, p. 149.
[11] Yoon, *Can You Hear Us?*, p. 150.
[12] Yoon, *Can You Hear Us?*, p. 164.

see her child once or twice a day. However, the woman ran away with the child after Liberation.... So the girl had to leave without her child.'[13]

Escape from the comfort stations in Singapore proved impossible for most comfort women. Some tried when they learned that they were not employed for the jobs they had been told they were brought to Singapore to do, but instead were engaged in sex work. 'Coo', when asked whether she had to do sex work as soon as she arrived in Singapore from Korea, responded: 'I don't know. I ran away that's why. However, you could not run far enough. The master would hire men to catch the runaways. I ran away from the soldiers. I was scared of them when they came into the room. I was shocked and horrified at first. I begged them to take me back to Korea.'[14] She describes how the comfort station 'was crowded with soldiers in the daytime. They were waiting in line. I locked the door from the inside and did not go out. But I could not keep doing that.'[15] 'Coo' remembers the difficulties of settling into the life of a comfort woman in Singapore. While the ordinary soldiers would visit in the daytime, the officers would come at night and often stay the night. 'Coo' says: 'If I cry, the officers would comfort me, "Don't cry, don't cry. Okay, I won't do it." Sometimes high officials would call me at night. It was too shameful even mentioning it. I tried to kill myself a few times.... Anyway, when the soldiers came, they formed a line. And we had to service them all the way every day. It would be better for us to be dead. I got into fights with soldiers a lot.'[16]

Despite the difficult conditions, where the Korean comfort women in Singapore could exercise some degree of agency, they did. Yi Sunok in her testimony relates how the private manager of her comfort station controlled her daily life, but she also indicates that the comfort women when they had their opportunity acted rather than remained passive. Her account is part of the 1993 oral history collection compiled by the Korean Council for the Women Drafted for Military Sexual Slavery by Japan and the Research Association on the Women Drafted for Military Sexual Slavery by Japan. Yi's comfort station in Singapore was a large single-storey wooden building surrounded by a fence. There was another comfort station just beyond the fence. Yi believed that it had been 'purpose-built'. Her comfort station had about 30 cubicles with an electric fan hanging from the ceiling above every two cubicles. Yi came to Singapore from China with a group of Korean women working under a female proprietor

---

[13] Yoon, *Can You Hear Us?*, p. 166.
[14] Yoon, *Can You Hear Us?*, p. 147.
[15] Yoon, *Can You Hear Us?*, p. 147.
[16] Yoon, *Can You Hear Us?*, p. 147.

or manager, who was called *Obasan* ('auntie' or older woman). The *Obasan* was an obese Korean woman in her fifties from Cholla province who had lived in Japan for many years. When describing the *Obasan*, Yi remembered how the *Obasan* knew the Japanese military police who visited the comfort station well and even got them to beat comfort women who were a nuisance to her, such as those who drank too much. The *Obasan*, according to Yi, also 'kept a sword and pistol in her room, and later she would sometimes wear a military cap. If the women didn't listen to her commands, she beat them severely. I was beaten on my abdomen and bottom.'[17]

Obedience from the comfort women was important for the *Obasan* who tried to control their lives. 'We could overhear *Obasan* and the proprietors talking between themselves as they went in and out of the house. They would say "These girls are obedient", "girls in such and such a place wouldn't listen to us", and "it is easy to work with the girls from Kyongsang provinces".'[18] Yet, Yi tells how she and some of the other comfort women banded together to find a way to return to Korea and escape from the control of the *Obasan*. Yi asked for help from Fujiwara, a Korean carpenter and civilian employee of the Japanese working in Singapore, and one of her regular customers. Fujiwara was from Kwangju in Cholla province, and she appealed to him 'saying I wanted to go home even if I died in the process'.[19] Fujiwara agreed to help her.

Yi knew that comfort women who had left Singapore to go back to Korea had died when their ships had been sunk by Allied planes or submarines, which was becoming more frequent as Japan drifted towards defeat in the war. She said, 'Even so, I desperately wanted to go home.' Fujiwara, who had connections because of his job, took Yi and five of her friends, who also wanted to leave, to meet a senior officer. They secretly slipped out of the comfort station for a short while, telling the others that if *Obasan* asked, to tell her that they had gone for a walk in the nearby forest. The officer they met inquired how long they had been comfort women, and Yi replied that they had been working for six years. He told them that he was short of nurses for wounded patients on a Red Cross ship that would leave for Japan in a fortnight. To his question concerning whether the six women could do this type of work, Yi and her friends replied, yes. Later an army official was sent to the comfort station to tell *Obasan* to let them go. Yi said that *Obasan* 'didn't like it, and muttered and moaned. But

---

[17] Keith Howard, ed., *True Stories of Korean Comfort Women* (London: Cassell, 1995), p. 118.
[18] Howard, *True Stories of Korean Comfort Women*, p. 120.
[19] Howard, *True Stories of Korean Comfort Women*, p. 121.

new Korean women arrived to replace us before we left.'[20] When Yi left in the winter of 1944, she remembers that she was farewelled by 'one of her regulars', a Japanese soldier called Haname, whom she said 'had proposed to me before I left Singapore, but I turned him down because I wanted to get back to Korea.'[21] Yi recalled Haname had 'said he would buy me whatever I most wanted and took me by car into the city. I chose a handbag.'[22]

Diary of A Brothel Manager of Cairnhill Road Comfort Station

The testimony of the Korean comfort women of Singapore gives significant insights into their lives at the comfort stations outside the town area. However, based on their vague descriptions of where they worked, it is hard to be certain exactly where their comfort stations were located. The discovery of the diary of a Korean male comfort station manager, known simply as Park or Bak, a very common Korean surname, reveals what life was like for the Korean comfort women of Cairnhill Road. Park's diary offers a good opportunity to corroborate the oral history testimony of the Korean comfort women who worked in Singapore. The diary was published in 2013 as *Ilbongun Wianso Gwanliin-ui Ilgi* [Diary of a Japanese Military Brothel Manager].[23] This diary was discovered in 2012 by Korean historian Ahn Byung-jik, Professor Emeritus at Seoul National University. He found it at a local museum in Paju known as the Time Capsule Museum. The diary had been sold to a bookstore after Park's death and purchased by the owner of the museum soon after. Ahn translated the diary into Korean from the original admixture of writing in Korean and Japanese phonetic script and kanji.

The diary of the brothel manager of the Cairnhill Road comfort station was published as a Korean-language book that proved popular. Excerpts of the diary were transcribed into Japanese and English by Kyoto University Professor Hori Kazuo, Kobe University Professor Kimura Kan, and Haraguchi Yoshio, a former history teacher at a Japanese high school. Sections of the diary have

---

[20] Howard, *True Stories of Korean Comfort Women*, p. 121.
[21] Howard, *True Stories of Korean Comfort Women*, p. 121.
[22] Howard, *True Stories of Korean Comfort Women*, p. 121.
[23] Park [name deliberately obscured to protect identity], *Ilbongun Wianso Gwanliin-ui Ilgi* [Diary of a Japanese Military Brothel Manager], trans. Ahn Byung-jik (Seoul: Isup, 2013). There is a Japanese version by Hori Kazuo, of Kyoto University and Kimura Kan, of Kobe University, who also provided English-language excerpts: https://drive.google.com/file/d/1xUn-lWuIoWDMqgByTDeo61Cm4z5GMfLh/view.

also been translated and published in Japanese books on the comfort women because of its controversial content. The diary has since become well known and controversial because it is seen as challenging the oral history testimony of the surviving comfort women and their belief that they were sex slaves who were all forcibly recruited. A lot depends on how and by whom the diary is read. In South Korea, the diary has often been viewed as evidence that the comfort women were under the strict control of the Japanese military. In Japan, the diary is seen as evidence that the comfort women were paid prostitutes working in privately-run brothels.

Park was a comfort station manager at Number 88 Cairnhill Road, or the Kikusui Club as it is known in his diary, from February to December 1944 when he was in Singapore. He had previously been running comfort stations in Burma. Park returned to Korea after leaving Singapore in December 1944. He lived from 1905 to 1979 and came from the Korean city of Taegu. He became a comfort station manager because his brother-in-law was involved in recruiting comfort women in Korea. In 1942, both went to Burma to be managers of comfort stations. Park mentions that he and other managers with their comfort women in Burma and Singapore were part of the Fourth Comfort Corps, which left Busan on 10 July 1942 for Singapore, and then onto Burma.[24] The existence of the Fourth Comfort Corps has long been contested as its existence would prove that the Japanese military was involved in setting up the comfort women system. Park's diary corroborates other evidence concerning the historical reality of the Fourth Comfort Corps. The diary 'confirmed that the fourth comfort corps had existed', Ahn Byung-jik said in the Japanese *Jiji Press*, adding, 'It has also become certain that the Japanese government had organized comfort teams and took women to the frontline.'[25]

Because Park died before the comfort women became a controversial issue, his diary is said to be a very reliable source. According to Japanese historian and political scientist Kimura Kan, the diary is much more credible than oral history evidence because it could not have been influenced by the heated debates over the circumstances of the comfort women.[26] Park's diary was 'highly credible', Kimura told the *Jiji Press*, 'noting that there was little possibility of alterations because the man had died before the comfort women issue became a source of contention'.[27] The debates over the diary have concerned whether the comfort

---

[24] Park, *Ilbongun Wianso Gwanliin-ui Ilgi*, diary entry for 6 April 1944.
[25] *Jiji Press English News Service*, 12 August 2013.
[26] *Japan Times*, 13 August 2013.
[27] *Jiji Press English News Service*, 12 August 2013.

women were forcibly recruited or not, as well as whether they were sex slaves, or more like prostitutes. Another controversial issue is whether the Japanese military was involved in setting up the comfort stations and running them, or whether private operators did so.[28]

Park, while not part of the Japanese military, certainly worked closely with it, and used its vehicles and facilities. In Singapore, there was an association of comfort station managers. Comfort stations were known as 'clubs' and their managers elected an association president and vice-president, who were invariably Japanese or Korean men.[29] However, while the comfort stations or 'clubs' were managed by men who were not military officers, according to an entry in Park's diary, all the managers of the comfort stations in Singapore were given 'instructions from a lieutenant of the Defense Headquarters who was in charge of the clubs'.[30]

Park's diary also confirms that there were days when many soldiers called on the comfort women, with each one having to serve 30–50 soldiers in long lines. On Sunday, 26 March 1944, Park's Kikusui Club at Cairnhill Road took in what was a record for the club since it had opened—1,600 yen for one day.[31] On 29 April 1944, the Emperor's Birthday holiday, the club made even more money—2,450 yen.[32] Given that ordinary soldiers probably paid 1.5 yen for a ticket to have sex with a comfort woman, non-commissioned officers 3 yen, and officers 6 yen, this indicates that there were indeed long lines of soldiers outside the comfort station at Cairnhill Road. Elsewhere in the diary, Park indicates that he usually had around 16 comfort women at the clubs he managed.[33] These entries are an indication of the type of sexual slavery that the women endured in what must have seemed like a sex factory, serving so many soldiers so quickly. He himself became rich from managing the comfort stations, if the money he remitted back to Korea mentioned in the diary is any indication.

---

[28] For the heated nature of the debate provoked by the diary, see among others, Choe Kil-song, *Chosen shusshin no choba hito ga mita ianfu no shinjitsu — bunka jinrui gakusha ga yomitoku 'ian-sho nikki'* [The truth of the comfort women as seen by a manager from Korea: A cultural anthropologist interprets the 'comfort station diary'] (Tokyo: Hatoshuppan, 2017). This book is by a Korean cultural anthropologist who worked in Japan for a long time. Choe was professor emeritus in the social sciences at Hiroshima University. He was born in South Korea in 1940 and educated at Seoul National University, but later received his PhD from the University of Tsukuba, Japan.
[29] Park, *Ilbongun Wianso Gwanliin-ui Ilgi*, diary entry for 25 March 1944.
[30] Park, *Ilbongun Wianso Gwanliin-ui Ilgi*, diary entry for 19 September 1944.
[31] Park, *Ilbongun Wianso Gwanliin-ui Ilgi*, diary entry for 26 March 1944.
[32] Park, *Ilbongun Wianso Gwanliin-ui Ilgi*, diary entry for 29 April 1944.
[33] Park, *Ilbongun Wianso Gwanliin-ui Ilgi*, diary entry for 9 January 1943.

However, Park's diary suggests that the comfort women had more agency than previously thought from the oral history accounts of the comfort women. The most well-known example of agency is when 16 women from his comfort station called *Ichifuji-ro* at Insein, Rangoon, Burma, went to see a movie on their day off while Park stayed at the premises because of a toothache. However, the movie was shown at a Japanese military railroad unit, not a private cinema hall.[34] In the *Can You Hear Us?* oral history project, 'Goo', a Korean comfort woman, also recounts how she and other comfort women in an isolated Sumatran town went to the local cinema.[35] In another entry, Park described how two comfort women left a comfort station in Burma to marry and live with their partners, but later returned when ordered to do so by Army Logistics, which was in charge of the comfort women in Rangoon.[36]

The diary demonstrates that despite being in a difficult situation and the controls exercised over them, the comfort women sought to make choices over their own lives where they could do so. In Singapore, Park described how one of his comfort women who was pregnant went to hospital to have her baby on 5 September 1944. She took a leave of absence from work at the seventh month of her pregnancy.[37] He also describes comfort women of the Cairnhill Road Kikusui Club returning home. Park records that on 20 July 1944 when two comfort women at the Kikusui Club requested to return home, the owner, his friend Nishihara Kikujirou, allowed them to do so.[38] He gives an indication that some comfort women also seem to have saved considerably from their earnings. On 27 October 1944, at the Central Post Office, he remitted from the Singapore branch of the Yokohama Specie Bank 600 yen for one comfort woman of his Cairnhill Road Kikusui Club.[39]

However, Park's diary also reveals that there was little that he did not control in the lives of the comfort women. When the comfort women went out, Park usually accompanied them, and these events tended to be public rallies and celebrations of the Japanese Empire as well as more functional occasions, such as learning first aid.[40] It was Park who remitted their earnings to Korea and did the paperwork for their travel permits and employment transfers. He

---

[34] Park, *Ilbongun Wianso Gwanliin-ui Ilgi*, diary entry for 13 August 1943.
[35] Yoon, *Can You Hear Us?*, p. 241.
[36] Park, *Ilbongun Wianso Gwanliin-ui Ilgi*, diary entries for 29 July and 10 August 1943.
[37] Park, *Ilbongun Wianso Gwanliin-ui Ilgi*, diary entries for 4 July and 5 September 1944.
[38] Park, *Ilbongun Wianso Gwanliin-ui Ilgi*, diary entry for 9 and 20 July 1944.
[39] Park, *Ilbongun Wianso Gwanliin-ui Ilgi*, diary entry for 27 October 1944.
[40] Park, *Ilbongun Wianso Gwanliin-ui Ilgi*, diary entries for 19 February, 8 March, and 23 September 1944.

even did the grocery shopping for his club. The recruitment of Korean women for the comfort stations of Singapore is largely absent from the diary because the year of 1942 is missing in his diary. Recruitment in 1944 seemed to have been about replacing the comfort women who had left. He records on 15 April 1944 that his rival comfort station manager Nishihara Takeichi, of the Taiyo Club, went back to Seoul in April 1944 to recruit comfort women for some of the clubs in Singapore and that he would return with them in July.[41] Women seemed to have been both coming from Korea and returning, but all under the control of their managers. Later on, in his entry for 31 August 1944, Park mentions receiving a postcard from one of the comfort women in the Kyoei Club of Singapore who had returned to Korea, telling him she had arrived home safely.[42]

Park's diary is undoubtedly compelling evidence that comfort women may have had more agency than assumed. Yet, as a source, it is written from the perspective of their 'boss' or 'master', who was working with the Japanese military. Park, as a comfort station manager, made a large amount of money out of the business and so was unlikely to be critical of the industry that he had so much financial interest in and which had enriched him considerably. It is not a diary of a comfort woman, and he does not give voice to the comfort women that he managed. His perspective as their 'boss' would obviously be different from his employees' perspectives. Nonetheless, Park's diary has raised the controversial question of whether many of the comfort women were sex slaves or were paid prostitutes working on contracts. Mark Ramseyer and a chorus of right-wing nationalists have mistakenly taken the diary as evidence that the women were paid prostitutes who worked on contracts.[43] Yet there is no mention in the diary of any contracts, as the opponents to Ramseyer's perspective have correctly pointed out.[44]

What Park's diary of the Cairnhill Road comfort station of Singapore does suggest is that not only did the experiences of the comfort women vary but so did that of the managers. When the women sought to exercise what little choice they had in the comfort women system, much depended on their immediate situation in what were inherently exploitative conditions. The lives of the comfort women depended on what type of person their manager was and

---

[41] Park, *Ilbongun Wianso Gwanliin-ui Ilgi*, diary entry for 15 April 1944.
[42] Park, *Ilbongun Wianso Gwanliin-ui Ilgi*, diary entry for 31 August 1944.
[43] J. Mark Ramseyer, 'Contracting for Sex in the Pacific War', *International Review of Law and Economics* 65 (March 2021), 105971, doi:10.1016/j.irle.2020.105971.
[44] Concerned Scholars, 'Responses by Concerned Scholars to the Problematic Scholarship of J. Mark Ramseyer', https://sites.google.com/view/concernedhistorians/home?fbclid=.

how he ran the comfort station, all of which could vary. An Allied Translator and Interpreter Section (ATIS) report, dated 15 November 1945 and entitled 'Amenities in the Japanese Armed Forces', in its collection of captured documents on the comfort stations of the Philippines, contained a translated Japanese military report indicating that some of the poor conditions could be due to the greed of individual managers. This document was a Japanese military police assessment of the comfort stations of Manila, dated 7 February 1944:

> Many managers are interested in nothing beyond their own profit and do their job with no other purpose. They exhibit no concern for the welfare of the geisha, maids or hostesses, nor bother themselves with their health or sustenance nor with such matters as bath facilities. Their selfish conduct requires restraint.[45]

Park appears to have been one of the better comfort station managers amidst many who were very bad in what was an intrinsically abusive system of exploitation. While Park did give one of his comfort women time off to have a baby, it was more common for the managers to insist on abortions. Also, Park appears to have remitted at least some of the money that the comfort women were supposed to receive. He does not do it often though. Other managers pocketed their earnings. Perhaps, it is no surprise that he received postcards from the comfort women when they returned to Korea. Yet, it should not be forgotten that he was still the 'boss' and 'master' who controlled the lives of the comfort women at Cairnhill Road Kikusui Club under the inherently exploitative and slave-like comfort women system established by the Japanese military in Singapore.

Takashi Fujiwara alias Takashi Nagase's Visits to Singapore Comfort Stations

Oral history testimony about life in the comfort stations, even from the Japanese who were closely associated with them in Singapore, raises further questions about how much agency these women could have had in such difficult circumstances. Even for Japanese civilians, being inside a Singapore comfort station could leave disturbing memories. Takashi Fujiwara alias Takashi Nagase, a Japanese civilian interpreter at the Japanese military camp

---

[45] See 'Appendix B. — Police Report on Manila Brothels' of the Research Report No.120 Amenities in the Japanese Armed Forces, Allied Translator and Interpreter Section (ATIS), AWM 55, 12/92 (Australian War Memorial, Canberra). See also Dolgopol and Paranjape, *Comfort Women*, p. 50.

on Pulau Blakang Mati (Sentosa), in his June 1987 oral history interview, confirms the wretchedness of life inside the comfort stations of Singapore for the Korean women.

Nagase was attached to the Japanese Army's Aviation Troops fuel depot on Pulau Blakang Mati. Like Park's diary, his interview was conducted well before the comfort women became a controversial issue after 1991. The Pulau Blakang Mati comfort station was established in November 1942, when 12 to 13 Korean comfort women were moved there for the Japanese soldiers on the island. According to Hayashi Hirofumi, the location of the comfort station was in a building on the south side of what is now the Images of Singapore/ Madame Tussauds tourist attraction.[46]

Reports on the management of this comfort station seem starkly different from Park's account of his running of the Cairnhill Road one. Nagase recalled troubling memories of the condition of the Korean women at the comfort station and how 'they told me their stories in tears':

> Some of the girls told me, with tears running down their cheeks, that in Korea, at first they were asked to work in some restaurants for the Japanese in Singapore...and they were sent to the island of Singapore. However, on this island [Pulau Blakang Mati or Sentosa], they were forced to become prostitutes for the Japanese Army.[47]

In particular, Nagase remembered a military officer in charge of the unit that the comfort station on Pulau Blakang Mati was intended to serve: 'The head of the Japanese unit was Lieutenant Miki who was a very bad man. Before the girls were distributed to the other soldiers, he "tasted" one by one every night. I believe they were all virgins.'[48]

Nagase also recollected visiting the Cairnhill Road comfort station where he saw 'one girl keep one room and [at] the door, so many soldiers, about 10 were standing already'.[49] He described his impressions of what he saw inside in some detail: 'One of them must have from 30 to 50 soldiers in a day. I think their health [was] quite destroyed. I heard one soldier taking

---

[46] Hayashi Hirofumi, 'Shingaporu no Nihongun Ianjo' [Comfort Stations of the Japanese Army in Singapore], *Senso Sekinin Kenkyu* [Studies in War Responsibility] 4 (1994): 37.

[47] National Archives of Singapore, *The Japanese Occupation 1942–1945* (Singapore: Times Editions, 1996), p. 79; and Takashi Fujiwara alias Takashi Nagase, interviewed by Daniel Chew, 8 June 1987, accession number 000789, reel 2, p. 11 (National Archives of Singapore).

[48] National Archives of Singapore, *The Japanese Occupation 1942–1945*, p. 79.

[49] Takashi Fujiwara alias Takashi Nagase, 8 June 1987, reel 2, p. 13.

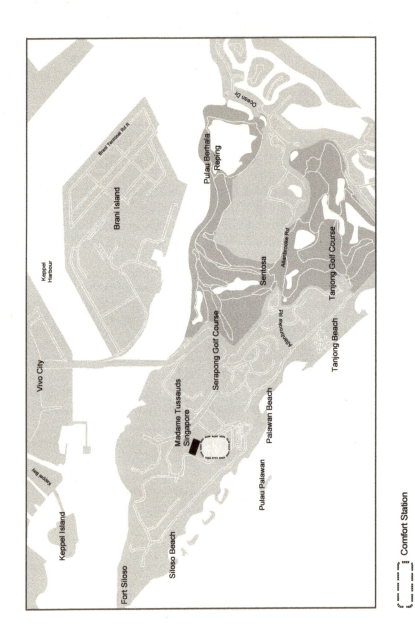

⌐ ¬ Comfort Station

Map 3.1 Pulau Blakang Mati (Sentosa) Comfort Station

only just a very short time, five minutes enough for them to do sex.'[50] Nagase commented that the burly soldiers queued up outside the terrace houses did not like Japanese civilians like himself being in the long queues, so he did not use the comfort stations. He therefore visited private prostitutes in Chinatown two to three times a month, costing $10 each time. With one Malayan dollar equivalent to one yen, Nagase's regular trips to local prostitutes cost a sum that was beyond what the wages of the ordinary soldiers could easily afford and which Nagase described as expensive for him too. The comfort stations of Singapore charged privates as little as one yen per visit and non-commissioned officers one-and-a-half yen.[51]

Even though Nagase was disturbed by the conditions of the Korean women in the comfort stations, he nonetheless rationalised forced prostitution using masculinist attitudes. Nagase mused: 'Anyhow excuse me, we were very, very young at that time and we didn't know [if we would] die tomorrow. So, all young soldiers were feeling death could come at anytime. So [we were] rather desperate. So we could do such things, I think. Without sex nothing [was] interesting.'[52] Nagase's memories of the Korean comfort women of Singapore confirm C. Sarah Soh's idea of the 'masculinist sexism' that went hand in hand with what she called 'Patriarchal Fascism' in the operation of the comfort station system. She uses the term 'masculinist to refer to those men and women who believe that men's sexual needs are biological and consequently concede to men their "natural right" to recreational sex with females'.[53] Soh's concept of 'Patriarchal Fascism' rested on the assumption that the state appropriated the bodies of these young women and offered them as 'imperial gifts' in order 'to reward the emperor's warriors with a regulated liberation from their battlefield duties, so that they may enjoy brief moments of rest and recuperation'.[54]

---

[50] Takashi Fujiwara alias Takashi Nagase, 8 June 1987, reel 2, p. 14.
[51] Miscellaneous records of the Southern Expeditionary Force (Tomi 8125 Butai) in Malaya and the Philippines, Allied Translator and Interpreter Section, ATIS, AWM 55 5/1 (Australian War Memorial, Canberra).
[52] Takashi Fujiwara alias Takashi Nagase, 8 June 1987, reel 2, p. 14.
[53] Chunghee Sarah Soh, 'Prostitutes versus Sex Slaves: The Politics of Representing the "Comfort Women"', in *Legacies of the Comfort Women of World War II*, ed. Margaret D. Stetz and Bonnie B.C. Oh (New York: M.E. Sharpe, 2001), p. 77.
[54] Soh, 'Prostitutes versus Sex Slaves', p. 74.

Many More Comfort Stations in Singapore?

The Nagase interview, the testimonies of the Korean comfort women, the oral history account by Tan Kek Tiam, and the diary of the military brothel manager at Cairnhill Road provide rare insights into what life was like inside the comfort stations of Singapore. However, for the Korean comfort women whose testimony was presented in this chapter, their comfort stations do not appear to be any of the ten that Hayashi Hirofumi has identified so far. This suggests that there are more, as Hayashi has commented when compiling his list. Further oral history testimony from Singapore witnesses gazing into a comfort station across the road from their own house, or looking out from their home behind a comfort station, suggests too that there were most likely many more than ten comfort stations in Singapore. But their testimony presents few insights into what happened inside them as the facilities were restricted to the Japanese military, or there were language difficulties between them and the comfort women. Nonetheless, it is worthwhile to briefly review some of these accounts to get a better sense of how local Singaporeans interacted with the sexually enslaved women and to assess its widespread scale.

Esme Woodford was aged 16 at the beginning of the Japanese Occupation and a schoolgirl at Katong Convent. In a December 2007 interview, she describes what she says was a comfort station across from her home on Onan Road that was staffed by Korean women. She says that there were no Chinese women, but she had no interaction with the comfort women as her father told his children 'to leave them alone'. Her father would regularly redirect lost Japanese soldiers who knocked on the door of the family home to the other side of the road.[55] Other residents in the area have also identified Onan Road in the Katong area as the site of a comfort station. Among these eyewitnesses was then Eurasian schoolboy Eric Charles Pemberton Paglar. In a September 2003 interview, Paglar said his father, a doctor, treated Japanese and Korean women from the Onan Road comfort station in his clinic nearby.[56] Thus, it is highly likely from corroborating these first-hand accounts that there was a comfort

---

[55] Esme Woodford, interviewed by Claire Yeo, 21 December 2007, accession number 003267, reel 1, pp. 14–5 (National Archives of Singapore).
[56] See Gay Wan Leong, interviewed by Tan Beng Luan, 16 March 1985, accession number 00535, reel 3, p. 34 (National Archives of Singapore); Gwee Peng Kwee, interviewed by Tan Beng Luan, 2 December 1981, accession number 00128, reel 9, p. 80 (National Archives of Singapore); and Eric Charles Pemberton Paglar, interviewed by Kelvin Kwek, 10 September 2003, accession number 002798, reel 4 (National Archives of Singapore).

station at Onan Road staffed by Korean women, although we cannot get any insights into what happened inside the comfort station.

Along Newton Road, where Japanese soldiers were billeted, there was another comfort station, according to Farleigh Arthur Charles Oehlers, a Eurasian doctor, who lived behind it on Lincoln Road. Oehlers in an April 1984 interview says that 'the house immediately behind ours, a very large house, two storey house, rambling old colonial house, had been converted into a comfort house by the Japanese. And they were filled with Korean girls. That was their recreation — Japanese soldiers.' Oehlers describes the limitations in interacting with the Korean women: 'And these Korean girls were, I mean, nice girls. I mean, they used to pop their heads out of the windows and have chats with us — my wife and myself. Not that we could understand them, but they could try and speak a little English to us.' He also recollects that in just one year of its operation, from 1942 to 1943, 'one girl had committed suicide by jumping from an upper floor window'.[57] Another oral history account by Indian businessman M.S. Varma from December 2003 also confirms the presence of a comfort station at Newton. Varma adds, 'We had in Singapore a lot of comfort houses.'[58]

Indeed there appear to be many first-hand accounts of numerous comfort stations, *ryotei*, and comfort women. However, interactions between Singaporeans and the sexually enslaved women proved difficult. Chew Chin Hin, who was a dental assistant at Tan Tock Seng Hospital, described in his interviews of April 2010 and February 2011, how 50 Korean comfort women came to the hospital to be treated for venereal diseases, mainly syphilis and gonorrhoea. They were housed in three wards of the Mandalay Road annex. Chew said that when they received dental treatment, he could 'hardly' communicate with them because of language difficulties. All he remembers is that these women were in their twenties and were sometimes visited by their 'Japanese boyfriends' on the hospital grounds outside the wards.[59] He had little communication with these comfort women, the comfort stations and *ryotei* being restricted areas. Local Singaporeans also remember having little to do with the Singapore Swimming Club and the Chinese Swimming Club on the

---

[57] Farleigh Arthur Charles Oehlers, interviewed by Low Lay Leng, 13 April 1984, accession number 000421, reel 3, p. 28 (National Archives of Singapore); and F.A.C. 'Jock' Oehlers, *That's How it Goes: Autobiography of a Singapore Eurasian* (Singapore: Select, 2008), p. 87.
[58] M.S. Varma, interviewed by Kelvin Kwek, 8 December 2003, accession number 002805, reel 24, p. 271 (National Archives of Singapore).
[59] Chew Chin Hin, interviewed by Mark Wong, 7 April 2010 and 15 February 2011, accession number 003499, reel 2 (National Archives of Singapore).

East Coast of Singapore after they were turned into *ryotei* for the officers.[60] Nonetheless, local Singaporeans remember many of these places in their oral history accounts of the Japanese Occupation.

While local Singaporeans observing the Japanese military's sex industry from the outside had limited interaction with the women of the comfort stations and the *ryotei*, their accounts complement testimony from inside them. Oral history accounts from inside the comfort stations of Singapore and the Park diary indicate that the comfort women were in a difficult situation, but if opportunities arose, and the women could exercise choice and agency, they did so. Park does not discuss this much in his diary, but he offers little to contradict the image of enslaved women serving long lines of Japanese soldiers in a sex factory-like system. His discussion of the record takings on certain days indicates that the poor conditions of the women having sex with 30–50 soldiers on busy days was not unusual. Also, from all the sources, including Park's diary, it appears that the Japanese military was ultimately in charge of the comfort women system even if various comfort stations in Singapore were operated by private managers. The discussion of what life was like inside the comfort stations of Singapore prompts a question to be explored in the next chapter: Where did most of these comfort women in Singapore come from?

---

[60] Kee Soon Bee, interviewed by Chong Ching Liang, 4 February 1998, accession number 001808, reel 4 (National Archives of Singapore).

Photo 1 Malaysian comfort women from Penang recovered on the Andaman Islands in 1945 (Source: Imperial War Museum).

Photo 2 Malaysian comfort women in 1945 on the Andaman Islands. The woman on the right is holding her child from her marriage before she was shipped to the Andaman Islands (Source: Imperial War Museum).

Photo 3 Jalan Jurong Kechil Comfort Station.

Photo 4 Terrace houses of the Cairnhill Road Comfort Station.

Photo 5 Kim Bok-dong (left), the last surviving Korean comfort woman of Singapore, with the comfort woman statue outside the Japanese Embassy in Seoul (Source: Getty Images. Photo taken by Woohae Cho).

Photo 6 Ho Kwai Min in 1940. She worked in the prewar Singapore sex industry and successfully resisted being forced into the comfort women system (Source: Feng Hui Bi and National Heritage Board, Singapore).

4
Korean and Indonesian Comfort Women in Singapore

The preceding chapter with its focus on the Korean comfort women at the Cairnhill Road as well as the Pulau Blakang Mati (Sentosa) comfort stations in Singapore leads to several salient questions. Were the comfort women of Singapore mostly Korean women? How significant was the presence of Korean comfort women compared to other nationalities at the comfort stations of Singapore? Were there particular nationalities of women that were also significant at the comfort stations of Singapore and how and why were they recruited? To answer these questions we need to look in greater detail at other comfort stations in Singapore apart from Cairnhill Road and Pulau Blakang Mati, where the comfort women appear to be predominantly Korean women.

Korean Comfort Women Come to Singapore

Cairnhill Road and Pulau Blakang Mati were not the only comfort stations in Singapore to have mostly Korean women. Japanese historians Shimizu Hiroshi and Hirakawa Hitoshi calculate that at the time of the Japanese surrender in August 1945, most of the 600 Korean women in Singapore were likely to have been comfort women.[1] Hata Ikuhiko, another Japanese historian, estimates that there were 500 Korean comfort women in Singapore at the time of Japan's surrender.[2] Both these estimates indicate that Korean women had a dominant presence at the comfort stations of Singapore. Chong Song-myong, in her testimony to the 1994 International Commission of Jurists, recalls that when she and other Korean comfort women were being moved by boat from Busan in Korea, about 200 out of the 400 women she estimates were on board

---
[1] Shimizu Hiroshi and Hirakawa Hitoshi, *Japan and Singapore in the World Economy: Japan's Economic Advance into Singapore* (London: Routledge, 1999), p. 140.
[2] Hata Ikuhiko, *Comfort Women and Sex in the Battle Zone*, trans. Jason Michael Jordan (Lantham, Maryland: Rowman & Littlefield, 2018), p. 110.

were dropped off in Singapore while the boat continued on its way to Burma, finishing its 40-day journey at Rangoon.[3]

Chong was describing a journey similar to that made by the infamous Fourth Comfort Corps, which left Busan on 10 July 1942 for Singapore, then went on to Burma, arriving at Rangoon on 20 August 1942. The convoy carried exactly 703 Korean comfort women and 90 operators of comfort stations and their family members, who were mainly Japanese.[4] The ships stopped at Taiwan and picked up 22 Taiwanese comfort women. They then stopped at Singapore. Upon reaching Burma, the comfort women were divided into groups of 20–30 for various comfort stations. Park, the manager of Cairnhill Road comfort station, was part of the Fourth Comfort Corps, which he writes about in his diary. He mentions that when he left Burma in early 1944 to go to Singapore, he met up again with another comfort station operator who was also in the convoy of the Fourth Comfort Corps. On 6 April 1944, Park happily writes in his diary after being in Singapore since February 1944: 'I found Mr. Tsumura working there.... He came here as the head of the Fourth Comfort Corps which left Busan two years ago.'[5]

Busan was a major port of departure where thousands of Korean comfort women were massed by their recruiters for their voyages to Southeast Asia and other parts of the Japanese Empire. This process is colourfully depicted by Pak Ok-nyon in the collection of interviews done from 1992 to 1996 that were later published in *Comfort Women Speak*. She recounts how her recruiter, promising her that she would work as a nurse in a military hospital, 'brought me a custom-made nurse's uniform, a pair of shoes, and a handbag and instructed me to come the following day to the Seoul Railway Station dressed in the new uniform.' Pak remembers: 'I went to the station with 50 other young girls who were also recruited from my community. At the station I was surprised to see

---

[3] Ustinia Dolgopol and Snehal Paranjape, *Comfort Women: An Unfinished Ordeal: Report of a Mission* (Geneva: International Commission of Jurists, 1994), p. 104.

[4] See 'Section II Amusements' of the Research Report No. 120 Amenities in the Japanese Armed Forces, Allied Translator and Interpreter Section (ATIS), AWM 55, 12/92 (Australian War Memorial, Canberra). See also Dolgopol and Paranjape, *Comfort Women: An Unfinished Ordeal: Report of a Mission*, p. 39.

[5] Park, *Ilbongun Wianso Gwanliin-ui Ilgi* [Diary of a Japanese Military Brothel Manager] trans. Ahn Byung-jik (Seoul: Isup, 2013). There is a Japanese version by Hori Kazuo, of Kyoto University and Kimura Kan, of Kobe University, who also provided English-language excerpts: https://drive.google.com/file/d/1xUn-lWuIoWDMqgByTDeo61Cm4z5GMfLh/view.

about ten thousand girls identically dressed like us.'⁶ Pak and the other girls (obviously numerous but not in the tens of thousands) were taken by train to Busan, put on a ship that stopped at Shimonoseki in Japan, then went to the front at the island of Rabaul, New Guinea. There the girls went to work in comfort stations. The promise of being a nurse seems quite a common means for recruiting comfort women. In the collection *Comfort Women Speak*, Yi Yong-ngo recollects that a career as a nurse in the military was also the promise made to entice her to join up.⁷

There are remarkable similarities between the various large groups of Korean comfort women who were recruited and shipped out of Busan to Japan's newly conquered territories in Southeast Asia and the South Pacific. Chong Songmyong's trip with hundreds of women to Singapore and then Burma sounds like that of the Fourth Comfort Corps. How the women were recruited for the Fourth Comfort Corps is representative of how other batches of Korean women were recruited and sent to serve the military in Japan's new far-flung empire. The process is revealed in a well-known Allied report on the Fourth Comfort Corps, which was first discovered in the National Archives and Records Administration of the United States by the Japanese Kyodo News Service in 1992. The report is usually referred to as 'APO 689 Prisoner of War Interrogation Report No. 49'. Dated 1 October 1944, it summarised the information gained from the Allied Japanese-language translators' interrogations of 20 Korean comfort women captured in Burma. This document on the Fourth Comfort Corps suggests that many of the Korean women who were sent south to serve the Japanese military were tricked into becoming comfort women:

> Early in May of 1942 Japanese agents arrived in Korea for the purpose of enlisting Korean girls for 'comfort service' in newly conquered Japanese territories in Southeast Asia.
>
> The nature of this 'service' was not specified but it was assumed to be work connected with visiting the wounded in hospitals, rolling bandages, and generally making the soldiers happy. The inducement used by these agents was plenty of money, an opportunity to pay off the family debts, easy work, and the prospect of a new life in a new land — Singapore. On the basis of these false representations many girls enlisted for overseas duty and were rewarded with an advance of a few hundred

---

⁶ Sangmie Choi Schellstede, ed., *Comfort Women Speak: Testimony by Sex Slaves of the Japanese Military* (New York: Holmes & Meier Publishers, 2000), pp. 81–2.
⁷ Schellstede, *Comfort Women Speak*, p. 96.

yen. The majority of the girls were ignorant and uneducated, although a few had been connected with 'oldest profession on earth' before.[8]

Japanese historian Yoshimi Yoshiaki in his classic account of the comfort women from 1995, *Jugun Ianfu*, discusses the Fourth Comfort Corps, arguing that these Korean comfort women who left Busan in July 1942 were rounded up at the 'suggestion' of the Japanese Army of Korea, but adds that most likely this occurred at the 'request' of the Southern Army.[9] Yoshimi documents that at this time in mid-1942, the Southern Army was also making requests to Nanking and Taiwan for comfort women to be sent to its theatre of the conflict—Southeast Asia. He notes that the Japanese armies occupying China and Taiwan acceded to these requests and sent comfort women and operators of comfort stations for the Southern Army. However, the numbers were not large compared to the numbers of comfort women from Korea. Even these women were mainly Korean women already stationed in China and Taiwan. Yoshimi says that once they arrived in Singapore, they were sent to the comfort stations of the island.[10]

After the initial large numbers of comfort women sent from Korea to the south in the early period of the war, smaller numbers were brought by individual operators. The testimonies of Korean comfort women who came later to Singapore suggests this trend. These women describe how they were part of smaller groups of comfort women following individual recruiters and operators to Singapore to work at these operators' comfort stations. This is evidenced by the experience of 'Coo' from the *Can You Hear Us?* oral history project of 2005–06. 'Coo' tells how at 18 years of age, after fleeing an arranged marriage and while sheltering at a Buddhist temple in Taegu, she was enticed by a man from Busan who promised her a chance to make money at Shimonoseki in Japan. Upon arriving at Shimonoseki, he handed her and four of her friends over to a Japanese man who said that he would find jobs for them at a factory. From Shimonoseki, she went with the Japanese man by train to Yamaguchi, where there were already 20 mostly Korean women, many crying as they were far from Korea. The Japanese man then travelled with 'Coo' and the

---

[8] United States Office of War Information, Psychological Warfare Team, Attached to U.S. Army Forces, India-Burma Theater APO 689 Prisoner of War Interrogation Report No. 49, in Dolgopol and Paranjape, *Comfort Women: An Unfinished Ordeal: Report of a Mission*, pp. 44–5.
[9] Yoshimi Yoshiaki, *Comfort Women: Sexual Slavery in the Japanese Military during World War II*, trans. Suzanne O'Brien (New York: Columbia University Press, 2000), originally published in 1995 in Japanese as *Jugun Ianfu*, p. 81.
[10] Yoshimi, *Comfort Women*, p. 82.

other women by ship, stopping over in Manchuria then sailing to Singapore. According to 'Coo', the women 'were absolutely clueless about their future'. She called the man 'master', and grew more and more in debt to him as they travelled to Singapore: 'He would give me money if I told him that I needed to buy something. Of course I had to pay every penny back. He's the one who made all the money.'[11] When 'Coo' and the other girls arrived in Singapore, 'we saw it was not a factory' and they were expected to provide sex for soldiers in a comfort station run by the Japanese man who had travelled with them.

'Doo', interviewed in the same oral history project as 'Coo', tells a similar story of deception when coming to Singapore. At 19 years of age, she was also fleeing a failed arranged marriage, working in factories and restaurants when she responded to an advertisement in the paper promising well-paid jobs. She turned up at an employment office in Seoul and was told that overseas 'jobs are waiting for me, that lots of girls are going there too. So I went, in hope that I will make money.'[12] 'Doo' was deceived into thinking she was going to do nursing, laundry, and cleaning for the Japanese military. She went to Busan and stayed there for a month, being fed and housed by the employment office. While in Busan she was told that she was going to Singapore. She boarded a military ship to Singapore with ten others and someone from the employment office. 'Doo' remembers that the comfort station operator, or her 'master', did not get on the ship until it stopped in Taiwan. She was on a warship with lots of soldiers and about 20 other girls. Only when 'Doo' arrived in Singapore did she learn that she had been brought to provide sex for the Japanese military: 'I pressed them for an answer; Why do you force us to serve soldiers sexually? Haven't you brought us here for the cleaning job? They couldn't care less about my crying.'[13]

Later on in the war, it was also common for comfort station managers to move their Korean comfort women to Singapore from their existing comfort stations in the Japanese Empire, such as from China. Once in Singapore, they simply established a new comfort station or re-staffed an existing one. Yi Sunok recollects that after being at the same comfort station in China for three years, 'Suddenly, one night *Obasan* [auntie, the name for their proprietor] distributed cotton sacks and told us to pack our things. Some girls remained, but some

---

[11] Ji-hyeon Yoon, ed., *Can You Hear Us? The Untold Narratives of Comfort Women: Oral Narrations of Japanese Military Comfort Women* (Seoul: In-hwan Park, Kindle Edition, 2014), p. 144.
[12] Yoon, *Can You Hear Us?*, p. 158.
[13] Yoon, *Can You Hear Us?*, p. 161.

volunteered in the hope of seeing Singapore. We heard new girls would be sent to replace us. I kept quiet, saying nothing, but the proprietor told me to go.'[14]

The large number of Korean women disembarking at Singapore in the early years of the war, according to Chong Song-myong's testimony, certainly indicates that they were distributed to a number of comfort stations rather than just confined at Cairnhill Road and Pulau Blakang Mati. Korean women were also present in large numbers at the Seletar (Sembawang) naval base comfort station.[15] Sources indicate that there were likely many comfort women working there because demand for their services could be very high at times when large warships docked at the naval base. Zhou Xuji, a local port worker at the time, writes that the local people living at West Hill Estate village near the Seletar (Sembawang) naval base at the thirteen-and-a-half mile point of Seletar Road (now Sembawang Road) were forced out of their homes and the comfort station created behind barbed wire.[16] Vasu Krishnan, an Indian clerical port worker at the base, describes the day that he saw the Japanese navy bring in 'all very pretty girls from Japan' to the 'big British bungalows outside the shipyard' in order to staff this comfort station.[17]

Kazuo Takahashi, a Japanese naval port official in Singapore, writes in his memoirs of the day in December 1943 when he was ordered to the Seletar (Sembawang) naval base to help the military doctor with 50 comfort women who had just come off a ship from Japan. They were assembled at the old British theatre of the naval base at Gibraltar Crescent. Takahashi recounts how he went through a list of 350 people from the newly docked ship to single out the 50 comfort women who would be stationed in Singapore. He noted that although they all had Japanese names, at least 20 out of the 50 women were Koreans with the others being Japanese. After the roll call was finished, the 50 were taken by car to their medical examination by the chief military

---

[14] Keith Howard, ed., *True Stories of Korean Comfort Women* (London: Cassell, 1995), p. 119.
[15] Hayashi Hirofumi, 'Shingaporu no Nihongun Ianjo' [Comfort Stations of the Japanese Army in Singapore], *Senso Sekinin Kenkyu* [Studies in War Responsibility] 4 (1994): 38.
[16] See the recollections of port worker Zhou Xuji, 'Xinjiapo Jungang Gongren Diyu Shenghuo Huiyilu' [The Hellish Life of Singapore Military Port Workers: A Memoir], in *Malayan Chinese Resistance to Japan 1937–1945—Selected Source Materials*, ed. Shu Yun-Ts'iao and Chua Ser-Koon, comp. Chuang Hui-Tsuan (Singapore: Cultural and Historical Publishing House, 1984), pp. 485–6. Cited in Hayashi, 'Shingaporu no Nihongun Ianjo', p. 39 and footnote 19 on p. 43.
[17] Vasu Krishnan, interviewed by Jesley Chua Chee Huan, 25 March 2011, accession number 003533, reel 5 (National Archives of Singapore).

doctor.[18] Keiji Oshiga, a Japanese naval employee, writes in his memoirs about getting on a truck to visit the comfort station where these women worked, which he says was located at the South Gate of the Seletar (Sembawang) naval base. Oshiga describes how the comfort women were dressed in the Japanese yukata, or bathrobe.[19]

These comfort women at the Seletar (Sembawang) naval base comfort station could serve on some days up to half the complement of a 1,500-manned warship. Only half the complement of a ship would go ashore as the rest would engage in ship maintenance so the ship could get under way faster. Warships would come in on a monthly basis for regular re-provisioning. Sailors coming off visiting warships would be given a landing allowance, condoms, and a discount coupon for a comfort station ticket. Sailors could not go onshore without these items, wrote Sato Ryuichi, a machinist on a naval cruiser, in January 1944. Sato reported long lines at the comfort station on the base. The sailors would leave their ship at eight in the morning and were expected to be back by five in the afternoon as their ship was re-provisioned. Regularly, four ships would be at the naval base with subsequent demands on the Korean and Japanese comfort women, as well as local Singapore Chinese women who worked with them at this comfort station.[20]

While the Korean women worked alongside Japanese women in the comfort stations, relations with the Japanese comfort women were often antagonistic. 'Coo' in her interview with the *Can You Hear Us?* oral history project describes the poor relations between the Korean and Japanese women in the sex industry of the Japanese military in Singapore. When asked if there were Japanese comfort women working with her, 'Coo' replied:

> Yes, Japanese girls too. I got into a fight with Japanese girls frequently. A certain girl from Kyushu, Japan, called me, 'Josenjing' (a derogatory word used to describe Koreans). So I beat her and shouted, 'You people robbed us of our country. Did we ever do that to your people?' She said that she will report me to the Military Police. When she did that she said she was beaten by a Josenjing. A Military Police [man] who was on guard duty came running at me, calling 'Bakayaro (you idiot).' Not

---

[18] Kazuo Takahashi's memoirs in the entry for Seletar at the website of the Women's Active Museum on War and Peace (WAM): https://wam-peace.org/ianjo/area/area-sg/.
[19] Keiji Oshiga's memoirs in the entry for Seletar at the website of the Women's Active Museum on War and Peace (WAM): https://wam-peace.org/ianjo/area/area-sg/.
[20] Hayashi, 'Shingaporu no Nihongun Ianjo', pp. 37–8.

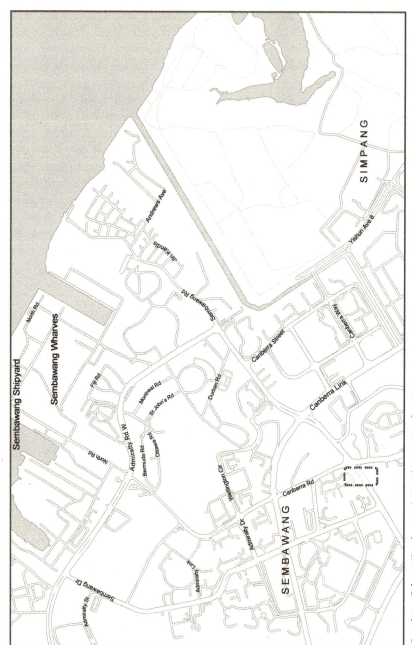

Map 4.1 Seletar (Sembawang) Naval Base Comfort Station

all Japanese women were bad. Some were gentle and nice. They were compassionate to other girls because we were all in the same boat.[21]

'Coo' tells how 'there many Japanese girls' in Singapore comfort stations, but their numbers were 'less than Koreans'. Also, among the comfort women working in Singapore, according to 'Coo', 'there were more older ones among the Japanese girls. The Korean girls were all young. They would send away those older girls later.'[22] The description given by 'Coo' of the Korean and Japanese comfort women tends to fit the general trend elsewhere. The Japanese comfort women were older as they tended to have had experience in prostitution before, whereas the Korean comfort women were younger as they tended to not have come from such a background.[23]

One activity in which the Korean and Japanese comfort women were forced to collaborate was putting on dancing shows when they had to go to officers' parties. 'Coo' described these parties at a theatre in Singapore:

> The Officers would drink and have fun. We danced in front of them. I and one of the other Korean girls were taught how to dance. Japanese girls danced too. We put on heavy makeup and danced in Kimonos on stage. The men would rush out to the floor shouting, 'Odore, Odorena (Dance. Let's dance).'[24]

Most of the time at the comfort station, instead of kimonos, 'Coo' said she just wore 'flower–embroidered short sleeves' and 'Mobe (work-pants or heavily-lined winter pants worn by women in rural areas)' or 'shong (slacks)'.[25] 'Coo' narrates how for the special Japanese dancing event at which she wore a kimono, an older Japanese woman managing the comfort station taught her how to dance and play the traditional Japanese stringed musical instrument, the samisen. When asked why she and one other Korean were chosen for this traditional Japanese dance, she replied: 'They chose the younger ones to teach. I think they chose us because there were not enough dancers.... We just went where we were told to.... I was tall and pretty then.'[26] 'Domijang' was the Japanese name given to her for the event. For 'Coo' and other Korean comfort

---

[21] Yoon, *Can You Hear Us?*, pp. 147–8.
[22] Yoon, *Can You Hear Us?*, p. 149.
[23] See, for example, among many other authors who make this point George Hicks, *The Comfort Women Sex Slaves of the Japanese Imperial Forces* (Sydney: Allen & Unwin, 1995), pp. 38–9.
[24] Yoon, *Can You Hear Us?*, p. 149.
[25] Yoon, *Can You Hear Us?*, p. 166.
[26] Yoon, *Can You Hear Us?*, p. 149.

women, it was very noticeable that there were many Koreans in Singapore engaged in the Japanese military's sex industry. 'Doo' remembers: 'There were a lot of Korean women in Singapore. They asked me, "How did you happen to come here?"'[27]

Korean Comfort Women and the Tanjong Katong Road Comfort Station

The considerable number of Korean comfort women in Singapore, noticed by 'Doo' and other Korean comfort women, was reflected in the large size of some of the comfort stations that were staffed by these women. According to a June 1983 interview with Robert Chong, a businessman who was a teenager during the Japanese Occupation, perhaps the largest comfort station that had mainly Korean women was a long row of shophouses along Tanjong Katong Road, between the junctions of Branksome Road and Wareham Road.[28] Othman Wok, a former cabinet minister in the Singapore government, in an interview with the Singapore press in August 1993, recollected that the comfort station did not extend as far back as what Chong remembers, and that the shophouses along Tanjong Katong Road between Wilkinson and Goodman roads were surrounded by 'wooden walls so no one could look inside'.[29] Lee Kuan Yew in his 1998 memoirs also remarked upon the size of the comfort station at Tanjong Katong Road, comparing it to Cairnhill Road:

> It [Cairnhill Road] was an amazing sight, one or two hundred men queuing up, waiting their turn. I did not see any women that day. But there was a notice board with Chinese characters on it, which neighbours said referred to a 'comfort house'. Such comfort houses had been set up in China. Now they had come to Singapore. There were at least four others. I remember cycling past a big one in Tanjong Katong Road, where a wooden fence had been put up enclosing some 20 to 30 houses.[30]

Memories of the Tanjong Katong Road comfort station reveal that it was indeed substantial.

---

[27] Yoon, *Can You Hear Us?*, p. 146.
[28] Robert Chong, interviewed by Tan Beng Luan, 11 June 1983, accession number 000273, reel 9, p. 104 (National Archives of Singapore).
[29] *The Straits Times*, 30 August 1993.
[30] Lee Kuan Yew, *The Singapore Story: Memoirs of Lee Kuan Yew* (Singapore: Singapore Press Holdings, 1998), pp. 58–9.

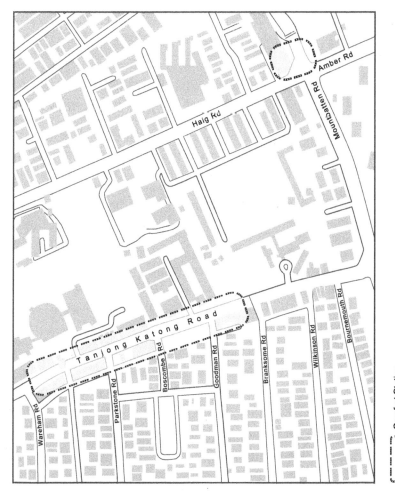

Map 4.2 Tanjong Katong Road and Katong Comfort Stations

The Katong area seems to have had a number of comfort stations and *ryotei* of all descriptions, not just the 'high-class' Chikamatsu, which was along the then shoreline near Amber Road. Lee Kip Lin, an architect who was a teenager at the time, recalled in his June 1984 interview another comfort station at a compound house on the corner of Mountbatten Road and Haig Road, where the 1970s Katong Shopping Centre was located when he gave his interview. This comfort station, Lee said, had only Indonesian women.[31] Robert Chong suggests that there may have been yet another comfort station in the area just down the beach at Tanjong Rhu.[32]

It was perhaps no surprise that the Japanese military chose the Katong area to situate some of its comfort stations and *ryotei* that provided sexual services. The area before the war had been the location of several illegal brothels that served the wealthy Chinese businessmen who lived in their weekend bungalows by the sea. Also, before the war, the Japanese business community of Singapore already had a *ryotei* in Katong with its own 'low-grade' geisha. This establishment was known as Tamagawa and employed many young geisha from Nagasaki. The other prewar *ryotei*, known as Shin Kiraku, was in the old red-light district around Hylam Street, which had been infamous as a place for Japanese prostitutes, or *karayuki-san*. After the official criminalization of prostitution by the British colonial authorities in 1930, these Japanese prostitutes continued their trade as 'hostesses' in these *ryotei*, providing sex for the customers. Once the war broke out, many of these women were detained by the British and interned in India along with the rest of the Singapore-based Japanese community.[33]

During the Japanese Occupation, the military took over additional buildings to set up their own brothels in order to add to these existing establishments. This did not go unnoticed by residents living in Katong. Gay Wan Leong, a student, in his interview of March 1985, remembered the geisha house and *ryotei* that the Japanese military set up on the corner of Joo Chiat Road and East Coast Road, opposite his aunt's home. He also recalled the brothels 'in front of my auntie's house at Onan Road, along Joo Chiat Road from East Coast Road corner, Joo Chiat Road right up to Fowlie Road. The whole area was [a] red-light area and there was a bicycle shop, a big bicycle shop in Joo

---

[31] Lee Kip Lin, interviewed by Low Lay Leng, 4 June 1984, accession number 000016, reel 8, p. 97 (National Archives of Singapore).

[32] Robert Chong, 11 June 1983, reel 9, p. 104.

[33] Shimizu and Hirakawa, *Japan and Singapore in the World Economy*, p. 139.

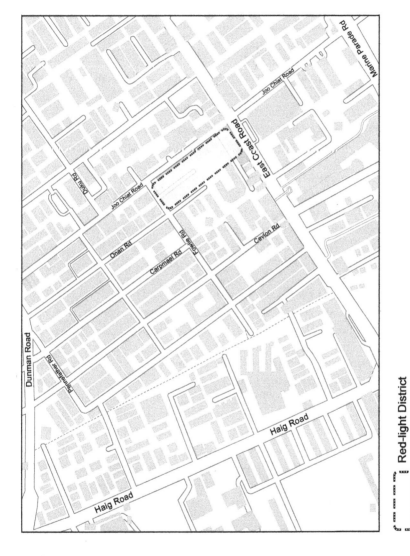

Map 4.3 Joo Chiat Road Japanese Red-Light District

Chiat Road—that was a geisha tea house.'[34] He recollected that both Japanese and local prostitutes worked in the red-light district, but only Japanese military officers and soldiers were allowed into the area, which was controlled by the issuing of passes. Gay said that the red-light districts had been set up to serve the soldiers and officers of the large Japanese military camps in the area because of the Kallang airfield's strategic importance.

The Tanjong Katong Road comfort station's size, and it being less secluded from the public than some of the other comfort stations, have meant that there has been a greater awareness of the presence of Korean women. Nonetheless these memories were still influenced by masculinist assumptions, which gloss over the bleak conditions for the women at the comfort station. Robert Chong recalls in his June 1983 interview that the Tanjong Katong Road comfort station was in his neighbourhood, near where large numbers of Japanese soldiers were stationed in their *butai*, or military units. He said, 'Comfort house for them is a very common thing among the rank-and-file and even the officers too. The way that they go to them it's not a sort of vice. To them it's a sort of relaxation or entertainment—their comfort house.' He mistakenly believed that the Tanjong Katong Road comfort station was little more than an ordinary brothel run by the women themselves, rather than a place of sexual enslavement. Interestingly, Chong could distinguish between Japanese and Korean women: 'And the comfort house is run by…Japanese women, but I believe they are mostly Korean women.'[35] His oral history interview took place in 1983—well before December 1991, when the comfort women became an international controversy—and made many who lived through the Japanese Occupation, such as Lee Kuan Yew, aware that most of the women they saw in the comfort stations were Koreans, not Japanese.

Chong's testimony on the Tanjong Katong Road comfort station brings out the soulless and mechanical nature of the comfort station, as well as the organised and systematic enslavement of the comfort women. When he was asked whether there was anything about the comfort station that resembled the trappings and decorations of ordinary brothels, Chong expressed his surprise at how stark and plain the comfort station was:

> They have no decorations, nothing. No signboards, everything. I mean no music, nothing. Just quiet. Only see the Japanese women up and down that's all, walking up and down. Not on the road. That means

---

[34] Gay Wan Leong, interviewed by Tan Beng Luan, 16 March 1985, accession number 00535, reel 3, p. 34 (National Archives of Singapore).
[35] Robert Chong, 11 June 1983, reel 9, p. 103.

they're walking, from upstairs they go downstairs, upstairs…. But all dressed in white. No make-up, nothing.[36]

Chong was also astonished by the plainness of the comfort women's white 'nurse's uniform' when compared to the figure-hugging cheongsams worn by the women in Singapore's prewar brothels. When asked if the women even wore a kimono, he responded:

> No kimono. Just ordinary…. Something like a nurse's uniform. That's all. They have no make-up, nothing. Simple, plain. A plain Miss. And the Japanese behave very well. They just take their turn, they just sit outside. They got to get a ticket.[37]

The long queue of Japanese soldiers was also astonishing to Chong, as were the changes to the shophouses creating long corridors for waiting soldiers. The Japanese altered the shophouses along Tanjong Katong Road so that the same procedures that were practised at comfort stations in China and other places were also followed at Singapore comfort stations:

> They have a corridor—a row of shophouses. Upstairs. Upstairs they have a corridor…. The shophouses, they have the downstairs and upstairs. Upstairs, they go upstairs. They get the coupons, the tickets, and they queue up for their next interview. More or less waiting their turn to see a doctor. They will sit quietly. Doesn't seem happy. I don't know what they're thinking of. Just waiting next for their turn and off they go. And next one coming. That's all. I don't see they feel comfortable. Nothing in it.[38]

The re-arranging of the interiors of the shophouses by the comfort station managers to accommodate the long lines of Japanese soldiers waiting to enter the cubicles of the comfort women was remarked upon by some of the owners of the shophouses. These owners often expressed their bewilderment when returning to their homes and noticing that the comfort station operators had knocked down sections of walls so as to create long corridors for the lines of soldiers. They also created rows of cubicles with futons for the comfort women to have sex with the soldiers, as well as to live, keep their few belongings, and sleep.[39]

---

[36] Robert Chong, 11 June 1983, reel 9, p. 104.
[37] Robert Chong, 11 June 1983, reel 9, p. 104.
[38] Robert Chong, 11 June 1983, reel 9, p. 105.
[39] Cheong Pak Yean, interviewed by Kevin Blackburn, 25 January 2019. Cheong was the owner of one of the shophouses at Jalan Jurong Kechil that were turned into a comfort station during the Japanese Occupation.

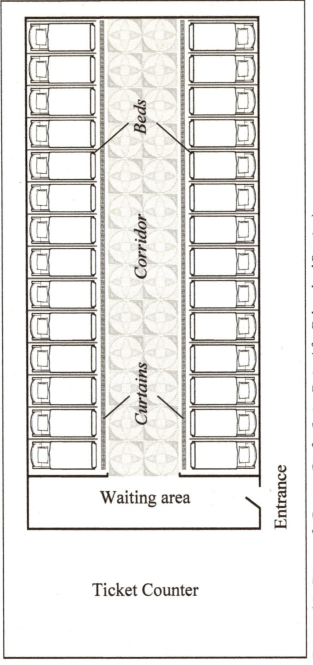

Diagram 4.1 Diagram of a Common Comfort Station Design (after Dolgopol and Paranjape)

The comfort station that Chong describes at Tanjong Katong Road, with its cubicles and long lines of Japanese soldiers waiting outside, undoubtedly had implications for the health of the women, as Takashi Fujiwara alias Takashi Nagase commented on about the women at Cairnhill Road and Pulau Blakang Mati in Chapter Three. The comfort women were given regular health screenings, but these tests were only for venereal diseases and not for their overall health. Mitsuyoshi Nakayama, a Japanese doctor who examined comfort women in Manchuria, in an interview with the Japanese newspaper *Asahi Shimbun* in August 1992, described the procedure that doctors went through with the comfort women: 'Surgeons only checked the women for visible symptoms caused by diseases such as gonorrhoea and syphilis. Some women possibly had internal diseases such as endometritis (an inflammation of the membrane lining the uterus) or clogged oviducts. We did not examine the women for these diseases. I think many of them have become unable to bear children.'[40] Another Japanese doctor who spoke to *Asahi Shimbun* on this topic, was Ken Yuasa. He examined comfort women in Anhui province in China and also noted damage to the uterus of the comfort women. Yuasa argued that 'through weekly medical check-ups, military surgeons came to realize how badly the women suffered from providing sex to such a large number of men. Few surgeons used military brothels.'[41]

Yoshimi describes how the comfort women often remarked in their testimony that it was very difficult for them to refuse the men in the long lines, as they were beaten if they did not do what soldiers requested. It was not just the comfort women who were unnerved by the long lines of soldiers. Yoshimi cited an account from the memoirs of a Japanese veteran who was a young officer when he first visited a comfort station at Nha Trang in Vietnam. He found the experience disconcerting, factory-like, and grotesque:

> It was a comfort station often talked about. The none-too-simple reality of it was that, rather than being stimulated, I felt I had been exposed to some grotesque world. Standing in line in broad daylight, doing it right under the nose of the people waiting for their turn, and the vivid image of men coming out one after another with their pants still half open. This ritual proceeded in conveyor-belt fashion in an atmosphere of a particular sort of tension, and rather than raising my spirits, made me, who knew nothing of the forbidden fruit of the tree of knowledge, flinch.[42]

---

[40] Dolgopol and Paranjape, *Comfort Women: An Unfinished Ordeal*, p. 49.
[41] Dolgopol and Paranjape, *Comfort Women: An Unfinished Ordeal*, p. 49.
[42] Yoshimi, *Comfort Women*, p. 140.

Thus Chong's portrayal of the Tanjong Katong Road comfort station conforms to the descriptions of comfort stations in other parts of the Japanese Empire, such as the Nha Trang comfort station in Vietnam. These stories reinforce C. Sarah Soh's argument about how the comfort stations were different from brothels. Soldiers went to comfort stations to quickly and 'hygienically' relieve their sexual urges rather than enjoy themselves as at a brothel. A comfort station was in the eyes of the Japanese military not 'a place of hedonistic pleasure because it ought to be a public toilet'.[43] She asserts that the perception among the soldiers of the comfort station 'as a public toilet epitomizes a phallocentric essentialist perspective on male sexuality'.[44]

Indonesian Women at the Comfort Stations of Singapore

While there are many memories of Korean women at the comfort stations of Singapore, it appears that when more comfort women were required at the comfort stations later in the war, the Japanese military brought in Indonesian women. Indeed the most noticeable group apart from Koreans in the comfort stations was Indonesian women.

Robert Chong mentions Indonesians working as comfort women at Tanjong Katong Road and Katong comfort stations. They appear to have been brought in from Java in the later years of the war.[45] Lee Kip Lin also recalls the large number of comfort women from Korea and Java in the Katong area. Lee was living nearby at Amber Road with his mother and father. In his interview of June 1984, Lee remembers that near Tanjong Katong Road, there was a large compound house where many Javanese comfort women worked and lived:

> you would see these women [Korean women] walking about the place. They had of course also another batch of prostitutes. And these were the saddest of them, Javanese women brought over from Java. And it appeared that they were brought out under the pretence that they would be trained as nurses. So they enrolled into this so-called nursing service and found themselves in Singapore to serve in brothels. It was very sad.

---

[43] Chunghee Sarah Soh, 'Prostitutes versus Sex Slaves: The Politics of Representing the "Comfort Women"', in *Legacies of the Comfort Women of World War II*, ed. Margaret D. Stetz and Bonnie B.C. Oh (New York: M.E. Sharpe, 2001), p. 77.

[44] Soh, 'Prostitutes versus Sex Slaves: The Politics of Representing the "Comfort Women"', p. 77.

[45] Robert Chong, 11 June 1983, reel 9, p. 104.

They were all housed in a compound house which stood at the corner of Haig Road and Mountbatten Road. Today the site is occupied by a shopping complex. What is it called? Katong People's Park is it? It was exactly there.[46]

Othman Wok, a former cabinet minister in the Singapore government, corroborated Chong's and Lee's account of the very noticeable numbers of Indonesian women at the comfort stations at Katong and Tanjong Katong Road and supplied additional detail. He recalled in an interview in June 1993 that at Tanjong Katong Road, 'there were Indonesian and Korean girls in white uniforms like nurses. People told me this place was for prostitutes.'[47] When he worked as a clerk in the Water Department at Keppel Harbour from 1944 to 1945, he saw Indonesian comfort women leaving the boats at the harbour after arriving from Java: 'Sometimes, I saw 30 to 50 girls on board some of the ships that carried Indonesian labourers who were being sent to work on the Death Railway.'[48] The images of 'men in black and beautiful Indonesian girls in white uniforms' were still vivid for Othman Wok.[49] He observed: 'These girls, aged between 14 and 20, were dressed in white uniforms, like nurses. I asked one of them what they were doing and she told me they were sent here to be nurses.'[50] Othman Wok recollected: 'The Indonesian women said, "We are going to be nurses!" What they really ended up being was comfort girls for the Japanese. They were literally kept prisoner in a row of houses at Katong Road.'[51]

The bleak life of the Indonesian comfort women at the Katong and Tanjong Katong Road comfort stations is further confirmed by E.J.H. Corner, a botanist working at the Botanic Gardens during the Japanese Occupation and who wrote of his memories in 1981. He remembered when they arrived in the early months of 1944 with the male Indonesian labourers: 'As for the women, if young and pretty, they went to the camp for prostitutes near Katong where the wailing of those women for help — "*Tolong, Tolong*" [help, help] — rent the hearts of passers-by.'[52]

---

[46] Lee Kip Lin, 4 June 1984, reel 8, p. 97.
[47] *The Straits Times*, 30 August 1993.
[48] *The Straits Times*, 30 August 1993.
[49] Othman Wok, 'Working with Death', in H. Sindhu, ed., *The Bamboo Fortress: True War Stories* (Singapore: Native Publications, 1991), p. 181.
[50] *The Straits Times*, 30 August 1993.
[51] Othman Wok, 'Working with Death', p. 181.
[52] E.J.H. Corner, *The Marquis: A Tale of Syonan-to* (Singapore: Heinemann Asia, 1981), p. 126.

Official Indonesian sources and testimony from the Indonesian women themselves after the war confirms that they had indeed been told that they were to be trained as nurses at colleges and were promised good wages, and that they could return to their villages. However, it was all false. Postwar records indicate that from late 1943 through to 1944, there were three groups of young women, totalling 219 in all, recruited by the Japanese in three separate drives to fill comfort stations in Malaya, Borneo, and Singapore. A group of 89 were sent from Jakarta to Kuching in Sarawak to work as comfort women there. A second group was sent from Surabaya to Jakarta then to Singapore. They only stayed a month in Singapore before being sent by boat to Labuan Island off Borneo, but half of the 80 young women perished when the boat hit a mine and sank in the seas off Labuan. The third group of about 50 from Jakarta was sent directly to Singapore where they ended up working in the Tanjong Katong Road and Katong comfort stations.[53]

There was another comfort station in Singapore with a considerable number of Indonesian women—the one on Pulau Bukom serving the Imperial Japanese Navy. According to an interview from February 1987 with Sukaimi bin Ibrahim of the Malay community living on the island, this island comfort station was completely staffed by Indonesian women who had been forced into providing sex for the Japanese sailors. These women had come with the *romusha* or forced labourers from Indonesia, who also worked on the island for the Japanese navy. Sukaimi bin Ibrahim himself had migrated from Java in the 1930s and had been an early member of the prewar Malay nationalist party known as Kesatuan Melayu Singapura. After the war, he joined the United Malays National Organisation (UMNO). While working at the Pulau Bukom comfort station, the women from Indonesia communicated their plight to Sukaimi bin Ibrahim and the Malays living on Pulau Bukom.[54]

The Indonesian comfort women and *romusha* of Pulau Bukom told Sukaimi bin Ibrahim that the Japanese military had deceived them with promises of receiving higher education if they left their families and went to Singapore. The Indonesians were all young men and women of schoolgoing age. The young men laboured carrying oil drums from the oil depot on the island until they started to lose weight and fall sick from lack of food. Some of them died. The Indonesian comfort women told Sukaimi bin Ibrahim that they despised the Japanese military for tricking them, yet felt they had little choice but to

---

[53] *The Straits Times*, 10 November 1946.
[54] Sukaimi bin Ibrahim, interviewed by Ong Lean Kim, 16 February 1987, accession number 000704, reel 9 (National Archives of Singapore).

accept their conditions on Pulau Bukom, as at least they received the basic necessities to keep alive. The women seemed to have been aware of the fate of Indonesian labourers whom the Japanese had brought to Singapore and had simply abandoned when they did not need them or when they fell sick. These *romusha* starved and died on the streets of Singapore.[55]

The deceptive practice of offering young educated Indonesian women from well-to-do families the chance to study overseas or to pursue an occupation, such as nursing, appears to have been used around 1943 to 1944 to recruit Indonesian girls to become comfort women for the Japanese military overseas. Renowned Indonesian novelist and writer Pramoedya Ananta Toer documented the lives of Indonesian comfort women who were tricked in this manner and sent from Java to the Eastern Indonesian island of Buru. He was on the island as a political prisoner of the Suharto regime in the 1970s and learned of the island's comfort women from fellow Javanese who had been exiled to the island. After the war was over, the young comfort women had stayed on the island because they felt too ashamed to return to their families. It was not until after the comfort women became a controversial issue in the 1990s that Pramoedya felt that he should perhaps try to publish what had been a disorganised manuscript he had put together on these comfort women in 1979. In 2001, this manuscript was published as a book called *Perawan Remaja dalam Cengkeraman Militer* [Young Virgins in the Military's Grip].

Pramoedya describes how in 1943, the Japanese military administration went through an elaborate pretence of registering boys and girls aged 15 to 17 at school on the pretext of taking steps to further their education.[56] Seven Sumedang schoolgirls aged 13–14 were recruited on the promise of being schooled as far away as Japan.[57] In reality, the girls were sent overseas to serve as comfort women and the boys as *romusha*. Pramoedya documents how the *Sendenbu* [Japanese Propaganda Department] demanded that the local Indonesian regents help recruit the young on the pretext of helping the war effort and preparing Indonesian youth for independence by becoming more educated and skilled. The Indonesian regents passed the demands onto the sub-district heads, who then passed the demands onto the village headmen. There was thus considerable local Indonesian involvement in the deception.

---

[55] See the account of many Indonesian labourers starving and dying outside the Raffles Museum in the Singapore town area in Corner, *The Marquis: A Tale of Syonan-to*, pp. 126–7.
[56] Pramoedya Ananta Toer, *Perawan Remaja dalam Cengkeraman Militer* [Young Virgins in the Military's Grip], originally published in 2001 (Jakarta: KPG, Kepustakaan Populer Gramedia, 2015), p. 7.
[57] Pramoedya, *Perawan Remaja dalam Cengkeraman Militer*, p. 10.

However, Pramoedya noted that this was 'all done under supervision of the *kempeitai*', the Japanese military police, and 'entirely controlled by the army'.[58]

Pramoedya delineated three factors that were crucial in persuading the teenagers, in particular the girls, to accept going overseas to Japan and Singapore for further study. Firstly, the 'girls' hearts were full of noble ideals to go forward and serve the people'. Secondly, 'the suffocating living conditions made it easy for the young girls and their families to delude themselves', 'so it was easy to enter the trap'. Thirdly, and 'this is more important, was the role of parents serving the Japanese administration in the bureaucracy', who persuaded their teenagers to go overseas.[59] Among these factors, he particularly emphasised the parents' fear of the Japanese.[60] Pramoedya insisted that 'the teenage virgins left the village and family on dangerous voyages, not of their own volition, but because of their parents' fear of the Japanese threat.'[61] He added that he felt that the Japanese military chose virgin teenage girls both to 'fulfill the sexual fantasies of Japanese soldiers' and because 'they would be less likely to resist and would be more helpless'.[62]

Comparing the Experiences of the Korean and Indonesian Comfort Women Who Came to Singapore

Some readers have viewed Pramoedya's book as a novel, but others have seen it as an exercise in historical documentation. William Bradley Horton, a historian of the Indonesian comfort women, regards the book as a historical work, making the wry comment that 'it seems safe to say that much of his data about women in Buru is salvageable for the writing of history'.[63] Horton views the deception used in the recruitment of Indonesian comfort women that was highlighted by Pramoedya as adding complexity to the all too often black-and-white Indonesian discourse of the comfort women simply being abducted by the Japanese, who are stereotyped as evil perpetrators. Horton agrees that local Indonesians were also involved in persuading these young women to be recruited: 'Many of these particular women were probably recruited with the

---

[58] Pramoedya, *Perawan Remaja dalam Cengkeraman Militer*, p. 11.
[59] Pramoedya, *Perawan Remaja dalam Cengkeraman Militer*, p. 12.
[60] Pramoedya, *Perawan Remaja dalam Cengkeraman Militer*, p. 14.
[61] Pramoedya, *Perawan Remaja dalam Cengkeraman Militer*, p. 15.
[62] Pramoedya, *Perawan Remaja dalam Cengkeraman Militer*, p. 15.
[63] William Bradley Horton, 'Pramoedya and the Comfort Women of Buru: A Textual Analysis of *Perawan Remaja dalam Cengkeraman Militer* (Teenage Virgins in the Grasp of the Military)', *Journal of Asia-Pacific Studies* (Waseda University), no. 14 (March 2010): 85.

excuse of some kind of schooling (including the safe-sounding profession of midwife at a/the hospital in Ambon), and various pressures like the demand for loyalty and need to struggle for victory in the war, as well as the potential loss of their fathers' positions.'[64] Horton pursued this line of thought, claiming that 'it is not already clear exactly who was involved in the recruiting of the girls, although certainly the Javanese bureaucracy was involved in many cases.'[65] He contends that the parents of the girls had to give their approval and that among them there was some awareness that the young women were not going to further their education in Japan or Singapore for a career: 'There are a few hints that parents were not always willing to allow their 14 year old girls [to] go away, and there is at least one hint that a Javanese woman far away from the port cities understood the fate that awaited these girls.'[66] Horton concludes that 'it is clear that in each of these cases the families at least pretended to believe that these girls would obtain an education. It could well have been that understanding that allowed them to live at peace, both psychologically and with the realities of Java under Japanese occupation.'[67]

The work of Horton and other scholars, such as Yamamoto Mayumi and Kawata Fumiko, reveals how Indonesian women were recruited into Indonesian comfort stations.[68] Horton makes the point that recruitment of women into prostitution for the Japanese military in Indonesia was similar to that elsewhere in the Japanese Empire, namely Korea, where deception played a key role. The experience of the Indonesian women in the comfort stations at Katong, along Tanjong Katong Road, and on Pulau Bukom tends to confirm the argument that there was a variety of ways through which women were brought into the sex industry of the Japanese military, but deception was a key strategy used many times in different contexts.

To analyse these deceptions, Horton compares the euphemisms used in other parts of the Japanese Empire for the recruitment of comfort women and those used in Indonesia, arguing that a viable research strategy would be 'to examine the use of euphemisms related to prostitution, and to see how they

---

[64] Horton, 'Pramoedya and the Comfort Women of Buru', p. 84.
[65] Horton, 'Pramoedya and the Comfort Women of Buru', p. 84.
[66] Horton, 'Pramoedya and the Comfort Women of Buru', p. 84.
[67] Horton, 'Pramoedya and the Comfort Women of Buru', p. 84.
[68] For a clear and concise summary of the research on Indonesian comfort women, see William Bradley Horton, 'Comfort Women', in Peter Post, William H. Frederick, Iris Heidebrink, and Shigeru Sato, eds, *The Encyclopedia of Indonesia in the Pacific War* (Leiden: Brill, 2010), pp. 184–96. See also Kawata Fumiko, *Indoneshia no 'Ianfu'* [The Comfort Women of Indonesia] (Tokyo: Akashi Shoten, 1997).

were used to "trick" women in different contexts'.[69] Horton notes that 'work by women in restaurants and bars was equated with prostitution by many Europeans interviewed after the war. This also seems to have been a euphemism used by the Japanese in their efforts to recruit women for brothels, and probably was used by other procurers.'[70] He adds: 'This is not surprising given the close relationship between, and the licensing of, brothels, geisha-houses, restaurants, tea-houses and their employees in Japan. In pre-war Kwantung and Taiwan geisha and *shakufu* (women serving sake), as well as prostitutes, were checked regularly for venereal disease, while waitresses were one of the major sources of prostitutes in Japan itself.'[71] In Indonesia, as in Singapore and other parts of the Japanese Empire, working in restaurants was a euphemism for providing sexual services for the Japanese military. Horton adds: 'The largest, best organized brothels in Indonesia, while they may have been located in former hotels, were frequently attached to restaurants and served as general entertainment quarters for the (usually Japanese) military or civilian clients. Movement from one to another, especially from restaurants to brothels, seems to have been common.'[72] Horton affirms: 'The recruiting strategies for Indonesian women of work as actresses or study to be nurses have their own cultural logics.'[73]

The recruitment of the Indonesian comfort women using deception is an interesting parallel to the range of methods of recruitment of the Korean comfort women. Sociologist Caroline Norma makes the point that Korean women were predominant in the comfort stations of the Japanese Empire because there existed in Korea an extensive and well-entrenched prewar system of trafficking women into prostitution that involved many Korean traffickers and procurers, who would use a range of techniques, especially deception, to recruit women. Norma argues that the 'overrepresentation of Korean women among comfort station survivors is in part due to their mass organization in civilian prostitution before and during the war'.[74] She adds that the 'nature of the causal link between Japanese imperialism and the creation of the comfort station system' itself 'turns on colonial civilian sex industry development'.[75]

---

[69] Horton, 'Comfort Women', p. 196.
[70] Horton, 'Comfort Women', p. 196.
[71] Horton, 'Comfort Women', p. 196.
[72] Horton, 'Comfort Women', p. 196.
[73] Horton, 'Comfort Women', p. 196.
[74] Caroline Norma, *The Japanese Comfort Women and Sexual Slavery During the China and Pacific Wars* (London: Bloomsbury, 2016), p. 153.
[75] Norma, *The Japanese Comfort Women and Sexual Slavery During the China and Pacific Wars*, p. 153.

Norma surmises that 'because it reveals an institutional basis to the history of military sexual slavery going back further than the eight years of war', it 'should strengthen the contemporary case for justice for survivors'.[76]

Just as there were established prewar trafficking networks of Korean women, so too in Singapore there existed prewar organised trafficking of women from Indonesia. In the 1930s, Singapore Malay and Chinese port workers and customs officials were involved in the procuring of young women of around 20 years old from Java but also other parts of Indonesia, such as Sumatra and the Riau islands. They obtained Chinese Indonesian women as well as Javanese women. At times, they also trafficked women into Singapore from Thailand. One Malay customs official told of his involvement in an interview in September 1985. He described how they smuggled women into Singapore with the help of Javanese seamen who concealed the women on the ships that they were working on.

Indonesian women were brought in for men who requested beautiful brides and mistresses, but many women were trafficked into prostitution and brought to their 'bosses' at places such as Perumal Road in Little India and Palembang Road in the Malay enclave of Kampong Rochor.[77] Some also worked in the well-known Johore Road red-light district. The Javanese seamen were paid $20–$30 for each woman brought to Singapore. Sometimes hundreds of women would be requested. When the women alighted from Java, if the seamen were asked by other customs officials who the women were, the seamen would just say that they were their wives. The customs officials could also be bribed.

The Malay customs official involved in trafficking Indonesian women explained the attraction in Java of coming to Singapore for a better life rather than staying in poverty: 'People there really admired Singapore' and 'they wanted to go to Singapore, and their parents also liked the idea of going to Singapore' to work or to marry. If the opportunity arose, the Indonesian women would exercise whatever agency they could given their conditions. In his interview, the Malay customs official added that many of these women were well dressed and 'spoke cleverly' in both Javanese and Malay. According to him, 'they were smart enough to know that if they left us, there would be other opportunities they could find.... They would look for rich people and

---

[76] Norma, *The Japanese Comfort Women and Sexual Slavery During the China and Pacific Wars*, p. 153.
[77] Anon 4, interviewed by Mohd Yussoff bin Ahmad, 17 September 1985, accession number 000598, reel 13; and see interview 27 September 1985, reels 19–21 (National Archives of Singapore).

follow them', and 'here they could try to find jobs'.[78] He described the Javanese prostitutes they were trafficking through the port as being well known for their 'gentleness' and 'kindness'.[79] The women worked in prostitution for five to six years before some married out of the business and had children, while others succumbed to illness.

The Malay customs official contextualised this human trafficking of Indonesian women by describing how Chinese and Malay customs officials as well as other port workers were also helping agents to bring in Chinese women from Hong Kong and Canton for prostitution rackets run by Chinese gangsters. European women were also brought through the port for prostitution in Singapore.[80] However, trafficking women for prostitution in Singapore meant operating beyond the realms of the law. Prostitution in Singapore was made illegal in 1930 after being licensed in the decades going back into the late nineteenth century. Yet, even though the traffickers operated outside of the law in the 1930s, the old trafficking networks of young women proved remarkably persistent.

Although coming from very different societies, the Korean and Indonesian comfort women of Singapore, as they worked sometimes side by side, shared many similarities in their recruitment and conditions of work. Examining the comfort stations of Singapore reveals that the Korean women were predominant in numbers, but Indonesian women, according to memories of the local Singapore population, were also very noticeable in their presence at the comfort stations of Singapore. Indonesians made up the staff of whole comfort stations, namely those at Katong and Pulau Bukom. The recruitment of both groups of comfort women through Korean and Indonesian co-operation, as Horton suggests, offers insightful parallels. The Indonesian comfort women were pressured by their parents to take up the offer of nursing. There were Korean women who were similarly trafficked into prostitution by well-established Korean networks which had procured them and sent them into the Japanese military's sex industry. The experience of the comfort women in Singapore tends to confirm the work of scholars, such as Horton, who emphasise the variety of the ways in which the comfort women were recruited and conditions in which they worked.

---

[78] Anon 4, interviewed by Mohd Yussoff bin Ahmad, 17 September 1985, accession number 000598, reel 11 (National Archives of Singapore).

[79] Anon 4, interviewed by Mohd Yussoff bin Ahmad, 27 September 1985, accession number 000598, reel 21 (National Archives of Singapore).

[80] Anon 4, interviewed by Mohd Yussoff bin Ahmad, 27 September 1985, accession number 000598, reels 19–21 (National Archives of Singapore).

5
The Comfort Women Returning to Live in Postwar Society

At the end of the war, many in Singapore noticed that the Japanese military's sex industry had produced major changes in the lives of women. Captain Sasaki Masao, a long-time Japanese resident of Singapore from the prewar period, observed in his interrogation when he was captured by the Allies late in the war that the prostitution of women was far more widespread than ever before. Prostitution involved more women across many ethnic groups, including many Singapore women. Sasaki said: 'The inmates of the brothels are Chinese, Malayan [Malay], Korean, Japanese, Indian, and Eurasian. In my opinion the brothels were the biggest change made by the Japanese in Singapore.'[1] Sasaki's observations indicate the scale of the Japanese military's sex industry, given that before the war, Singapore already had a reputation as a centre for prostitution. A 1941 colonial report on prostitution concluded that 'one of Singapore's foremost industries is prostitution and all that goes with it, and that at the moment this profession must be employing, either full or part time, many thousands of individuals'.[2]

This chapter traces how many of these women involved in the Japanese military's sex industry in Singapore preferred either to not tell their families about their experiences or to not return to their homes and communities to face scorn and humiliation. In Singapore, the returning British colonial authorities rounded up many of these Singapore women who continued to work in prostitution on the streets and put them into a home for the 'rehabilitation'

---

[1] Cited in Christopher Bayly and Tim Harper, *Forgotten Armies: Britain's Asian Empire and War with Japan* (London: Penguin, 2005), p. 410. For Sasaki Masao, see Box 139/XL 10130: Report of interrogation of Japanese Prisoner of War who lived in Malaya, Burma, Singapore for years before the war (National Archives and Records Administration, United States of America, with a copy held at the National Archives of Singapore).
[2] Extract, 1/17 in Prostitution in Singapore, 1941, CO 273 667/50657 (The National Archives, Kew).

of prostitutes in order to turn them into 'good wives'. When these women were discussed in early postwar Singapore society, it was in terms of how they were 'fallen' women.[3] This discussion of these women suggests what feminist author Dale Spender has written concerning how women were subordinated by a language that was controlled by men.[4] Does the way these women were talked about in Singapore society soon after the end of the war confirm Spender's point that 'language and the conditions for its use structure a patriarchal order'?[5]

The Postwar Lives of the Indonesian Comfort Women in Singapore

After the war, representatives from the Indonesian Republic sought to locate and return the Indonesian comfort women. In July 1946, Maria Ulfah Santoso, the Indonesian Republic's Minister for Social Affairs, asked Allied Headquarters, South East Asia Command, in Singapore for permission to send Indonesian Red Cross representatives to Singapore to trace and recover the 219 Indonesian young women and girls who had been taken by the Japanese to become 'nurses'.[6] In August 1946, Nyonya Hidayat, of the Indonesian Red Cross, arrived in Singapore at the invitation of the South East Asia Command to look for the young women.[7] By November 1946, 75 per cent of the 219 women had been found after a widespread public campaign to locate them.[8] However, only 20 out of the 50 at the Tanjong Katong Road and Katong comfort stations wanted to be repatriated to Indonesia. The rest had married local men or kept working in areas such as 'hostessing', fearing the abuse that they would be subjected to at home once it became known that they had been comfort women for the Japanese soldiers.[9]

The testimony of the Indonesian comfort women who wanted to remain in Singapore revealed their apprehensiveness about returning to the societies they came from in Java. Speaking about their experiences in January 1947, these women described how they had been tricked into becoming comfort women. They used what Dale Spender has called the language of patriarchy to portray themselves as having become 'fallen women' from 'respectability'. One young

---

[3] *Sunday Tribune*, 13 January 1946.
[4] Dale Spender, *Man Made Language* (London: Routledge and Kegan Paul, 1980), p. 12.
[5] Spender, *Man Made Language*, p. 57.
[6] *Indian Daily Mail* (Singapore), 24 July 1946.
[7] *Malaya Tribune*, 3 August 1946; and *The Straits Times*, 25 September 1946.
[8] *The Straits Times*, 10 November 1946; and *Sunday Tribune*, 26 January 1947.
[9] *Sunday Tribune*, 26 January 1947.

woman called Mariam said they were lured 'from respectable families on the promise of "higher education"'.[10] Another woman aged 25, from Bandung, recalled when interviewed in January 1947: 'We come from good families... many of us came to Singapore to better our prospects, but we were sadly disillusioned. We were made "comfort girls" by the Japs — I know it's ugly to talk about our past life but there it is, simple and plain. We were forced to become bad.'[11] They felt that they would be rejected if they returned to their families. Some of the women were working as dance hostesses and preferred the freedom of that life to going back to their families in Indonesia with their strict expectations of being 'chaste' and 'pure'. The young Indonesian women from the Tanjong Katong Road and Katong comfort stations lamented in January 1947:

> We love dancing and we like Singapore very much.... We doubt whether we'll ever return to Java. The Japanese are to blame for the tragedy in our lives. How can we go home now and face our family? We prefer to remain here and start life anew.[12]

The issue was discussed by *Comrade*, the newspaper of the veterans of the communist-led guerrilla resistance from the war, the Malayan People's Anti-Japanese Army (MPAJA). In September 1946, *Comrade* commented on the fate of the Indonesian comfort women: 'Many of them, it seems, now have become professional prostitutes, and because of the shame that would be brought on their families in Java if they go home, they refused offers to transport them back to Indonesia', while only 'some had settled in good homes and married'.[13] The Singapore colonial Social Welfare Department confirmed this predicament of the Indonesian women in its 1946–47 report on prostitution and the trafficking of young women: 'Although the British Military Administration endeavoured to repatriate as many as possible of these imported girls, many of them either could not or would not return to their homes.'[14]

Other Indonesian comfort women eventually preferred to marry Malay men in Singapore rather than return to their families in Indonesia. Othman Wok recalled in his 1993 interview that initially, at the end of the war, 'some of the

---

[10] *Sunday Tribune*, 26 January 1947.
[11] *Sunday Tribune*, 26 January 1947.
[12] *Sunday Tribune*, 26 January 1947.
[13] *Comrade*, 29 September 1946.
[14] Colony of Singapore: Report to U.N.O. For Period 30th June 1946–30th June 1947 in Trafficking in Woman and Girls File, Social Welfare Department, Number SWD 241 Vol. 1, Microfilm Number MSA 3448 (National Archives of Singapore).

girls did escape and went to a village near Tanjong Katong Road. The village head said they asked the fishermen to send them back to Indonesia.'[15] However, the women soon began to rethink any plans they had to return home and considered the possibility that their families would not accept them. Othman Wok described what happened: 'After the war, many of these girls escaped to a nearby Malay kampong at Amber Road with the help of the young men of that village. Disgraced, they did not want to go back to Indonesia, and many married the locals.'[16]

The Indonesian women who had worked at the comfort station of the Imperial Japanese Navy on Pulau Bukom also did not want to return home to Java because they felt ashamed and believed that their families would reject them. According to an interview from February 1987 with Sukaimi bin Ibrahim, of the Malay community on the island, these women on Pulau Bukom told him: 'It would be better if we died outside our homeland than if we went back with our bodies defiled.'[17] He remembered that these women chose instead to become part of his own Malay kampong community at Pasir Panjang, across the sea on the main island of Singapore. These former Indonesian comfort women soon comprised 90 per cent of an Indonesian arts society at Pasir Panjang set up by Sukaimi bin Ibrahim.[18] Thus, a significant number of young Indonesian women stayed in Singapore and successfully became part of the Malay community, which already had many Javanese migrants.

The language used by the Indonesian women and others to describe themselves illustrates what feminist writer Dale Spender has written about the relationship between women, language, and male control. The Indonesian comfort women claiming that they had become 'bad' women reflects Spender's ideas that male dominance created a language to control the lives of women. Spender asserts that to describe themselves, 'women have been obliged to use a language which is not of their own making'.[19] She writes that 'the monopoly over language is one of the means by which males have ensured their own primacy, and consequently have ensured the invisibility or "other" nature of females, and this primacy is perpetuated while women continue to use, unchanged, the

---

[15] *The Straits Times*, 30 August 1993.
[16] Othman Wok, 'Working with Death', in *The Bamboo Fortress: True War Stories*, ed. H. Sindhu (Singapore: Native Publications, 1991), p. 181.
[17] Sukaimi bin Ibrahim, interviewed by Ong Lean Kim, 16 February 1987, accession number 000704, reel 9 (National Archives of Singapore). For the quote, see also *The Straits Times*, 30 August 1993.
[18] Sukaimi bin Ibrahim, 16 February 1987, reel 9.
[19] Spender, *Man Made Language*, p. 12.

language which we inherited.'[20] Examining the groups of comfort women from different ethnic groups and nationalities in Singapore also reveal how they were described and controlled in the postwar period using a language that reflected a male-controlled order of society.

The Korean Comfort Women's Return Home

The end of the war was an anxious time for the comfort women as they contemplated returning to their homes. The many Korean women in Singapore were disliked by not just the Japanese but also the local population because of the mistaken perception that they were willing prostitutes of the Japanese military. In October 1945, one of the owners of the terrace houses of the Cairnhill Road comfort station wrote to the Singapore press about his unhappiness that the Korean comfort women were still residing in the buildings: 'The Koreans who followed in the wake of the former Japanese invading Hordes are still resident in comfort in houses at Cairnhill Road, one of the best residential quarters of the city, while the former occupiers of those houses continue to live in misery and in unhygienic hovels in the congested areas into which they were driven when the Japanese ejected them in 1942.'[21] The owner added, in complete indifference to what many of the Korean comfort women had been through: 'Why must they be pampered at the expense of the long-suffering house owners and citizens of this colony?'[22]

Perhaps as a response to this anger, in December 1945, *The Straits Times* carried a short story and a picture of comfort women growing vegetables on a farm with the caption: 'New Job for Comfort Girls'. The story noted that 'Japanese comfort girls have been put to work on the land'.[23] Implicit in the account was the assumption that hard labour and growing their own food would 'reform' these women, who were seen to have lived off sexually consorting with members of the Japanese military. The Singapore artist Liu Kang's early postwar work reflects these disdainful attitudes when he portrayed the comfort women as willing and happy sex partners of the Japanese military and called

---

[20] Spender, *Man Made Language*, p. 12.
[21] *Malaya Tribune*, 20 October 1945.
[22] *Malaya Tribune*, 20 October 1945.
[23] *The Straits Times*, 10 December 1945.

them 'known prostitutes' in his comic book of the Japanese Occupation *Chop Suey* in early 1946.[24]

Historian Hayashi Hirofumi's work on the comfort women of Singapore suggests that around the time when Japan surrendered, the Japanese military turned the Korean comfort women into nurses for their hospitals, perhaps as an attempt to conceal the widespread existence of the comfort women system. He argues that in this process of the women being re-assigned to hospitals, 'some women were abandoned locally by the Japanese military, while others were able to return to Japan and the Korean Peninsula'.[25] Hayashi discovered evidence of the military turning the comfort women into nurses from an intercepted and translated Japanese document at the National Archives and Records Administration in the United States. This was an encrypted message sent by the Japanese Commander-in-Chief of the Southern Expeditionary Fleet on 18 August 1945 to naval stations across Southeast Asia. It was intercepted and deciphered by the Allies, and reads: 'Relative to Naval Consolation Establishments in Singapore, as of 1 August the employees [Japanese] have been given employment in (Naval) Hospital #101. The larger number of the girls have been made assistant nurses. Please take steps similar to these.'[26] Another document discovered by Hayashi, this time at the Japanese Self-Defense Agency's National Institute for Defense Studies, reveals a similar message by the Japanese army in Indonesia on 20 August 1945 to make its comfort women nurses at its hospitals. This message asks the recipient after having read it to burn the copy of the message, so perhaps there could have been some element of concealment by the Japanese military.[27]

In his research, Hayashi traced the life of a Korean woman who went through this transition from comfort woman to nurse at the orders of the Japanese military. Han Cho-soo was a comfort woman in Jakarta who on 1 August 1945 was suddenly 'proclaimed a nurse' with the 5th Army Hospital and transferred to Singapore. This would indicate that she was a comfort woman made into a nurse. Han was also among the list of 'absences' in a document from the

---

[24] Liu Kang, *Chop Suey: A Selection from a Host of Gruesome Events that Occurred in Malaya during the Japanese Occupation* (Singapore: Global Arts & Crafts, 1991), originally published in 1946, p. 15.

[25] Hayashi Hirofumi, 'Shiryo shokai kangofu ni sa reta "ianfu-tachi"' [Introduction of materials on 'Comfort women' who were made nurses] in Women's Active Museum Testimonials from North and South Korea and Japan, 2010. See http://hayashihirofumi.g1.xrea.com/paper99.htm.

[26] Hayashi, 'Shiryo shokai kangofu ni sa reta "ianfu-tachi"'.

[27] Hayashi, 'Shiryo shokai kangofu ni sa reta "ianfu-tachi"'.

5th Army Hospital in Jakarta but had since died in Singapore. Hayashi cites research work surveying the 'List of Absences' directory of the Japanese army, and notices that among them were 314 Korean women identified as 'nurses' or 'employees'. The transfers in the 'List of Absences' occurred gradually over August 1945 when Japan surrendered. These absences thus appear to be Korean comfort women who became nurses at the end of the war. Hayashi also found Han Cho-soo's name engraved on a memorial to the Southern Army's 'hospital-related deceased' in Singapore's Japanese Cemetery. Hayashi concludes: 'It is not possible to determine for sure whether she was a comfort woman, but it is likely. This is a monument and not a tomb. But if the memorial includes the name of a "comfort woman", it is very rare for such monuments to have the names of comfort women engraved upon them.'[28] Thus, it is likely that the Japanese Cemetery of Singapore has a memorial to a comfort woman. Hayashi thinks that the Japanese military's attempt to make comfort women nurses may have been an 'attempt to conceal the presence of comfort women' from the Allies, but it could also have been an attempt to integrate them officially into the Japanese military registers so they would be taken together with military personnel and repatriated together by the Allies.[29]

Hayashi's conclusions are confirmed by the testimony of Kim Bok-dong, who was a Korean comfort woman in Singapore at the time of the Japanese surrender. She says that the Japanese military absorbed her and many of her fellow comfort women at her comfort station in Singapore into the army hospitals as nurses. Kim recounted that 'in Singapore after the war the Japanese tried to cover up the existence of these comfort stations by turning us into nurses at army hospitals'.[30] She and the other comfort women were held on the island of Singapore in the Jurong internment camps with the Japanese. Kim worked as a nurse with surrendered Japanese soldiers for a year until she was gathered together with the other Koreans and repatriated to Korea.

Kim, fearful of disapproval from the Korean society, did not tell her family about what had really happened to her in her eight years away since she had been taken away on the pretext of working in a factory. She recalled: 'Although I was reunited with them, they had no idea what I had gone through. How could I tell them about my experiences? As a woman I had things done to me that were unfathomable. So I couldn't say anything to anybody. They had all thought

---

[28] Hayashi, 'Shiryo shokai kangofu ni sa reta "ianfu-tachi"'.
[29] Hayashi, 'Shiryo shokai kangofu ni sa reta "ianfu-tachi"'.
[30] Kim Bok-dong gave her last interview on the YouTube channel *Asian Boss* in October 2018: https://www.youtube.com/watch?v=qsT97ax_Xb0.

that I had gone to work at a factory.'³¹ Eventually, her mother asked her several years later why she did not want to marry. Kim recalled: 'But because I did not want to get married even though I was getting older, my mother wanted to find out why I did not want to get married. She pushed me to be honest with her. So I confessed that given all the abuse that had been done to my body, I didn't want to screw up another man's life. It should just be my problem. So I told her I couldn't get married. Once [she] found out, my mother also could not talk about it to anyone and became very distressed. Eventually she suffered a heart attack and passed away as a result.' Her mother had kept Kim's secret for fear of male disapproval in the family.³²

Some Korean comfort women returning from Singapore, while not telling their families and communities about their experiences because they would have faced disapproval, kept in touch with one another in the years following the end of the war. Yi Sunok recollected in an interview she gave in 1993 that after returning to Korea with her friends from her comfort station in Singapore, they remained close for over six years. Yi remarks: 'during those years Sadako and Masako often visited me, but then Masako died following an operation. She had been one year older than myself and had she still lived, she would have registered at the Korean Council with me.' The Korean Council for the Women Drafted for Military Sexual Slavery by Japan in the 1990s built on these close links between some of the Korean comfort women and took up their cause, demanding recognition, an apology, and compensation from the Japanese government. However, with the passage of time, the close association between the comfort women who returned from Singapore grew weaker. Yi says: 'Some of those who were comfort women with me still live in Kyongju, but it seems they have not registered. I don't know where Sadako is now, nor how she makes a living.'³³

Postwar Condemnation of Local Singapore Comfort Women

The disapproval that Kim Bok-dong and other Korean comfort women faced when they returned home was similar to the reception experienced by local Singapore women who had been forcibly recruited by the Japanese military and sent to comfort stations. N.I. Low and H.M. Cheng in their 1947 book on the Japanese Occupation *This Singapore (Our City of Dreadful Night)* described

---

[31] Kim Bok-dong, October 2018, https://www.youtube.com/watch?v=qsT97ax_Xb0.
[32] Kim Bok-dong, October 2018, https://www.youtube.com/watch?v=qsT97ax_Xb0.
[33] Keith Howard, ed., *True Stories of Korean Comfort Women* (London: Cassell, 1995), pp. 122–3.

the fears of local Singapore comfort women returning to Singapore after being taken from their families and sent to comfort stations in Indonesia:

> On 6 March, 1946, six months after the collapse of Japan, a party of fifteen girls landed in Singapore. They had served as 'comfort' girls in Java for nearly four years. Said one to the man whose duty it was to receive them at the wharfside, 'Will my father have me back?'[34]

These fears seemed well grounded given the unfavourable perceptions of the former comfort women in the public imagination and the prevalence of what Dale Spender has referred to as patriarchal language applied to them by male leaders in Singapore. Many community leaders and figures in the colonial state held them in disdain. Chen Su Lan, a leader of the Chinese community, expressed these disproving opinions when he complained in the Singapore Advisory Council to the British Military Administration in November 1945 about the dramatic increase in the number of prostitutes on the streets soliciting. He believed that many of these women were left over from the comfort stations and *ryotei*, and were unable or unwilling to return to their families. He had little sympathy for the women, seeing them as 'fallen' women even though he knew that many had been tricked into providing sexual services for the Japanese. Although 'victims', they still represented for him 'a demoralisation of Singapore womanhood'.[35]

In early postwar Singapore, to remove these women from public, Chen even wanted a ban on young women dancing and waitressing because many women had been drawn into prostitution through these activities under Japanese rule—and he believed that this practice persisted. In December 1945, in the Singapore Advisory Council to the British Military Administration, Chen gave his account of how the Japanese Occupation had encouraged the prostitution of Singapore women as they took up waitressing jobs:

> In dealing with the question of waitresses, I am treading on delicate ground which angels fear to tread. In March 1942, when I was hiding on an island outside of Singapore, the first Chinese newspaper I read contained a Japanese advertisement calling for a certain number of army prostitutes for their fighting forces. This was followed a month

---

[34] N.I. Low and H.M. Cheng, *This Singapore (Our City of Dreadful Night)* (Singapore: City Book Store, 1947), p. 13.
[35] Chen Su Lan, *British Military Administration, Malaya, Advisory Council, Singapore Report of Proceedings*, 14 November 1945, p. 19, in Singapore Advisory Council, File Number BMA (H) HQ CH 36-45, Microfilm Number NA 869 (National Archives of Singapore).

later by a less vulgar advertisement, calling for '30 pretty girls' for the swimming club. Knowing what the enemy had done in all occupied territories, especially China, I saw that this was the thin edge of the wedge of the Japanese demoralising knife that was to cut into the vitals of Malayan womanhood. My fear was amply justified, for when I returned two months later, Singapore was in a topsy-turvy condition socially.... Later, and during the whole period of the occupation, a girl could easily get a job, leaving her brothers loafing in the streets. A husband had to take care of the baby, whereas the wife made hundreds of dollars under the Japanese.[36]

In his speeches on prostitution in Singapore that he made soon after the war, Chen went on to outline in detail the legacy of the prostitution of Singapore women in the restaurants that had been set up to provide sexual services during the Japanese Occupation. He saw key components of this sex industry continuing into the postwar period, particularly the practice of female staff offering sex at the 'low-grade' restaurants:

We rejoice and say the Japanese have gone; but are they gone? The seed they sowed has grown into a vile fruit, and the Japanese national policy of making women in the occupied regions chattels for the gratification of the lust of men has amply succeeded. They have lost in the field of battle, but they have won in the field of moral degradation and social degradation. Those highly painted waitresses who were seen at the Jap-sponsored restaurants in the period of the occupation are still there. They are not there as mere plate-washers; but as baits to attract customers; and as such how can they resist the temptation and the almost inevitable sequence of making one further step into a house of ill-fame? Therefore if we wish to tackle the question of prostitution and venereal disease scientifically and correctly, we must not forget the waitresses, who are a danger to society...there should be an age limit whereby a woman under 30 should not be employed as a waitress. Most of the young waitresses should be at home or in schools.[37]

---

[36] Chen Su Lan, *British Military Administration, Malaya, Advisory Council, Singapore Report of Proceedings*, 12 December 1945, p. 59, in Singapore Advisory Council, File Number BMA (H) HQ CH 36-45, Microfilm Number NA 869 (National Archives of Singapore).

[37] Chen Su Lan, *British Military Administration, Malaya, Advisory Council, Singapore Report of Proceedings*, 12 December 1945, pp. 59–60 in Singapore Advisory Council, File Number BMA (H) HQ CH 36-45, Microfilm Number NA 869 (National Archives of Singapore).

Chen believed that the number of prostitutes in Singapore in 1945 had increased 'tenfold' from the prewar period.[38] He described how after the war many of these women congregated along Jalan Besar, posing 'a danger' in 'morally corrupting' men who were walking along the street. Chen said, 'Anyone who takes the trouble to go down Jalan Besar any night would like to see street soliciting stopped at once for the sake of men who happen to pass there. Any man who passes by there with no intention of doing anything immoral may be attracted to one of these women. So it is to safe guard these men who perhaps have never been to a woman before, that this measure is intended.'[39]

'To safe guard' these men from the prostitutes streetwalking, Chen proposed amendments to the prewar Women and Girls' Protection Ordinance to enable the police to arrest and detain these women who were soliciting on the streets. Before the war, there had been no laws against prostitutes on the streets. He elaborated that under the prewar ordinance, 'a prostitute is not a criminal. She is presumed to be a passive agent while her keeper is the active agent in the act of prostitution. She is the victim and her keeper the aggressor. For this reason no provision is made for the punishment of the prostitute, even when she becomes the active agent and the aggressor, but when she steps beyond the bounds of propriety and social decency, as in street soliciting, the law must step in and call a halt to the illegal practice.'[40] To deal with the widespread increase in street soliciting that had resulted from the Japanese Occupation, Chen insisted on inserting into the Women and Girls' Protection Ordinance the clause: 'Any women who is a habitual prostitute who loiters in a street, pavement, back-lane, or public places, or who exposes herself in such a part of a dwelling or in such a manner to attract passers-by for the purposes of prostitution shall be deemed to have committed the offence of street soliciting unless the contrary is proven.'[41]

---

[38] Chen Su Lan, *British Military Administration, Malaya, Advisory Council, Singapore Report of Proceedings*, 13 December 1945, p. 72, in Singapore Advisory Council, File Number BMA (H) HQ CH 36-45, Microfilm Number NA 869 (National Archives of Singapore).

[39] Chen Su Lan, *British Military Administration, Malaya, Advisory Council, Singapore Report of Proceedings*, 23 January 1946, p. 134, in Singapore Advisory Council, File Number BMA Ch.A 49-1945, Microfilm Number NA 870 (National Archives of Singapore).

[40] CCAO and Lieutenant Colonel Broome, *British Military Administration, Malaya, Advisory Council, Singapore Report of Proceedings*, 23 January 1946, p. 95, in Singapore Advisory Council, File Number BMA Ch.A 49-1945, Microfilm Number NA 870 (National Archives of Singapore).

[41] Chen Su Lan, *British Military Administration, Malaya, Advisory Council, Singapore Report of Proceedings*, 23 January 1946, p. 134, in Singapore Advisory Council, File Number BMA Ch.A 49-1945, Microfilm Number NA 870 (National Archives of Singapore).

Chen's amendment making it possible to round up and detain prostitutes working on the streets was enthusiastically taken up by the leader of the British Military Administration, Major-General H.R. Hone, Chief Civil Affairs Officer (CCAO). During the debate on Chen's amendment, Lieutenant Colonel R.N. Broome, Advisor, Chinese Affairs, recalled how the police in prewar Singapore could sometimes round up 20–30 prostitutes streetwalking along Bras Basah Road on one night, but they had to be released because none of the existing ordinances covered them. Broome was satisfied that Chen's amendment meant streetwalking prostitutes could be rounded up and detained.[42]

Male community leaders outside of the Singapore Advisory Council were of a like mind as Chen and the officials of the British Military Administration. V.K.G. Nair, journalist and social commentator, expressed similar sentiments in the press. His letter to the press was provocatively entitled: 'Ex-Japanese Prostitutes in British Singapore'. He wrote that 'the hundreds of prostitutes who ply their trade in the streets of Singapore after sunset' was 'one of the many legacies left behind by the Japanese'.[43] While acknowledging that the 'large majority of these unfortunate girls are therefore victims of circumstances', he declared, 'This evil has now taken such deep root in society that it has to be viewed from a new angle.'[44] For Nair, this new angle meant rounding up the women and putting them in a home, as it did for Chen and other male leaders of the community examining the issue. Nair, like his male counterparts, was aware that many of these women had been comfort women. He singled out three factors why there were so many prostitutes in early postwar Singapore:

> The increase in the number of prostitutes compared with pre-war days may be due to three factors: Firstly, the Japanese forced a number of young girls into 'Comfort' homes; secondly, the acute poverty that prevailed during the occupation period; thirdly, the mysterious disappearance of thousands of male supporters during the Jap terror regime.[45]

Chen and Nair were just two of many male leaders in the community in Singapore who from 1945 to 1947 publicly voiced their moral disapproval of the Singapore women formerly engaged in sex work with the Japanese

---

[42] CCAO and Lieutenant Colonel Broome, *British Military Administration, Malaya, Advisory Council, Singapore Report of Proceedings*, 23 January 1946, pp. 95–6, in Singapore Advisory Council, File Number BMA Ch.A 49-1945, Microfilm Number NA 870 (National Archives of Singapore).
[43] *The Straits Times*, 13 August 1946.
[44] *The Straits Times*, 13 August 1946.
[45] *The Straits Times*, 13 August 1946.

military. Lim Chin Hian, yet another social reformer, also contended that 'prostitutes seem to abound in every nook and corner today' and that 'during the occupation men dared not go out at night for fear of being collared by the Japanese, but nowadays, if any young man is not careful, he will be collared by these ex-Japanese prostitutes.'[46]

In early postwar Singapore, women who had any links with the Japanese, especially those who had sexual liaisons with them, were treated with disdain. Women who continued their life of military sexual liaisons with soldiers from the returning British army were treated with particular disapproval. These social critics sometimes hid behind pejorative nom de plumes in the press, such as 'Ashamed Chinese'. He, like others, started by acknowledging that 'during the Japanese regime many young Asiatic girls — through force of circumstances in some cases — went about with Japanese officers.'[47] 'Ashamed Chinese' even agreed that many of these prostitutes became mistresses of Japanese officers and officials 'to escape being rounded up by the Japanese M.P.s and turned into "comfort girls" for the Japanese Army', whom he also acknowledged were servicing up to 40 Japanese soldiers a day.[48] Yet, 'Ashamed Chinese' stridently complained that after the war these women simply switched from being mistresses and prostitutes for the Japanese to being mistresses and prostitutes for the British military. He was not alone in complaining about this trend. Male public opinion in Singapore, as expressed by male leaders, was particularly unsympathetic to women in this position, which reflected notions of the 'fallen' women who consorted with the Japanese during the war and with the British after the war.[49]

Often these critics blamed the 'fallen' women for the increase in venereal disease during the Japanese Occupation. According to Dr Lyall, the Senior Medical Officer of the Social Hygiene Hospital that attended to cases of venereal disease, the women who were involved in the sex industry for the Japanese military were to blame for the fifteen-fold increase in venereal disease.[50] Nair in his crusade against the prostitutes from the Japanese Occupation even declared: 'I refer to the hundreds of prostitutes who ply their trade in the streets

---

[46] *The Straits Times*, 24 August 1946.
[47] *The Straits Times*, 24 August 1946.
[48] *The Straits Times*, 24 August 1946.
[49] *The Straits Times*, 28 June 1947.
[50] *Sunday Tribune*, 25 January 1948. See also the assessment in Po Leong Kuk and Girls Welfare, File Number BMA 255-45, Microfilm Number MSA 013 (National Archives of Singapore); and Middle Road Hospital, File Number DMS 17-45, Microfilm Number MH 214 (National Archives of Singapore).

of Singapore after sunset. These women are one hundred per cent infected, and apart from the spreading of V.D. the sight of these painted dolls behaving shamelessly in public is a blot on the fair name of Singapore.'[51]

Women's Opinions on the Comfort Women of Singapore

Male leaders, such as Chen Su Lan, who condemned these women, had an easy and draconian solution. They wanted them rounded up and sent to a home for prostitutes. Some female community leaders objected to this proposal. Women's opinions about the postwar legacies of the comfort stations and *ryotei* were publicly and forthrightly put forward by Lee Kiu. The only woman on the Singapore Advisory Council to the British Military Administration, she had been a member of the communist guerrilla force, the Malayan People's Anti-Japanese Army, and was a member of the communist front political party, the New Democratic Youth Party. Lee Kiu was described by Victor Purcell, the British Military Administration's Chief Chinese Affairs Adviser, as a 'young Chinese coolie girl of 26 [actually born in 1923, so even younger] with a neo-Jacobin toilette', who was relentless in her advocacy for the downtrodden in her early postwar social work. Purcell held a patronising view of her in the Advisory Council: 'Miss Lee Kiu is the energetic indomitable often obstinate woman leader that the proletariat throws up from time to time.'[52] She later left Singapore and Malaya for life in China as the Communist united front strategy gave way to armed insurrection and the Malayan Emergency.[53]

For Lee Kiu, the emancipation of women was an important component of Marxism's emphasis on the liberation of the oppressed. She fought for equal pay and paid maternity leave for women labourers.[54] She was also a founder of the Singapore Women's Federation, which had a membership of 3,000.[55] One of the few female Chinese leaders to have emerged from the war, and very active in social welfare relief, Lee Kiu was chosen by the British Military Administration to represent the views of Chinese women on the Singapore

---

[51] *The Straits Times*, 13 August 1946.
[52] Malaya's Political Climate IV Period 10th November to 30th November, 1945, p. 49, WO 203/5032 (The National Archives, UK). See Christopher Bayly and Tim Harper, *Forgotten Wars: The End of Britain's Asian Empire* (London: Penguin, 2008), p. 118.
[53] For a biographical account, see Lee Kiu (Li Qiu), 'Yige Ma Gong Dangyuan de Huiyilu' [Memoirs of a Malayan Communist], *Journal of the South Seas Society* 55 (December 2000): 83–112.
[54] *The Straits Times*, 25 November 1945.
[55] *The Straits Times*, 23 October 1946.

Advisory Council. Her views were different from her male colleagues regarding what should happen to the women who had worked in the sex industry of the Japanese military and remained in prostitution.

From late 1945 to early 1946, amid the calls by her male colleagues to round up these women and then force them into institutions, such as the prewar Poh Leung Kuk home, so that they were out of sight, Lee Kiu argued against the approach of Chen and his male counterparts:

> To take drastic steps against prostitutes or to send them to the Po Leung Kok [Poh Leung Kuk] or some Homes will not tackle the problem at its roots. We must devise some measures to deal with this whole problem. At present, a large number of girls are employed as waitresses in cafes and coffee shops and if we drive them out of employment, many would become prostitutes because there is nothing for them to do. Or if we send them to homes that would not solve the problem at all. I would suggest that these women-waitresses and prostitutes be recommended for some work in various industries so that they have some work to do. If they have a livelihood they would not work as prostitutes and waitresses any more. We have to open up more factories and offer work for the women. At the same time, we must promote social recreation so that they young people can spend their time in a proper manner.[56]

The British Military Administration had initially appeared to value the views of women. In September 1945, Major-General H.R. Hone, Chief Civil Affairs Officer (CCAO), asked Rosalind Foo of the Young Women's Christian Association (YWCA) to conduct 'a survey into the present position of women and girls in this country and to suggest ways in which they might be helped'.[57] He instructed: 'Our interest at this moment is not in professional prostitutes or those who are acting as such of choice; but in those girls who have been forced into such a way of life by the Japanese and the economic conditions during the occupation.'[58] However, the instructions from the British Military Administration indicated a preference for rounding up the women and placing them into the prewar premises of the Poh Leung Kuk home for detained prostitutes, which simply acted as a place for detention although the stated

---

[56] Miss Lee Kiu, *British Military Administration, Malaya, Advisory Council, Singapore Report of Proceedings*, 14 November 1945, p. 21, in Singapore Advisory Council, File Number BMA (H) HQ CH 36–45, Microfilm Number NA 869 (National Archives of Singapore).

[57] CCAO to Miss Begg, 30 September 1945, Item 27, in Social Welfare BMA 27–45, Microfilm Number NA 869 (National Archives of Singapore).

[58] CCAO to Miss Begg, 30 September 1945, Item 27, in Social Welfare BMA 27–45, Microfilm Number NA 869 (National Archives of Singapore).

purpose was 'rehabilitation'. Poh Leung Kuk had taught the girls and women skills, such as needlework, so they could work as amahs or maids in Chinese homes. It also arranged marriages between the inmates and 'suitable' Chinese coolies who were seeking a bride.[59] However, over time it developed a reputation as a place of detention. Rosalind Foo seems to have been hired to help carry this out.[60]

Not surprisingly, it was Chen's ideas of institutionalising the local prostitutes who formerly worked in the Japanese military's sex industry that were favoured by the male British colonial officials. Worried about their troops contracting venereal disease, the British armed forces were putting pressure on Brigadier P.A.B. McKerron, Deputy Chief Civil Affairs Officer (DCCAO), who represented the British Military Administration in the Singapore Advisory Council. McKerron announced that the British armed services were 'equally interested in the suppression of prostitution and the elimination of venereal disease'.[61] He mentioned that both himself and Colonel Dr W.J. Vickers, the British Military Administration's Deputy Director Civil Affairs (Medical), had attended several conferences with the armed forces making strident representations on prostitution and venereal disease. McKerron noted: 'We propose to deal with all brothels when we find them and break them up, and we propose also to deal with street soliciting...because the Services are equally anxious, if not more anxious, to see that this sort of thing shall cease.'[62] McKerron suggested having a women's wing of the police force to round up these prostitutes from the Japanese Occupation who in the early postwar period were soliciting on the streets.

Victor Purcell, the British Military Administration's Chief Chinese Affairs Adviser, and the other male members of the Singapore Advisory Council just wanted the women removed from the streets. Purcell sounded sympathetic to Lee Kiu's objections to the idea: 'As Miss Lee Kiu says, prostitution is basically

---

[59] *Singapore Free Press and Mercantile Advertiser*, 30 April 1929.

[60] Victor Purcell to DCCAO, *Subject: Women and Girls, Welfare, 5 October 1945*, in Social Welfare BMA 27–45, Microfilm Number NA 869 (National Archives of Singapore).

[61] Brigadier McKerron, *British Military Administration, Malaya, Advisory Council, Singapore Report of Proceedings*, 14 November 1945, p. 22, in Singapore Advisory Council, File Number BMA (H) HQ CH 36–45, Microfilm Number NA 869 (National Archives of Singapore).

[62] Brigadier McKerron, *British Military Administration, Malaya, Advisory Council, Singapore Report of Proceedings*, 14 November 1945, p. 22, in Singapore Advisory Council, File Number BMA (H) HQ CH 36–45, Microfilm Number NA 869 (National Archives of Singapore).

economic and whatever we may do apart from attacking the basic cause is palliative. Nevertheless we cannot await the final solution without approaching the problem and attempting to improve the present situation.'[63] But in the end, for Purcell, as for the other men on the Singapore Advisory Council, rounding the women up and putting them into a home was a far easier option: 'The immediate problem in Singapore is to find somewhere the girls and women who have been victims of the Japanese regime and are now destitute or have to resort to prostitution can find refuge and start life again.'[64]

During the Singapore Advisory Council debates about the young prostitutes still working on the streets after the Japanese Occupation, Lee Kiu persisted against male opposition to argue for solutions that would respect the rights of the women:

> I have been to Bras Basah Road and to areas along Jalan Besar making personal investigations and I have seen numerous cases of these prostitutes on the road being insulted by menfolk. I can see very clearly that their life is not a happy one. Now that the factories are not yet re-opened, what sort of work can they take up? I am opposed to the proposal that all prostitutes be arrested because once they are arrested they will be brought before the court and fined and when they are released they will take up the profession again. That is not a fundamental solution. The only solution open to us is to get them employment by re-opening the factories.[65]

However, Lee Kiu conceded to her fellow male members of the Singapore Advisory Council that something needed to be done quickly rather than wait for factories to be set up. Instead of detaining the prostitutes at another Poh Leung Kuk home, she proposed setting up a Girls' Training School that would give them six months of training in skills to take up other employment. Lee Kiu reasoned that 'we cannot arrest all of them and keep them there' and that 'if we arrest one group into the Po Leung Kok [Poh Leung Kuk] home another

---

[63] Victor Purcell, *British Military Administration, Malaya, Advisory Council, Singapore Report of Proceedings*, 14 November 1945, p. 23, in Singapore Advisory Council, File Number BMA (H) HQ CH 36–45, Microfilm Number NA 869 (National Archives of Singapore).
[64] Victor Purcell, *British Military Administration, Malaya, Advisory Council, Singapore Report of Proceedings*, 14 November 1945, p. 23, in Singapore Advisory Council, File Number BMA (H) HQ CH 36–45, Microfilm Number NA 869 (National Archives of Singapore).
[65] Miss Lee Kiu, *British Military Administration, Malaya, Advisory Council, Singapore Report of Proceedings*, 23 January 1946, p. 96, in Singapore Advisory Council, File Number BMA Ch.A 49-1945, Microfilm Number NA 870 (National Archives of Singapore).

group would come out and there would be no end of arrest.'⁶⁶ She advocated that the 'home be run in the same way as a boarding school' and that its 'syllabus may include reading, general knowledge, needlework, cookery, housekeeping, nursery work, other handwork, discipline training, physical exercise, etc.' She further urged: 'Do not adopt the detention measure in the management of the home. The inmates can ask permission from the person in charge to go out. Take the inmates to visit factories, creches, hospitals and other places of educational value, such as cinemas. Equip the women with tools for recreation, musical instruments, books etc for the amusement of the inmates after studying hours.'⁶⁷

Rounding Up the Young Singapore Prostitutes from the Japanese Occupation

Concessions were made to Lee Kiu's concerns over the women who still remained on the streets as prostitutes after the Japanese Occupation. The proposed home for them would be primarily a training school and a place for 'rehabilitation' and learning skills. In December 1945, Lieutenant Colonel R.N. Broome, Advisor, Chinese Affairs, announced that the British Military Administration would be setting up a Girls' Training School for 'the reclaiming of girls brought into prostitution under the Japanese regime'.⁶⁸ In March 1946, the British Military Administration allocated the sizeable sum of £20,000 to this project. The Singapore Social Welfare Council, which comprised both colonial officials and community representatives engaged in social work, announced that the school was for the 'many girls' who 'have been forced in the period of the Japanese Occupation into prostitution either directly by the

---

⁶⁶ Miss Lee Kiu, *British Military Administration, Malaya, Advisory Council, Singapore Report of Proceedings*, 13 December 1945, p. 72, in Singapore Advisory Council, File Number BMA (H) HQ CH 36–45, Microfilm Number NA 869 (National Archives of Singapore).

⁶⁷ Miss Lee Kiu, *British Military Administration, Malaya, Advisory Council, Singapore Report of Proceedings*, 13 December 1945, p. 73, in Singapore Advisory Council, File Number BMA (H) HQ CH 36–45, Microfilm Number NA 869 (National Archives of Singapore).

⁶⁸ Colonel Broome, *British Military Administration, Malaya, Advisory Council, Singapore Report of Proceedings*, 12 December 1945, pp. 66–7, in Singapore Advisory Council, File Number BMA (H) HQ CH 36–45, Microfilm Number NA 869 (National Archives of Singapore); and *Malaya Tribune*, 13 December 1945.

Japanese or indirectly by the conditions during the occupation'.[69] Proponents of the school within the Singapore Social Welfare Council argued that it 'need not be confined to these girls, and for the future its work will be rather prevention to save girls', as the school was also aimed at preventing 'the girls from falling into such a way of life, by offering them a preferable alternative — though its immediate aim is rehabilitation'.[70] The Singapore Social Welfare Council declared that the Girls' Training School 'would give girls a short but intensive and comprehensive course in domestic economy, so that when a girl leaves she will be able to assume full responsibility for running a home and care of the children' either as a domestic servant or when starting her own family and home.[71]

The colonial government acted to deal with the noticeable numbers of women left in prostitution from the Japanese Occupation by formally setting up by June 1947 a Women and Girls' Section in its Social Welfare Department. The Social Welfare Department's 1947 report to the United Nations on the trafficking of women and girls into prostitution outlined the legacy of the Japanese military using local women in their comfort stations that was being dealt with by this section of the department:

> One of the results of the Japanese Occupation from the anti-vice point of view, was the very considerable increase in prostitution. This is not surprising in view of the extensive use made by the Japanese authorities of recognised brothels for the use of their military personnel. These so-called 'comfort houses' were staffed by local girls who were either induced or coerced into them or by the importation of girls from the N.E.I. [Netherlands East Indies] and elsewhere, ostensibly for service with the Japanese army as nurses, etc…. On the surrender of the Japanese Army in Singapore, those brothels were closed…many local girls who had been compelled to take up prostitution to stave off starvation were endeavouring to earn a living in this way on the streets.[72]

---

[69] Scheme Submitted to the Welfare Council by the Sub-committee to consider the Rehabilitation of women and girls to the Singapore Social Welfare Council, Meeting 26 July 1946 in Social Welfare BMA 27-45, Microfilm Number NA 869 (National Archives of Singapore).
[70] Scheme Submitted to the Welfare Council by the Sub-committee.
[71] Scheme Submitted to the Welfare Council by the Sub-committee.
[72] Colony of Singapore: Report to U.N.O. For Period 30 June 1946–30 June 1947 in Trafficking in Woman and Girls File, Social Welfare Department, Number SWD 241 Vol 1, Microfilm Number MSA 3448 (National Archives of Singapore).

Many of the women feared going back to their communities as social outcasts. They had little choice but to continue to work in the sex industry. The Social Welfare Department's solution was the rounding up of these streetwalkers.

From 1 January 1947, the young prostitutes from the Japanese Occupation were collected from the streets and then housed in the newly built Girls' Training School premises at Pasir Panjang. The Social Welfare Department declared that 'under statutory powers the Women and Girls' Section can detain girls under 18 years of age who are being trained as prostitutes, are habitually in the company of prostitutes, or are in fact prostituting'.[73] The department's 1947 annual report described how the conditions of work of these women resembled those in the sex industry of the Japanese military during the war with sex in small cubicles: 'The juvenile street walkers normally rent small cubicles without air or light and their earnings are small when the rapacity of the amahs, landlords and bullies has been satisfied.'[74] However, missing was the Japanese military's emphasis on condoms. Social workers in the department reported that of the 60 juvenile prostitutes between the ages of 13 and 17 detained in 1947, all had venereal disease.

The procedures of detaining these young prostitutes were similar to those in the prewar period. Before the war, girls would be detained and cured of venereal disease in the Hospital for Social Hygiene at Middle Road, then placed in the Poh Leung Kuk home until they were 18 years old or when their welfare could be taken care of outside of the institution. There were attempts to make sure the new Girls' Training School avoided the bad reputation of Poh Leung Kuk as a place of detention for prostitutes, instead of as a place for learning new skills for further employment.[75] In contrast to the Poh Leung Kuk home, the girls at the training school attended many more courses in cooking and buying food, dressmaking, needlework, care of infants, laundry work, household cleaning, and maintenance.[76] They also received an elementary education and were encouraged to play sports and games such as badminton and swimming.[77]

---

[73] *Social Welfare Singapore 1947: The Third Annual Report of the Department of Social Welfare* (Singapore: Colony of Singapore, 1948), p. 25.
[74] *Social Welfare Singapore 1947*, p. 25.
[75] Scheme Submitted to the Welfare Council by the Sub-committee; and see *Social Welfare Singapore 1947*, pp. 25–7.
[76] D.R. Horne, Memorandum Girls' Training School, 26 September 1946, Item 18A, in Social Welfare BMA 27-45, Microfilm Number NA 869 (National Archives of Singapore).
[77] *Social Welfare Singapore 1947*, pp. 26–7.

The new Girls' Training School received the support and co-operation of the Singapore Women's Federation under its president Yang Peh Fong and its advisor Lee Kiu, although they did have some reservations. Both of them cautioned that they thought it 'unwise for the authorities to arrest prostitutes', recommending that 'educational methods should be adopted and suitable jobs recommended to them so as to alleviate their sufferings'.[78] Ann Wee, an early social worker in the Social Welfare Department, believed that the imbalanced ratio of males to females in colonial Singapore meant these young women from the Girls' Training School were able to marry and establish families because of the shortage of women as potential wives for 'young artisan men' who were too poor to obtain a wife 'from other sources'.[79]

Colonial officials in the Social Welfare Department believed that all that these girls required were homemaking skills, which they learnt at the Girls' Training School. However, within a year it was clear that the idea of taking the young prostitutes off the streets and putting them into the Girls' Training School was not working as well as hoped. The 1947 report of the Social Welfare Department was frank in admitting that 'while the process of detection is not difficult, but rehabilitation is a most arduous, and, in many cases, unrewarding task. The resentment against authority which a girl is bound to feel when she is detained can only be increased by rigorous detention, and the chances of thus re-directing a girl's life along more satisfactory lines are negligible.'[80]

Many young women simply absconded and escaped from the Girls' Training School. Reports of the Social Welfare Department regularly mentioned numerous escapes by the young prostitutes. The 1947 report of the department observed that the 'Home is surrounded by barbed wire and the gate is kept locked but this is more to keep undesirables out than the girls in. There have been many escapes during the year, and the staff have had many disappointments, much anxiety and constant hard work'.[81] The report concluded that staff were often left hoping that 'when a girl escapes, the memory of a period of orderly living and genuine human affection may not entirely be erased, and may prove a starting point from which, she will, as an individual, plan to shake herself free from her unfortunate environment.'[82]

---

[78] *Sin Chew Jit Poh*, 21 March 1946, a translation is in Social Welfare BMA 27-45, Microfilm Number NA 869 (National Archives of Singapore).
[79] Ann Wee, *A Tiger Remembers: The Way We Were in Singapore* (Singapore: NUS Press, 2017), p. 57.
[80] *Social Welfare Singapore 1947*, p. 26.
[81] *Social Welfare Singapore 1947*, p. 26.
[82] *Social Welfare Singapore 1947*, p. 26.

The matron, who was from China with a background in running homes for young prostitutes, as well as the assistant matron, and a teacher reported what they noticed about the behaviour of the 30 to 35 girls at the home.[83] The personalities of the girls had been influenced by years of a life of prostitution, which ill suited them for the elementary education they were given:

> These girls start with the handicap of being entirely untaught upon arrival. Their way of life has been one which encouraged idleness and discouraged thought and initiative. The change consequent on detention frequently causes hysterical out-bursts. The nervous tension to which they are subject occasions laughter and tears with little or no intervening periods of calm. Their former way of life has produced the exhibitionists in each one, and the appearance of strangers has a most unsettling effect. For these reasons the slight mental discipline required for elementary education, imposes a great strain, and makes for slow progress.[84]

Despite the failure of 'rehabilitating' the young prostitutes in its first year of 1947, the second year in 1948 proved to have greater success for staff at the Girls' Training School. The process of detaining the young prostitutes and sending them to the Girls' Training School at Pasir Panjang continued with 48 raids carried out and 103 prostitutes detained. Fifty were sent to the Girls' Training School or transferred to the Salvation Army home.[85] By early 1949, the social workers' evaluation of the results were more positive after the 'initial problems and disappointments' in 1947.[86]

In 1948, a new and more successful approach was found to 'rehabilitate' the young prostitutes by experimenting with more personalised treatment. There was a realistic recognition among officials that 'the young prostitute removed under warrant from Singapore's disorderly houses is a difficult subject and needs individual handling of a specialised kind.'[87] They outlined how it was difficult for them to connect with the young prostitutes because of the attitudes that many had developed streetwalking:

---

[83] *Beginnings, The First Report of the Singapore Department of Social Welfare. June to December, 1946* (Singapore: Government Printer, 1947), p. 39; and see *Social Welfare 1948: The Fourth Annual Report of the Department of Social Welfare* (Singapore: Colony of Singapore, 1949), p. 31.
[84] *Social Welfare Singapore 1947*, pp. 26–7.
[85] *Social Welfare Singapore 1948*, p. 31.
[86] *Social Welfare Singapore 1948*, p. 30.
[87] *Social Welfare Singapore 1948*, p. 30.

> The girl committed to the home by the Protector will, in most cases, have been sold as an infant or a young child to a procuress and will have been brought up with no other in view but to make herself attractive to men and a source of profit to her purchaser. Genuine interest and affection will have been entirely absent from her experience and she will have acquired a cynical and deep-rooted suspicion of any motives which are not clearly obvious to her. Also these girls are, almost without exception, entirely illiterate and are thus dependent on the least satisfactory influences for their knowledge of human behaviour. The newcomer to the home is usually an exhibitionist and displays a grotesque and pathetic sophistication.[88]

The person who developed the approach that produced results that impressed the social workers in the Social Welfare Department was 'the Chinese matron of this home, who has had experience of kindred work in the devastated provinces of China'. The department reported that the matron 'has introduced a system of treatment which is producing gratifying results. The keynote of this treatment is, by means of a sympathetic individual approach coupled with the strictest discipline, to turn the girls into children again. This method has induced reasonable contentment in place of emotion and hysteria.'[89]

The matron's approach to 'rehabilitating' the young prostitutes entailed three steps. The matron and her staff started by developing the girls' trust on a one-to-one basis: 'The first step in training is to win the confidence of the individual girl.' Social workers from the department observed that 'through constant frank talks, understanding and firm discipline, interesting activities and, by setting an example of hard work, the matron and the staff have slowly succeeded in bringing a feeling of security into the girls' lives.' This crucial first step impressed the social workers from the department, who commented on the changes they saw in the young former prostitutes: 'Their mistrust and fear of punishment is thus slowly broken down and their co-operation is secured in the process of rehabilitation.'[90]

The social workers of the Social Welfare Department explained the next step for the 'rehabilitation' of the young prostitutes from the Japanese Occupation was building 'a foundation upon which some education can be built up'. Along with lessons in Mandarin, English, and arithmetic, the girls were given simple talks on anatomy, the functions of the body, germs, and disease. The talks began with imparting knowledge of venereal diseases, which the girls had

---

[88] *Social Welfare Singapore 1948*, p. 30.
[89] *Social Welfare Singapore 1948*, p. 31.
[90] *Social Welfare Singapore 1948*, p. 31.

been treated for at the Social Hygiene Hospital, but of which they had only a poor understanding previously. The teachers used a practical and relevant approach to pique the girls' interest in education. This led them to the Girls' Training School library, which had many 'simply written books in Chinese about V.D., and its consequences, the facts of life, the understanding of oneself and mother craft, as well as books bearing on other aspects of the home, such as needlework, poultry rearing, gardening and games, swimming and physical activity'. Education for the girls was kept very practical and focused on day-to-day activities. The social workers summed up the astonishing results of this approach in the second step: 'To these girls, semi-illiterate, books and instruction which centre round themselves and the simple life they live in the home have great appeal. No special persuasion is needed to make them settle down in the afternoons in their library. Those with experience of this type of girl will realise that this is a very remarkable fact.'[91]

The third and last step that the Chinese matron used was to provide them with vocational education so they could earn a living and become economically independent. The matron and the teachers tried 'to stimulate the desire to earn one's own living' by visits to factories, welfare centres, telephone offices, and printing offices, as well as other places the women would be able to work after leaving the school. The social workers remarked on how 'these visits have proved popular and it is believed by opening up vistas that are completely new to the girls they will have a beneficial influence on their outlook.'[92] By the end of the 1940s, the social workers were optimistic about the transition that the young prostitutes from the Japanese Occupation were making at the Girls' Training School:

> The girls who now sit quietly in the library after tea, who leave the house unescorted to go for walks and shopping expeditions in the neighbourhood, who make their own clothes, who tend to their own flowers and poultry, who display a pleasant and natural demeanour who in many respects behave like ordinary children, are very different from the strident, hysterical, prenaturally aged beings who first entered the home.[93]

This seemingly successful 'rehabilitation' of the young prostitutes who had worked in the Japanese military's sex industry during the war brought to an end the public discussion about these women. By the 1950s, concern over the young prostitutes remaining from the war was replaced by other concerns over a

---

[91] *Social Welfare Singapore 1948*, p. 31.
[92] *Social Welfare Singapore 1948*, p. 31.
[93] *Social Welfare Singapore 1948*, p. 31.

new generation of younger prostitutes who were being brought into Singapore from China by unscrupulous immigration agents.[94] Social workers in the Social Welfare Department during the 1950s, such as Ann Wee, recall no longer seeing these Singapore women who were a living legacy from the Japanese military's sex industry.[95] By 1950, these young women, forced into prostitution due to poverty or coercion during the Japanese Occupation, began to disappear from the records of the Social Welfare Department.[96] Many women who had worked in the Japanese military's sex industry keenly felt the postwar campaigns against them. Like their counterparts in Korea, these women would have also had every incentive to keep silent about their pasts.

In conclusion, there are common threads from the early postwar experiences of the Indonesian, Korean, and Singapore women who worked in the Japanese military's sex industry. All had to deal with societies that were largely unsympathetic to their plight. Colonial authorities and community leaders were particularly alarmed by the number of Singapore women who had become prostitutes during the Japanese Occupation and after the war continued to make a living streetwalking. The large sex industry that the Japanese military had fostered in Singapore had undoubtedly created this postwar situation, which absorbed the resources of the colonial authorities in the immediate years after the end of the war. The creation of the Girls' Training School at Pasir Panjang in order to provide these young prostitutes from the Japanese Occupation with training so that they could take up alternative employment and settle down into their own homes seems to have had sufficient success. By the early 1950s there was little discussion of Singapore women who had become involved in the sex industry of the Japanese Occupation.[97] However, given the discussion of their plight in the mid to late 1940s, it was very likely that these women chose to remain silent about their experiences in order to re-integrate into society rather than remain ostracised. Records indicate that by the early 1950s women who

---

[94] *Report of the Social Welfare Department 1950* (Singapore: Colony of Singapore, 1951), pp. 20–6.
[95] Ann Wee, interviewed by Kevin Blackburn, 26 November 2019. See the records in Trafficking in Woman and Girls, Social Welfare Department, SWD 241 Vol. 1, Microfilm Number MAS 3448 (National Archives of Singapore).
[96] See the records in Trafficking in Woman and Girls, Social Welfare Department, SWD 241 Vol. 1, Microfilm Number MSA 3448 (National Archives of Singapore); and Traffic in Woman and Children Annual Report, CSO 7180-47, Microfilm Number MSA 3447 (National Archives of Singapore).
[97] See the *Report of the Social Welfare Department 1950*, pp. 21–3; and *Report of the Social Welfare Department 1951* (Singapore: Colony of Singapore, 1952), pp. 5–8.

had entered prostitution out of the circumstances of the Japanese Occupation were no longer noticeable among Singapore women engaged in prostitution. The early postwar discussion over the women and their experiences illustrates Dale Spender's point that male-controlled language helped perpetuate and reinforce the women's subordination in society. By marrying and settling down into families the women escaped the opprobrium and censure for being 'fallen' women, as long as they kept quiet about their pasts and appeared as 'good wives'. These circumstances appear conducive to creating a silence about these women. However, what has been surprising is the longevity of this silence, which will be explored in the next chapter.

6

The Silence of the Local Comfort Women of Singapore

This chapter pursues the explorations of Chapter 1 in examining the reasons why local Singapore comfort women maintained a silence in the 1990s despite local journalists asking them to tell their stories, especially during the 50th anniversary commemorations of the Second World War. Diana Wong in her assessment of the memory of the Japanese Occupation makes the point that until the 1990s there existed a 'memory suppression' in Singapore of what happened during the period. It was only during the 50th anniversary commemorations that public memory of the Japanese Occupation became prominent as the Singapore government sought to incorporate the suffering of the local population under the Japanese into a narrative of national survival.[1]

Until the 1990s, the narratives of the Second World War in Singapore tended to be divisive accounts based on the different experiences of the various ethnic groups of Singapore. However, in the 1990s the state developed what Wong calls a 'survivalist' narrative to remember the Japanese Occupation. This way of commemorating the Japanese Occupation focused on remembering common suffering and surviving the challenges, which fitted into an overall 'survivalist' narrative of Singapore history that the state was promoting. Wong describes the 50th anniversary commemorations of the Second World War as an 'orgy of commemorations' orchestrated by the state. This leads to two questions. What attempts were there to bring to light the memories of local Singapore comfort women during this period of commemoration in the 1990s? How was the search for these memories of the women carried out?

---

[1] Diana Wong, 'Memory Suppression and Memory Production: The Japanese Occupation of Singapore', in *Perilous Memories: The Asia-Pacific War(s)*, ed. T. Fujitani, Geoffrey M. White, and Lisa Yoneyama (Durham: Duke University Press, 2001), pp. 218–38.

The Search for Local Singapore Comfort Women by the English-Language Press

Chapters 1 and 5 have demonstrated that the international controversy over the Korean comfort women in December 1991 caused the issue to re-emerge in Singapore after it had disappeared as a topic of public discussion in the early 1950s as the young prostitutes from the Japanese Occupation left the Girls' Training School and either took up jobs in the workforce, or married and had families. From 1992 onwards, *The Straits Times* investigative journalist Phan Ming Yen worked with Japanese historian Hayashi Hirofumi to document the location of the comfort stations of Singapore in a series of newspaper articles.[2] When it became public knowledge that there were comfort stations in Singapore and yet no former local comfort women had come forward to give testimony, Phan posed the question in a headline of *The Straits Times* on 30 August 1993: 'Were there Singaporean Comfort Women?'[3]

Phan contacted local historians, who expressed their doubts about the existence of local Singapore comfort women. Ernest Chew, a National University of Singapore historian and Dean of the Faculty of Arts and Social Sciences in the early 1990s, was sceptical: 'I am not aware of any written documented research on the Singapore side and there has been no scholarly work done on the Singapore experience. One has to rely mainly on oral history sources.'[4] Military historian Ong Chit Chung, of the History Department at the National University of Singapore and a ruling People's Action Party Member of Parliament, expressed even stronger doubts: 'In my own research, I have not come across cases of Singaporean comfort women.'[5] He added, 'There is no documented evidence of Singaporeans being comfort women but there is always the possibility.'[6]

However, Phan concluded in his piece that 'various sources in Singapore, who declined to be identified, have said they had friends or relatives who were once comfort women but decline to elaborate.'[7] Phan later recalled that in the 1990s, he and his colleagues at *The Straits Times* discovered that while there were local Singapore comfort women still living, they refused to give testimony for fear of public disapproval. Phan's colleague at *The Straits Times*, Eurasian

---

[2] *The Straits Times*, 30 August 1993.
[3] *The Straits Times*, 30 August 1993.
[4] *The Straits Times*, 30 August 1993.
[5] *The Straits Times*, 30 August 1993.
[6] *The Straits Times*, 30 August 1993.
[7] *The Straits Times*, 30 August 1993.

journalist Raoul Le Blond, mentioned to him that he had contact with a woman who had been in the Japanese military's sex industry but was reluctant to go public over her experience.[8]

In other words, the local Singapore comfort women still had reservations about ending their own silences that they had initiated in the early years after the war when they were ostracised and discriminated against for being part of the Japanese military's sex industry. William Bradley Horton's work on Indonesian women suggests reasons for such a reluctance amongst some former comfort women to tell their stories in public. Horton argued that the process of obtaining information from a comfort woman could prove to be damaging for her, 'at least in terms of her position in society'.[9] A former comfort woman risked losing the very social position she had achieved in her society and her family if she publicly revealed her past in the brothels of the Japanese military. In many Asian societies, even if she would have received sympathy as a 'victim', there was a strong likelihood that public revealing of her past would invite subtle yet damaging unvoiced aspersions about her 'sordid past'. She could be transformed from 'a good wife' to a 'fallen' woman in the society in which she had been able to live and achieve a degree of social status because she had concealed her past in the Japanese military's brothels. When examining oral history work done with comfort women, Horton emphasised that they may have nothing to gain from giving testimony and interviews, but everything to lose: 'More importantly, though, such work entails the risk of damaging the social position of those women and reviving memories which they may have tried to leave behind.'[10] In the 1990s, there were indications in Singapore that much of what Horton raised about the circumstances of the comfort women in Indonesia was also applicable.

Chapter 1 indicates that local Singapore comfort women would have been reluctant to provide testimony after hearing Lee Kuan Yew's widely reported 1992 statement that the Korean comfort women had 'saved the chastity of many Singaporean girls', which implied that Singapore women were not involved in the Japanese military's sex industry. His words carried considerable weight in Singapore, with few daring to contradict him. Singapore in the 1980s and 1990s was still a male-dominated society led by conservative leaders. This was evidenced by Prime Minister Lee Kuan Yew's statements on the role of

---

[8] Phan Ming Yen, interviewed by Kevin Blackburn, 1 February 2020.
[9] William Bradley Horton, 'Pramoedya and the Comfort Women of Buru: A Textual Analysis of *Perawan Remaja dalam Cengkeraman Militer* (Teenage Virgins in the Grasp of the Military)', *Journal of Asia-Pacific Studies* (Waseda University), no. 14 (March 2010): 79.
[10] Horton, 'Pramoedya and the Comfort Women of Buru', p. 85.

women in society that he made in 1983 and 1986. He expressed regret that his government's policies to educate women had created a society in which many university graduate women remained unmarried, mainly because Singapore men preferred wives who were inferior in terms of educational levels.

In a December 1986 speech at the National University of Singapore, Lee said he believed that the reason 65 per cent of graduate Singapore men married non-graduate women 'reflects the old cultural biases of men for wives who are seen to be controllable'.[11] Lee said he would have preferred that educated women in Singapore be like those in Japan, where there was social pressure on women to educate themselves not in order to take up careers like their male counterparts but in the arts, languages, and home economics, so that they could marry and complement their husband's careers as well-educated wives and mothers. He even praised former Japanese Prime Minister Kakuei Tanaka for spreading around what Lee thought were Tanaka's superior genes by having many children with his multiple mistresses. Lee appeared to recall with nostalgia the days when Chinese men did the same before the marriage laws removed polygamy.[12]

In his National Day Rally Speech in August 1983, Lee famously spoke about bringing back practices that had historically subordinated women in a modern form to make sure that well-educated women remained mothers: 'Equal employment opportunities, yes, but we shouldn't get our women into jobs where they cannot, at the same time, be mothers.... You just can't be doing a full-time heavy job like that of a doctor or engineer and run a home and bring up children.'[13] Lee admitted: 'It is too late for us to reverse our policies and have our women go back to their primary role as mothers, the creators, protectors of the next generation. Our women will not stand for it. And anyway they have already become a too important factor in the economy.'[14] He argued that 'therefore we must further amend our policies and try to reshape our demographic configuration so that our better educated women will not be lost in the next generation.'[15] This meant introducing policies which gave preference in government services and financial benefits to graduate mothers

---

[11] Lee Kuan Yew, 'Lee Kuan Yew On Marriage, Education, and Fertility in Singapore', *Population and Development Review* 13, no. 1 (1987): 181.
[12] Lee, 'Lee Kuan Yew On Marriage, Education, and Fertility in Singapore', pp. 179–85.
[13] *The Straits Times*, 15 August 1983.
[14] *The Straits Times*, 15 August 1983; and Lee, 'Lee Kuan Yew On Marriage, Education, and Fertility in Singapore', pp. 179–85.
[15] *The Straits Times*, 15 August 1983; and Lee, 'Lee Kuan Yew On Marriage, Education, and Fertility in Singapore', pp. 179–85.

over less educated women, and the setting up of a government unit organising social gatherings for graduate men and graduate women to meet.

Male dominance in Singapore society was reflected in the reactions to Lee's speech by two significant Singapore women's organisations, the Singapore Council of Women's Organisations and the Singapore Women's Association. While many women strongly voiced their disagreement with Lee Kuan Yew's ideas, these two women's organisations expressed some agreement and went further, arguing that childbirth was national service for women, just as all males performed national service by undergoing regular military training. The Singapore Council of Women's Organisations, representing 22 women's organisations and 93,000 women members, planned a seminar entitled 'Childbirth is National Service'.[16]

Not surprisingly, Singapore women writing during the 1980s and 1990s regularly described their own society as a modern-day patriarchy. In 1986, Shamala Kandiah, at the National University of Singapore, saw her lot and that of other Singapore women as living in a society where 'underlying the facade of equality is a patriarchal ideology which keeps male domination alive'.[17] Singapore historian Kho Ee Moi sees this situation only fading in the twenty-first century when institutional changes were made. These included the removal of the one-third quota for women entering medical school, which had been based on the belief that female doctors would marry and drop out of the profession. Also removed were measures that prevented women in the public service from having their husbands covered for medical insurance, which had been grounded in the assumption that women would not be supporting their husbands. She argues that in the 1980s and 1990s state policy and discourse was aimed at 'putting women back in the homes'.[18]

When working at the Singapore *Straits Times* in the 1990s trying to track down former local Singapore comfort women to tell their stories, Phan recalls that the conservative patriarchal nature of Singapore society, reflected in its leadership, did not help in persuading the local Singapore comfort women to come forward to tell their stories.[19] Singapore also appears to have lacked a strong

---

[16] *The Straits Times*, 17 August 1983.
[17] For a mid-1980s assessment of Singapore society as patriarchy, see women's studies writer at the National University of Singapore Shamala Kandiah, 'Women in a Patriarchy: The Singapore Case' (National University of Singapore, Academic Exercise, 1986), p. 8.
[18] Kho Ee Moi, 'Economic Pragmatism and the "Schooling" of Girls in Singapore', *HSSE Online* 4, no. 2 (2015): 62–77; and Kho Ee Moi, *The Construction of Femininity in a Postcolonial State: Girls' Education in Singapore* (New York: Cambria Press, 2013).
[19] Phan Ming Yen, interviewed by Kevin Blackburn, 1 February 2020.

feminist movement that was prepared to push back assumptions preventing former comfort women from speaking out and discussing their experiences.

The type of organisations that were critical for the comfort women of other countries to speak out were absent in Singapore. Scholars writing on the comfort women have identified supportive feminist humanitarian organisations as crucial for many of the Korean comfort women to publicly recall their memories in a conservative Asian society.[20] In South Korea, feminist academic Yun Chung-ok had been essential in researching the lives of the comfort women and setting up supportive women's organisations to help them in their attempts to obtain justice. In Japan, Matsui Yayori played a similar role in setting up the Women's Active Museum on War and Peace, which was dedicated to the cause of the comfort women. These women and many other feminist activists, such as Nakahara Michiko, were instrumental in helping the comfort women come forward.[21]

In Singapore, unlike in South Korea and Japan, there was no supportive feminist movement calling for local Singapore comfort women to tell their stories from 1992 onwards. The initial focus of the Singapore women's movement was many of the policy issues that had emerged from Lee Kuan Yew's speeches in the 1980s, rather than a broad agenda that included the prostitution of women, both in the present and the past. The main Singapore women's rights and feminist organisation was the Association of Women for Action and Research (AWARE), which was in the 1990s a new group, having been formed only in 1985. AWARE had directly emerged from a group of professional women who were critical of Lee Kuan Yew's ideas that they should not concentrate as much on their careers as marriage and motherhood. It arose from a December 1984 forum at the National University of Singapore to discuss Lee's policy proposals called 'Women's Choices, Women's Lives'.[22]

The comfort women was an issue that was put on the agenda of Singapore's fledgling feminist organisation AWARE in the early 1990s when it arose

---

[20] C. Sarah Soh, *The Comfort Women: Sexual Violence and Postcolonial Memory in Korea and Japan* (Chicago: University of Chicago Press, 2008), pp. 40–6, 71–2, 232–4.

[21] See Pyong Gap Min, *Korean "Comfort Women": Military Brothels, Brutality, and the Redress Movement* (New Brunswick: Rutgers University Press, 2021), pp. 19–85; and Eika Tai, *Comfort Women Activism: Critical Voices From the Perpetrator State* (Hong Kong: University of Hong Kong Press, 2021).

[22] Lenore Lyons, *A State of Ambivalence: The Feminist Movement in Singapore* (Leiden: Brill, 2010), p. 37.

as an international controversy.[23] But lacking the resources and focus of its counterparts in South Korea and Japan, AWARE did not pursue it. It continued to be seen as an issue concerning women in other countries—Korea, Japan, Indonesia, the Philippines, and Taiwan—but not in Singapore. Phyllis Chew, one of several AWARE presidents in the 1990s, recollects that AWARE was then more interested in the middle-class concerns of its members, who were mainly professional women, rather than issues surrounding sex work or contentious historical matters concerning the comfort women.[24] This was perhaps not surprising. AWARE appears not to have been in a position to pursue issues which went beyond its resources as well as the key concerns of its middle-class membership. The work of sociologist Lenore Lyons on the AWARE of the 1990s documents how its attempts to reach out to working-class women, as well as women who only spoke Mandarin and Malay, were not sustained in the 1980s and 1990s despite indications that these women were receptive to the advocacy role of AWARE when they were contacted during gatherings.[25] Chinese- and Malay-speaking working-class women were the very section of society that local Singapore comfort women were likely to be found in rather than among the middle-class, English-educated women that comprised the membership of AWARE.

In the 1990s, there were limited prospects for political and civil society groups in Singapore to take up the comfort women issue. Political scientists Diane K. Mauzy and R.S. Milne confirm that in the 1990s, AWARE was 'viewed as an organization that chooses its issues with care so as to avoid direct confrontation with the government'.[26] The People's Action Party (PAP) dominated the political landscape and eschewed activism of any kind. Singapore civil society was only slowly emerging in the 1990s out of decades of state dominance.[27] In contrast, in Malaysia, it was the activist youth wing

---

[23] George Hicks, *The Comfort Women: Sex Slaves of the Japanese Imperial Forces* (Sydney: Allen & Unwin, 1995), p. 197.

[24] Phyllis Chew, interviewed by Kevin Blackburn, 20 November 2019.

[25] Lyons, *A State of Ambivalence*, pp. 57, 105–7.

[26] Diane K. Mauzy and R.S. Milne, *Singapore Politics Under the People's Action Party* (London: Routledge, 2002), p. 160; and see Lenore Lyons, 'Internalised Boundaries: AWARE's Place in Singapore's Emerging Civil Society', in *Paths Not Taken: Political Pluralism in Post-war Singapore*, ed. Michael D. Barr and Carl A. Trocki (Singapore: NUS Press, 2008), pp. 248–63.

[27] See Terence Lee, 'Gestural Politics: Civil Society in "New" Singapore', *Sojourn: Journal of Social Issues in Southeast Asia* 20, no. 2 (2005): 132–54; and Terence Lee, 'The Politics of Civil Society in Singapore', *Asian Studies Review* 26, no. 1 (2002): 97–117; and Mauzy and Milne, *Singapore Politics Under the People's Action Party*, pp. 157–68.

of the ruling United Malays National Organisation (UMNO) and its socially conscious coalition partner, the Malaysian Chinese Association (MCA), which were willing to take up the cause of local comfort women. They promised support in obtaining compensation from the Japanese government. These organisations were able to uncover former comfort women with the aid of the Malaysian Malay and Chinese press. Similar activist-orientated political wings were absent in Singapore.[28]

The Malay Press's Attempts to Tell the Stories of Local Singapore Comfort Women

During the 1990s, there was an attempt in Singapore by journalists to reach out to the comfort women in their own languages. However, contacting local Singapore comfort women in their own languages proved difficult. In the Singapore Malay press, just as with the Singapore English-language press, no local comfort women came forward to tell their stories. Instead, in the Malay press, women from Malaysia appeared telling their stories.[29]

Hani Mustafa, of the Singapore Malay-language newspaper *Berita Harian*, recalls the problems she had as a journalist trying to find Malay comfort women in Singapore who were willing to talk about their experiences. She discovered in interviews with locals who worked for the Japanese military that 'in Singapore not many local women were recruited. Most were from Korea.' A Malay driver for the Japanese military told her that 'he had seen a few local comfort women, but the numbers are small'. In addition, she felt that it was 'not easy for women to come forward to share their stories as comfort women' in Singapore during the 1990s because of the continuing stigma. Hani Mustafa then turned to Malaysia to find stories about the comfort women. She recalled that in contrast to Singapore, 'in Malaysia it was different, as there was a call by the ruling United Malays National Organisation (UMNO)'s youth wing to help them get compensation', and thus the former comfort women registered with the group because 'many were very poor and I believe the compensation would have helped relieve their financial problems'.[30]

Hani Mustafa explored some of the reasons why it was difficult to find comfort women in Singapore in the feature story that she eventually published

---

[28] Nakahara Michiko, 'Comfort Women in Malaysia', *Critical Asian Studies* 33, no. 4 (2001): 581–2.
[29] *Berita Harian*, 8 September 1995.
[30] Hani Mustafa, interviewed by Kevin Blackburn, 4 December 2019.

in *Berita Harian*'s special September 1995 issue for the 50th anniversary of the end of the war. She started her feature with Lee Kuan Yew's 1992 statement that implied that there had been no local comfort women, only Koreans who 'saved the chastity' of Singapore women. Just like her counterpart in *The Straits Times* had done in 1993, she asked Ong Chit Chung, a military historian and member of the ruling People's Action Party, about the existence of local comfort women. This time, over two years after his first interview with Phan of *The Straits Times*, Ong seemed more inclined to concede that there were local Singapore comfort women, but they had chosen to remain silent. Ong speculated that the Japanese military most likely had not wanted to make the existence of comfort women public during the war, and thus did not want to recruit many local women, which would have made the comfort women very noticeable in Singapore. He mentioned that it was very likely that among the Malaysian comfort women, there were women taken from Singapore. His responses to Hani Mustafa's questions reveal that he had had some discussions within the Singapore government and bureaucracy over the possibility of there being local Singapore comfort women who could make claims against the Japanese government, but 'until now we have never heard stories of sexual enslavement in Singapore'.[31] He elaborated that it appeared that in Singapore both 'those women who may want to confess and the Singapore government do not want to make a claim for compensation regarding this matter'.[32] Ong added: 'The war crimes against these women were also not recorded, and thus there was no official discussion' about local Singapore comfort women.[33] He concluded by saying: 'So it's hard to get clear evidence of sex slaves here.'[34]

Unable to obtain an interview with a Singapore comfort woman, Hani Mustafa eventually settled on telling the story of Malay comfort woman Sadiah Mat, aged 65, from the Malaysian state of Kelantan for *Berita Harian*'s 50th anniversary of the end of the war feature. She travelled all the way to Kelantan to interview Sadiah. In 1942, Sadiah, then 12 years old, went with her father when he was taken to Burma by the Japanese military to work on the Burma-Thailand Railway as a forced labourer. Her family consisted of just herself and her father. After her father died working on the Burma-Thailand Railway, Sadiah was taken by the Japanese to a comfort station in Burma for sex work alongside 50 Korean, Chinese, Indonesian, and Malayan women in 10 narrow

---

[31] *Berita Harian*, 8 September 1995.
[32] *Berita Harian*, 8 September 1995.
[33] *Berita Harian*, 8 September 1995.
[34] *Berita Harian*, 8 September 1995.

rooms with mats at a longhouse near where Japanese troops were stationed. The overwhelming majority of the women were Korean.

At first, Sadiah was unaware of why the Japanese had taken her. When she arrived, she noticed that the other women were not wearing clothes, just torn shorts or panties. She was taken to a room and left there by herself. A few minutes later, a Japanese soldier came in and started taking off his shirt. She recalled that as the soldier raped her, 'I kept screaming as hard as I could but the soldier ignored it.' She added: 'Shocked and confused, I was raped by the soldier several times, after which several other soldiers came in and started raping me alternately.'[35] Sadiah added: 'I remember when I was sick and my body was shivering, but the Japanese officer who guarded the house did not care about it. I was dragged into the room and was raped by some Japanese soldiers waiting in the room.'[36]

Initially, Sadiah resisted being raped, but after being beaten every time for resisting, 'I later accepted the fact that I would not be able to resist the Japanese and surrendered every time they approached.'[37] She recalled that 'most of the women were Korean, but it's hard to remember who was there and who was not there because every day there was a new face and every day there was a murder.'[38] Sadiah recalled being perplexed by the voices of women screaming from either being raped or beaten by Japanese soldiers. A Japanese doctor was assigned to the home twice a month to make sure no one got pregnant or sick. The doctors gave them tablets to prevent venereal disease, but they caught it anyway. According to her, if a woman fell pregnant, she could be killed by the Japanese military.

Sadiah was one of four Malay women who worked in the longhouse. One of them hanged herself, but Sadiah and the two others eventually escaped in 1945 with the help of Omar Ahmad, a forcibly conscripted Malay worker on the Burma-Thailand Railway. Sadiah later married her rescuer, Omar, and they had nine children together. Her two fellow escapees, Meriam Said and Mariam Ibrahim, were still living next to Sadiah and Omar in Kampung Kedai Buloh, a fishing village at Kota Bharu, the capital of Kelantan.[39] Sadiah and Omar's house was described by Hani Mustafa as a 'dilapidated hut which always gets water inside it when it rains'.[40]

---

[35] *Berita Harian*, 8 September 1995.
[36] *Berita Harian*, 8 September 1995.
[37] *Berita Harian*, 8 September 1995.
[38] *Berita Harian*, 8 September 1995.
[39] *Berita Harian*, 8 September 1995.
[40] *Berita Harian*, 8 September 1995.

In much need of money, they had all registered with the Malaysian ex-labourers on the Burma-Thailand Railway Association (Persatuan Bekas dan Warisan Buruh Paksa Malaya 1942–46) to obtain money from the organisation's compensation claim against the Japanese government.[41] The Association claimed unsuccessfully from the Japanese government $30,000 for each labourer and $150,000 for each comfort woman (both sums were in Singapore currency). A total of 300 former Malaysian comfort women and 2,700 Malaysian ex-labourers were registered with the Association in 1995.[42] The poverty that Sadiah was living in encouraged her to tell her story as a comfort woman and make a claim for compensation. In the years after Hani Mustafa told Sadiah's story, there continues to be no testimony of local Singapore comfort women in the Malay press.

The Chinese Press's Attempts to Tell the Stories of Local Singapore Comfort Women

On the 50th anniversary of the end of the war in August and September 1995, the journalists of the Singapore Chinese press, like their counterparts in the Malay press, also tried hard, using all their contacts, to bring to light the testimonies of local Singapore comfort women who were Chinese. They too failed. The story they ran was that of the son of a woman who worked in a kitchen of the Tanjong Katong Road comfort station. Huo Yue Wei, a *Lianhe Zaobao* journalist, asked in the story: 'Were women forced to become Japanese comfort women in Singapore?' She answered her question by stating the view voiced by the military historians in Singapore at the time, which was that 'the

---

[41] For an account of the organisation, see Mat Zin Mat Kib, 'Persatuan Bekas Buruh Paksa dan Keluarga Buruh Jalan Keretapi Maut Siam-Burma 1942–46 Persekutuan Tanah Melayu 1958–1973: Satu Tinjauan Sejarah Perkembangannya' [The All Malaya Association of Forced Labourers and Families of Forced Labourers of the Burma-Siam Death Railway, 1958–1973: A Survey of its Development], BA thesis, School of Humanities, Universiti Sains Malaysia, 1988. See also his book, Mat Zin Mat Kib, *Persatuan Buruh Keretapi Maut Siam-Burma* [The Association of Labourers on the Burma-Siam Death Railway] (Kuala Lumpur: UPENA, 2005). The organisation declined in the 1970s, but was revived in the mid-1980s and made attempts in the 1990s to lodge compensation claims against the Japanese government. See *Japan Times*, 14 August 1991; and E. Bruce Reynolds, 'History, Memory, Compensation, and Reconciliation: The Abuse of Labor along the Thailand-Burma Railway', in *Asian Labor in the Wartime Japanese Empire*, ed. Paul H. Kratoska (Singapore: NUS Press, 2006), p. 331. Association documents were transferred to Chin Gin Lin of Paloh, Malaysia, and accessed via his daughter-in-law, Ann Chin and son, Chin Chen Onn.

[42] *Berita Harian*, 8 September 1995.

possibility certainly exists. However, it is understandable that no local woman has been willing to testify.'[43]

Huo in her *Lianhe Zaobao* feature told the story of Fu Yao Hua, aged 65, a retired bank employee, who when he was 12 years old helped his mother in a kitchen of the Tanjong Katong Road comfort station buildings for several months. Six months after the fall of Singapore, Fu Yao Hua's mother was at the market one day and met a Hainanese chef who was just looking for an assistant. At that time, his mother was recently widowed, so she immediately seized the opportunity and recommended herself. She brought her son to live with her at the comfort station to run errands and buy things, and to save on living expenses.

Fu recalled that the comfort station was located in a row of a dozen 1930s shophouses along Tanjong Katong Road, between Branksome Road and Goodman Road. The front of the shophouses downstairs was blocked off, except for a few stairs to let people in and out. He recalled small doors upstairs allowing unimpeded access to Japanese soldiers. On the first day of her job, his mother solemnly warned Fu to behave and be quiet and that he must never go out of the kitchen and into the other rooms, known as the 'restricted area', otherwise she would be 'beheaded'. When he first arrived, Fu did not understand what was happening in the rooms of the 'restricted area'. His job was very simple—to buy a bottle of beer or chocolates from the grocery store when needed. Occasionally, in moments of levity, one or two comfort women in the rooms would ask him to enter the 'restricted area' and give them gentle strikes to their backs to relieve back pain.

In Fu's memories, these comfort women worked at the comfort station for only a short while and were in their twenties or thirties. He said that they wore long gowns with wide sleeves that looked like Japanese-style pyjamas. Fu remembers that at the comfort station, the Koreans used Japanese when talking to each other. Those who called for his help gave simple instructions in the Hokkien dialect.

Interestingly, Fu recollected that the comfort women sometimes went out for trips. When they did go out, the women would put on a lot of make-up and wear beautiful kimonos before hailing a rickshaw. Fu recalled, 'It was like watching a movie.'[44] This recollection corroborates what Korean comfort women who worked in Singapore have also said in their oral history testimonies about dressing up in formal kimonos to go out and entertain

---

[43] *Lianhe Zaobao*, 13 August 1995.
[44] *Lianhe Zaobao*, 13 August 1995.

Japanese officers at traditional Japanese musical and dancing performances held in private theatres. This aspect of the lives of the comfort women in Singapore was described in Chapter 4.

Despite the occasional gaiety when the women dressed up to go out, for Fu, there was mostly an atmosphere of fear in the comfort station. Fu said it seemed like the comfort station was open all day until late into the early hours of the morning, with Japanese soldiers entering and exiting continuously, and drunk people making loud noises. He recalled that occasionally he would hear the sound of someone being whipped and beaten in the middle of the night. He described an incident that revealed his fear working at the comfort station for the Japanese military. One day he was called to go back into the rooms in the 'restricted area', but no one was there. Out of curiosity, he handled a swan-shaped glass ashtray on a table but accidentally broke it. Fu was so scared that he ran from the room and went to the kitchen to tell his mother. His mother was also terrified and told him to leave immediately and go back to his uncle's house. Fu left, but after crossing Tanjong Katong Road, he hid in the shrubs and trees opposite the comfort station, cried for a while then walked to his uncle's house in dismay. How the matter was resolved later, he did not know, but after that day he dared not go back to the comfort station, and his mother later left. Fu's account was the closest that Singapore readers came to hearing oral history from a Singaporean who was in a comfort station of Singapore. In the years after, there was no local testimony from inside the comfort stations, notably none from any Singapore women.

Ho Kwai Min and Explaining the Silence of Local Singapore Comfort Women

Why local Singapore comfort women did not come forward in the 1990s when Singapore journalists were asking them is perhaps best explained by what happened when the silence that surrounded sex work was partly broken by Ho Kwai Min. She was a former Chinatown Cantonese 'high-class' prostitute who successfully escaped attempts to enslave her in the Japanese military's sex industry. Her testimony about her wartime experiences has been discussed in Chapter 2.

On 24 November 1992, the weekly local Chinese television current affairs show, *The Tuesday Report* aired a documentary on the prewar female entertainers for wealthy men known as the *pipa tsai*, who were among the Cantonese prostitutes of Chinatown. The documentary was called *Pipa Meng* [Pipa Dream]. In this documentary, Ho Kwai Min was both open and selective in her recollections. She described providing sexual services to her high-paying Chinese businessmen clients before and after the war, but said nothing about what her life was like during the Japanese Occupation.[45] The producer of the documentary Wang Li Feng and the scriptwriter Feng Bi Hui knew Ho. Both were very supportive of her and later became her closest friends, as she had very few surviving family members as she grew older. These two women in the Chinese television industry helped Ho in her declining years, and after she died in 2017, at the age of 95, they were involved in fulfilling her wish of donating her estate to her preferred charities.

According to the documentary makers, Ho's 'beauty, and talent in performing was well known in the old Cantonese red-light district of Chinatown, comprising the three streets of Teck Lim Road, Keong Saik Road and Jiak Chuan Road [known as the "Blue Triangle"]. She was always mingling with those who were rich and high-ranking.'[46] Ho had ceased working in the sex industry at the age of 26 in 1948, after being in the business for eight years. Afterwards, as an independently wealthy woman, she was well regarded as a philanthropist and a fundraiser for good causes. She had first raised money in 1940 for the China Relief Fund in its fight against Japan. In her later life, she donated to, and raised money for, the Kwong Wai Shiu Hospital and the Buddhist Singapore Soka Association. Because she suffered as a child in Guangdong, she also supported the Singapore Children's Society.

After seeing the documentary, Tan Beng Luan invited Ho to do an interview for the Oral History Centre at the National Archives of Singapore on 24 December 1992. The extensive interview that Ho gave proved to be an extraordinary historical source that revealed much about the underside of Singapore history and how despite difficult situations, women could still exercise choice and achieve a degree of autonomy. In the interview, Tan asked Ho whether she regretted doing such a public interview on television. Ho said she had no regrets at all. But when probed by Tan, Ho started to mention how some people had reacted after the documentary went on air. Ho noticed that some of her neighbours smirked or appeared disdainful of her after the documentary. In her Buddhist prayer group, there were also individuals who

---

[45] *The Tuesday Report: Behind the Red Lantern*, aired 24 November 1992 (National Archives of Singapore), https://www.nas.gov.sg/archivesonline/audiovisual_records/record-details/97d0d61f-964b-11e4-859c-0050568939ad.

[46] Fu Peilin, 'Yi gu "pipa zai" yue xiao yan yi ai renjian juan bisheng jixu 29 wan yuan gei san jigou' [The late "Pi Pa Girl", Yue Xiao Yan, donating her life savings of $290,000 to three organisations], Channel 8 online news, 4 May 2021, https://www.8world.com/news/singapore/article/tuesday-report-streets-of-memory-s2-e1-keong-saik-road-1466601.

reacted badly when finding out about her past. Ho recalled when she was at the airport, she saw a female acquaintance with her family. Instead of greeting her, the woman completely ignored her and showed scorn. In the interview, it was clear that after Ho publicly revealed her past in sex work, she had experienced some degree of social stigma.[47]

As a strong and independent woman with very few family members—only an adopted daughter and her family—Ho could shrug off this social stigma that arose from revealing her past in the sex industry, but this would not be the case for many other women. Ho's experience shows what ageing local Singapore comfort women in the 1990s could expect if they went public about their pasts. This is confirmed in another oral history interview done with Ho Teck Fan in March 2006, when he was asked about the local Singapore women who were at the Bukit Pasoh Road comfort station. The interviewer asked: 'After the war, have you heard or seen any of these women?' Ho replied: 'No, no one would talk about it. It is so shameful. Who would dare talk about it?'[48]

Yet, the 1990s when Singapore journalists Phan Ming Yen, Hani Mustafa, and Huo Yue Wei were writing in the English, Malay, and Chinese press, was the opportune moment for encouraging the comfort women to come forward to tell their stories. The publicity given to the comfort women issue was at its height and the prospect of apologies and compensation was good. In July 1995, Japan's Socialist Prime Minister Tomiichi Murayama set up the Asian Women's Fund, which was overseen by the Ministry of Foreign Affairs. The fund functioned until 2007, with the aim of compensating individual comfort women who applied with a sum of two million yen (USD 18,000). They would also receive a letter of apology from the Japanese government. Funds would also be made available for age care and medical facilities of the comfort women.[49]

However, many comfort women and the organisations that supported them boycotted the Asian Women's Fund because it was a private fund, sourced from donations and not an official compensating body of the

---

[47] Ho Kwai Min, interviewed by Tan Beng Luan, 24 December 1992, accession number 001393, reel 5 (National Archives of Singapore).
[48] Ho Teck Fan, interviewed by Lim Lai Hwa, 22 March 2006, accession number A003042, reel 9 (National Archives of Singapore).
[49] Kim Puja, 'The Failure of the Asian Women's Fund: The Japanese Government's Legal Responsibility and the Colonial Legacy', in *Denying the Comfort Women: The Japanese State's Assault on the Historical Truth*, ed. Nishino Rumiko, Kim Puja, and Onozawa Akane (London: Routledge, 2018), pp. 93–113.

Japanese government.[50] Of the 234 registered Korean comfort women, only 61 applied for compensation from the fund. Women from Korea, Taiwan, and the Philippines applied and received individual compensation, while funds were provided for facilities for medical and aged care in Indonesia and the Netherlands for their comfort women. Most of the women who applied came from the Philippines. They made up 211 of the 285 claims from women who were individually compensated.[51] Poverty seemed to be a factor behind the number of women from the Philippines applying for compensation.[52] Only 13 Taiwanese women applied. No Malaysian women applied. The Malaysian government was rumoured to have quietly withdrawn its support from its own comfort women claiming compensation from Japan in a misguided attempt to please the Japanese government.[53]

From her investigative journalism into Malay comfort women, Hani Mustafa gave a telling explanation of why Singapore women did not come forward to claim compensation. She commented that in Malaysia, many of the former comfort women, such as Sadiah Mat, lived in poverty and needed compensation, and hence joined organisations that were helping them gain compensation. Unlike Singapore women, Malaysian women were willing to risk their social status that they had regained during the decades of remaining silent after the war. They were willing to endure the stigma that came with revealing their pasts that Ho Kwai Min had experienced when she went public in 1992.[54]

Hani Mustafa's assessment of comfort women tends to confirm some of the conclusions that William Bradley Horton, a historian working on the Indonesian comfort women, made about the Javanese comfort women who had been taken to Buru Island and who were reluctant to come forward for fear of damaging their social position. Revealing their pasts came with real social costs that they were not prepared to pay.[55] Japanese historian Maki Kimura

---

[50] Kim Puja, 'The Comfort Women Redress Movement in Japan: Reflections on the Past 28 Years', in *The Transnational Redress Movement for the Victims of Japanese Military Sexual Slavery*, ed. Pyong Gap Min, Thomas R. Chung, and Sejung Sage Yim (Berlin: De Gruyter, 2020), pp. 50–1.
[51] Hata Ikuhiko, *Comfort Women and Sex in the Battle Zone*, trans. Jason Michael Jordan (Lantham, Maryland: Rowman & Littlefield, 2018), p. 253.
[52] C. Sarah Soh, 'Japan's National/Asian Women's Fund for "Comfort Women"', *Pacific Affairs* 76, no. 2 (2003): 228.
[53] Nakahara Michiko, 'Comfort Women in Malaysia', *Critical Asian Studies* 33, no. 4 (2001): 581–9.
[54] Hani Mustafa, interviewed by Kevin Blackburn, 4 December 2019.
[55] Horton, 'Pramoedya and the Comfort Women of Buru', p. 85.

has made a similar point in her research about Korean comfort women. She noticed that the act of these women giving testimony could undermine their social status among their families and communities. According to Kimura, these women, after coming forward with their testimonies in the 1990s, were still treated as 'fallen' women and gossiped about, particularly Korean women living in Japan. In these types of situations, the social cost of coming out as a comfort woman has been quite high.[56]

Comfort women in Singapore, too, would have very little to gain compared to their poorer Malaysian counterparts such as Sadiah. The compensation offered by the Asian Women's Fund would not have made up for the social cost of being publicly revealed in the eyes of their families and communities as 'fallen' women. Studies of prostitution in Singapore during the late 1980s and 1990s revealed that despite it being permitted and regulated in designated red-light areas, the stigma surrounding prostitution was so pervasive that current and former sex workers were often ostracised and treated as pariahs, so they in response carefully guarded their anonymity.[57]

Comfort women in Singapore may also have been reluctant to speak about involvement in the Japanese military's sex industry as their experiences may not have been as black-and-white as the forced abduction of virginal girls portrayed in Jing-Jing Lee's novel. Singapore women providing sexual services for the Japanese military might well have been more like the 50 Cantonese prostitutes who were forcibly rounded up and sent to comfort stations in Thailand and Peninsular Malaysia. Their lives during the Japanese Occupation might well have been more like that of Ho Kwai Min. In addition, the masculinist memories of women in the sex industry of the Japanese were still prominent. The women who worked in the sex industry during the Japanese Occupation would have recalled the public disapproval soon after the end of the war, which cast them as pariahs. They would have also remembered the lessons from their experiences in Pasir Panjang Girls' Training School of keeping quiet and integrating into families and communities.

---

[56] Maki Kimura, *Unfolding the 'Comfort Women' Debates: Modernity, Violence, Women's Voices* (London: Routledge, 2016), pp. 198–201.

[57] Connie Quah Bee Lian, 'Prostitution in Singapore Society', MSc thesis, National University of Singapore, 1991; and Jasmine S. Chan, 'Prostitution and Stigmatization: Perspectives on Deviance', Academic exercise, National University of Singapore, 1987. See also Jin Hui Ong, 'Singapore', in *Prostitution: An International Handbook on Trends, Problems, and Policies*, ed. Nanette J. Davis (Westport, Connecticut: Greenwood Press, 1993), pp. 243–72.

Local Singapore comfort women coming forward in the 1990s would also have had to face memories of the early postwar attitudes towards women who worked in the sex industry of the Japanese military. These were often recycled in published memoirs of the Japanese Occupation. Chin Kee Onn, who was a schoolteacher in Singapore when the island fell to the Japanese, expressed these disdainful attitudes to the women in his well-known book on the Japanese Occupation, *Malaya Upside Down*. It was first published in January 1946, but has had various reprints since then. Chin wrote:

> A new moral code came into existence. Prostitution was legalised and prostitutes increased. Young girls in their teens entered the sex-market by the thousand. It was a matter of pride to be the mistress of a Japanese, especially if he were an MP. Pimping became a fine art, and procurers knew how to exact the fullest advantage for themselves. According to medical opinion, venereal diseases came third as the most prevalent disease of the period.[58]

Any comfort women coming forward in Singapore would have had to endure the questions that such memories raised about their sexual backgrounds, including whether they were forcibly recruited or not.

The silence of local Singapore comfort women during what Diana Wong has called 'an orgy of commemoration' and memories on the 50th anniversary commemorations of the Second World War has remained. The commemorations of the 1990s, when the comfort women issue emerged and there was considerable interest, seems to have been the most opportune time for these women to have given their testimony. Women interested in compensation had a real prospect of receiving modest compensation from Japan out of the Asian Women's Fund that was set up in 1995. Although the Singapore women's movement and the government of Singapore were not as supportive and involved as their counterparts in other Asian countries, nonetheless there were interested journalists urging the women to tell their stories in the national media. Yet, despite the best efforts of these journalists across the different language groups, no woman chose to do so in the early to mid-1990s or has done so since. What has happened since then? To discover what has happened since the 1990s entails investigation of how the comfort women have since found their way into being represented in popular culture and as well in attempts to incorporate them into Singapore's heritage landscape.

---

[58] Chin Kee Onn, *Malaya Upside Down*, 3rd edition, originally published in 1946 (Singapore: Federal Publication, 1976), p. 176.

7

The Comfort Women of Singapore as 'Dark Heritage'

The history of the comfort women since the international controversy in December 1991 can be divided into overlapping phases. The initial phase has been categorised as a period that dealt with the human rights of the comfort women when action was focussed on asking the Japanese government for an apology. In 1993, the Kono Statement was issued by the Japanese government acknowledging the historical fact of the comfort women and apologising to them. Soon after, there was a greater focus on legal action against Japan to obtain compensation. Moving into the twenty-first century, with the passing away of many of the comfort women, the issue became less focussed on human rights and legal compensation, and more concerned with the commemoration of the comfort women and the marking and remembering of their experiences as heritage.[1] The comfort women of Singapore may follow this trend of being increasingly commemorated as what heritage studies calls 'difficult', 'painful', or 'dark' heritage, similar to the heritage associated with the Holocaust or the atomic bombings of Hiroshima and Nagasaki. What has been the development of the comfort women as an issue in Singapore from the 1990s to the present? How have the comfort women of Singapore been represented in culture and heritage in Singapore?

The Depiction of Comfort Women in Singapore Theatre

The impact of *Berita Harian* journalist Hani Mustafa's 1995 story of the Malaysian comfort woman Sadiah Mat was significant in Singapore, although it did not encourage local Singapore comfort women to speak out about their memories, as revealed in Chapter 6. Hani Musfata's powerful story of Sadiah's

---

[1] See Edward Vickers, 'Commemorating "Comfort Women" Beyond Korea: The Chinese Case', in *Remembering Asia's World War Two*, ed. Mark Frost, Daniel Schumacher, and Edward Vickers (London: Routledge, 2019), p. 175.

life was named the best newspaper feature in Singapore for 1995.[2] The life of Sadiah and the *Berita Harian*'s continued discussion of the comfort women (*hamba seks Jepun*, or Japanese sex slaves, as they were called in the Malay press) inspired playwright Khairi Razaai of Teater Kami to create his play *Hayat Hayatie* [Hayatie's Life]. The play tells the story of a 12-year-old Malay girl in Singapore who is forcibly recruited to become a comfort woman. In his play, Khairi Razaai dealt not only with the abuse of the Malay comfort women by the Japanese military, but also their years of silence after the war when they returned to their families, married, and had children. *Hayat Hayatie* was first staged in Singapore at the Blackbox as part of its 'Women Victims of War' theatre on 24–29 September 2002, around the time when there were a number of commemorative events marking the 60th anniversary of the fall of Singapore in 1942. The play was later restaged on 20–21 January 2017 at the Malay Heritage Centre, as one of a number of events marking the 75th anniversary of the fall of Singapore.[3]

Hayat Hayatie was created from Khairi Razaai's study of the oral history testimonies that had emerged since the comfort women had erupted as an international issue in December 1991. In 2002, when Khairi Razaai started rehearsing with his actors, to their astonishment, he did not have a script to give them. For his play, Khairi Razaai applied the techniques of 'devised theatre'. He and his actors began the process of creating a story from a study of the historical documents about the Malay comfort women. From this process of studying what had become known about the comfort women over the last decade, they devised the story, created the characters, and outlined the emotions that they wanted their characters to express.[4] Norsiah Ramly, a popular 37-year-old veteran stage and screen actress, played the role of Hayatie. She described how much she relied upon the historical accounts that were given to her, rather than prepared scripts that she was used to reading from her 17 years as an actress: 'Not only that, all the actors, including me, were asked to make a journal to record every feeling and process during our own study of the topic. The actors had to do their "homework" and self-study to create their own characters. I was shocked and stressed because before as an actress I was never told to do anything…before I was like a queen because everything was prepared.'[5]

---

[2] Hani Mustafa, interviewed by Kevin Blackburn, 29 November 2019. See *Berita Harian*, 1 March 1996.
[3] *The Straits Times*, 17 and 23 January 2017; and *Berita Harian*, 15 September 2002.
[4] *Berita Minggu*, 15 September 2002.
[5] *Berita Minggu*, 15 September 2002.

In the 2017 production, the actress who played Hayatie, Dalifah Shahril, aged 38, also remarked on how she used historical documents and oral history testimonies that had emerged about the comfort women since 1992. She had played Hayatie's adopted daughter Norita in the original 2002 production so she had been through the 'devised theatre' approach. Dalifah Shahril recounted how in 2017, as in 2002, she 'pored over newspaper articles about former brothels in Singapore and interviews with some survivors. It was sobering and eye-opening.' She affirmed, 'We went through so much, did so much research.... It's one of my favourite plays.'[6] When Dalifah Shahril won best theatre actress in Singapore for the year 2017 for her role as Hayatie, she reiterated, 'It's one of those plays that have a special place in my heart because I went through it from scratch. We did a lot of research, went to places used by the Japanese during their occupation of Singapore—we did a master's programme in this performance.'[7] In the play *Hayat Hayatie*, Dalifah Shahril had to play Hayatie in a variety of situations that reflected life in the comfort station, from scenes of brutal rape to the small pleasures of receiving mail. Reflecting on the nature of the character that she was playing, she said, 'You can literally see her pain, but she is so strong-willed.... She knows how to handle trauma and hardship.'[8]

The cast of *Hayat Hayatie* were almost all female Malay actresses. After going through the experience of creating the play, they and Khairi Razaai saw *Hayat Hayatie* as not only the story of a Malay comfort woman, but an attack on the society that forced these women into silence. After reading about the comfort women in the Malay press, Khairi Razaai said that he asked himself a question: 'I wondered what became of their lives after they moved back into society.'[9] The stories of the comfort women made him 'think about women who had suffered other forms of abuse. Were they able to move on and, if not, why not?'[10] Khairi Razaai and his actresses wanted 'to use history to understand the position of women in Malay society today'.[11] The parallel was drawn between how Hayatie had been forced into a Japanese brothel in the 1940s, while Norita, Hayatie's adoptive daughter in the play, suffers from domestic abuse in her marriage, causing it to end. Norita, who is a well-educated young woman, becomes an activist for the human rights of women and children. Khairi Razaai said of his

---

[6] *The Straits Times*, 8 March 2018.
[7] *The Straits Times*, 27 March 2018.
[8] *The Straits Times*, 8 March 2018.
[9] *The Straits Times*, 17 January 2017.
[10] *The Straits Times*, 17 January 2017.
[11] *The Straits Times*, 17 January 2017.

play: 'We want the audience to question what has changed for women and, if nothing has changed, to question why.'[12]

Khairi Razaai outlined how using the 'devised theatre' approach, rather than presenting the mostly female cast with a prepared script written by him, had produced a play that criticised the operation of male control over the lives of women in Singapore both historically and in the present day. He explained, 'The concept of "devised" theatre is not just about getting the right feeling and situation of the time, but it is also training our actors to create their own characters, not the script writer's.'[13] He saw himself as enabling and empowering his actresses to articulate their own criticisms of patriarchy in Singapore by telling a story that was 'close to the heart of society'.[14]

The critique by the play of the subordination of women in Singapore society was noticeable to audiences and reviewers. In 2002, Kelolaan Hanim Mohd Saleh, *Berita Harian*'s theatre reviewer, wrote: 'From one point of view, *Hayat Hayatie* does not just fill the theatre with sadness and anger, but audiences take away an awareness of women's human rights. If the character of Hayatie struggles with her feelings from being forced to serve the Japanese army in the war, her daughter, Norita, a human rights activist, fights for justice in today's context. The situation may be different, but the anger of these two women over the injustices reaches a similar climax.'[15] In 2017, Akshita Nanda, a *Straits Times* theatre reviewer, also affirmed: '1945 meant freedom from the Japanese for Hayatie and her cohorts', but 'they and their daughters remained vulnerable to domestic abuse which, if not sanctioned by society, was often overlooked.'[16]

Hayat Hayatie is the most detailed and comprehensive Singapore play on the lives of the comfort women, but it was not the first Singapore play to feature comfort women. In the 1990s, there were increasing attempts by Singapore directors and playwrights to tell stories of the lives of what director Ong Keng Sen referred to as the 'marginalised' in Singapore's past, such as his play about the lives of rickshaw pullers called *Workhorse Afloat* (1997).[17] Susan Tsang, a *Business Times* theatre reviewer in the 1990s, called it theatre that gives 'a voice

---

[12] *The Straits Times*, 17 January 2017.
[13] *Berita Minggu*, 15 September 2002.
[14] *Berita Minggu*, 15 September 2002.
[15] *Berita Minggu*, 15 September 2002.
[16] *The Straits Times*, 23 January 2017.
[17] *The Straits Times*, 27 June 1997. See William Peterson, *Theater and the Politics of Culture in Contemporary Singapore* (Middletown, Connecticut: Wesleyan University Press, 2001), pp. 151–2.

to the voiceless' from the past.[18] Ong Keng Sen's TheatreWorks production *Broken Birds*, staged at Fort Canning on 1–18 March 1995, experimented with telling the stories of the trafficking and enslavement of Japanese women known as the *karayuki-san* before the war. Many had been trafficked to Singapore and Malaysia as prostitutes. Ong said that his depiction of these women was inspired by seeing Shohei Imamura's 1975 documentary *Karayuki-san, the Making of a Prostitute*, which told the story of former *karayuki-san* Zendo Kikuyo, who was still living in Malaysia when Imamura located her for the documentary.[19]

Kuo Pao Kun's *The Spirits Play* from 1998 was probably the first time that a comfort woman was a major character in a Singapore play. Written in the 1990s, the play reflected how the comfort women issue was one of many intense dialogues that had emerged in the debate over Japan's war responsibility and its wartime atrocities, with an emphasis on an apology from Japan. Kuo said that he had been inspired to write the play as a number of dialogues between spirits from the war when walking in Singapore's Japanese Cemetery 15 years before. Walking among the graves and tombstones of ordinary people from very different backgrounds, such as prostitutes, businessmen, and soldiers, moved him to explore in theatre the horrors of war. He said he had rewritten the play many times.[20]

For *The Spirits Play*, Kuo chose as his characters five dead Japanese souls stranded in a graveyard on an island that resembled Singapore and unable to return home: a soldier, a mother who lost her son in the war, a girl who was a comfort woman, a general who had led his troops to capture the island, and a poet. *The Spirits Play* is highly regarded as a classic play in Singapore drama.[21] It was first staged on 10 June 1998 by Theatre Practice at the Victoria Theatre, restaged at the Victoria Theatre on 13 November 1998 by the same theatre company, and yet again on 22 November 1998 at a theatre festival in Hong Kong. All these performances were in Chinese. Only later was *The Spirits Play* translated into English, then on 17–19 August 2000 performed in the open at Fort Canning, using some of the location's wartime architecture as background. Later on 25 and 26 August 2000 it was also staged inside the Victoria Theatre with Ong Keng Sen directing the play as a TheatreWorks production.

---

[18] *The Business Times*, 27 February 1995.
[19] *The Business Times*, 27 February 1995.
[20] *The Straits Times*, 6 November 1998.
[21] C.J.W.-L. Wee and Lee Chee Keng, eds, *Two Plays by Kuo Pao Kun: Descendants of the Eunuch Admiral and The Spirits Play* (Singapore: SNP International, 2003).

The character of the comfort woman in *The Spirits Play* has attracted the most interest. However, the play's comfort woman has never been seen by the playwright or directors of the play as representing a local Singapore comfort woman. She has been seen instead as a Japanese woman. For the first staging of *The Spirits Play* in English, Ong chose for the role of the comfort woman, 'Bubu', a 39-year-old actress from Kyoto, Japan, who was both an AIDS activist and a prostitute. 'Bubu' had an interesting career. A fine arts graduate from the Kyoto City University of Art, she became a housewife for six years. Thereafter, she abandoned what she considered a restrictive life as a Japanese housewife, divorcing and embracing the life of an actress during which she became a sex activist and prostitute. According to Ong, he chose 'Bubu' for the part because her 'decision to be a sex worker serves as a good juxtaposition against comfort women of the past who were forced into the trade'.[22] Speaking on her participation in *The Spirits Play*, 'Bubu' said, 'I hope to explore what my relationship with those women mean to me. I want to use the opportunity of playing a spirit to see how I can communicate to the cast and the audience.'[23] On 19 August 2000, in conjunction with the performance, a talk was arranged with 'Bubu' and Yoshiko Shimada, a Japanese feminist and multimedia performance artist, whose artistic work dealt with comfort women. The dialogue was chaired by Dana Lam, President of the Association of Women for Action and Research (AWARE).[24] The dialogue reflected the play's focus on the Japanese and Korean comfort women.

The Spirits Play has received critical acclaim around the world as a work of art that examines the nature of war and atrocity.[25] In 1998, Kuo declared his interest in examining the debate over Japan's wartime atrocities: 'The phenomenon during World War II intrigues me. Why do civilised people like the Japanese and Germans simply go berserk and not for just one or two days?'[26] When asked why in his November 1998 restaging, he had added an extra 10 minutes of dialogue at the end of the play, including considerably more dialogue for the comfort woman, Kuo replied, 'The extra segment is the result of my attempt to further explore the reasons and the psychology of those who engage in such unbelievable atrocities.... However, I must admit that I still do not have an answer.'[27]

---

[22] *The Straits Times*, 12 August 2000.
[23] *The Straits Times*, 12 August 2000.
[24] *The New Paper*, 14 August 2000.
[25] *The Straits Times*, 7 November 2001.
[26] *The Straits Times*, 6 November 1998.
[27] *The Straits Times*, 6 November 1998.

In Japan, there was a reluctance to show *The Spirits Play* as it dealt with the debate over Japan's wartime atrocities. From October to November 2000, when his other plays were being shown at the Tokyo National Theatre as part of the Asian Art Festival, Kuo told the Singapore press that 'their original plan for this festival was to stage three different versions of *The Spirits Play*...but the plan was rejected by the conservative authorities.'[28] The title of the 20th Asian Art Festival was 'When Petals Fall Like Snow—The World Of Kuo Pao Kun, Playwright', yet *The Spirits Play* was not allowed to be performed.

It is easy to see why the Japanese authorities, who held a conservative view of the past, were reluctant to stage the play in Japan. Kuo's comfort woman, like his other characters in the play, is Japanese. In her dialogue, she speaks of answering the call of the Japanese military to become a comfort woman in order to patriotically offer her body for the pleasure of the warriors fighting for the Emperor.[29] This propaganda for brainwashing mainly Japanese and Korean comfort women has been well documented by historians and has been described as 'Patriarchal Fascism', whereby these women were 'imperial gifts' to the soldiers sacrificing their lives for the Emperor.[30]

Kuo's comfort woman character in her dialogue details this 'Patriarchal Fascism'. She was told by an officer to drop her charges against the soldiers who raped her when she was a nurse, and to understand the plight of these soldiers so she might consider becoming a comfort woman. She recalled him saying that soldiers 'are confronted with injury and death. They deserve some sensual happiness, some feminine comfort before they march to their deaths.'[31] He outlined the role of the comfort women serving such soldiers:

> We actually have thousands of patriotic sisters who fully understand our soldiers' needs, and voluntarily submit themselves to such needs in the various theatres of the war. With the purity of their maidenly heart and the warmth of their virginal bodies, they gave themselves wholeheartedly to the reinvigoration of the bodies, heart, and the spirits of our patriotic fighters, so they would have the highest morale to bravely go forward with great vigour to fight, and to die, for our motherland![32]

---

[28] *The Straits Times*, 9 October 2000.
[29] Wee and Lee, *Two Plays by Kuo Pao Kun*, pp. 28–9, 89–92, 100, 137–9.
[30] Chunghee Sarah Soh, 'Prostitutes versus Sex Slaves: The Politics of Representing the "Comfort Women"', in *Legacies of the Comfort Women of World War II*, ed. Margaret D. Stetz and Bonnie B.C. Oh (New York: M.E. Sharpe, 2001), pp. 72–7.
[31] Wee and Lee, *Two Plays by Kuo Pao Kun*, p. 90.
[32] Wee and Lee, *Two Plays by Kuo Pao Kun*, p. 91.

She recalled her response: 'I was convinced, I was persuaded. I was converted. And I voluntarily withdrew my charges. More than that, I expressed my fervent wish to serve the nation, the leader and the military without reservation.'[33]

However, the comfort woman soon realised the sexual exploitation that she and other comfort women had to endure. In a dialogue with the general when he justifies the comfort women system, she counters, 'But my brother, have you ever seen how our sisters suffered under the burdens of men crawling over them one after another, score after score, long line after long line? Unrelenting, never-ending, no warmth, no feelings, no tenderness, no love....'[34] The general remained adamant about his belief in the comfort women system, later saying he set it up for his soldiers: 'Because I wanted to reward them with carnal satisfaction so that they would march to the front to fight to die!'[35]

The third major play in Singapore theatre that was perceived by audiences and reviewers to incorporate a story of a comfort woman was *Hotel Singapore* from 2015.[36] Helmi Yusoff, a theatre critic for *The Business Times*, called *Hotel Singapore* 'an instant classic'. Many other critics agreed, and it won best Singapore play for 2015.[37] The play was staged on 29–30 August 2015 at the Singapore International Festival of Arts as part of the events marking 50 years of Singapore's independence. Set in a hotel room, the play starts in 1915 and tells one story per decade to finish in 2015. The play ran for 5 hours, telling 11 stories with a cast of 80 actors speaking 7 languages. The characters chosen were marginalised or ordinary people not usually depicted in the textbooks of Singapore history, including a character who is usually referred to as a Malay comfort woman from the Japanese Occupation, transgender prostitutes of 1970s Bugis Street, a Malay man being racially profiled post 9/11, and a Chinese mother trying to accept that her daughter is marrying an Indian man.

Hotel Singapore was staged by the Wild Rice theatre company and directed by Ivan Heng and Glen Goei, with a script by Alfian Sa'at and Marcia Vanderstraaten. The play was wildly popular and Wild Rice restaged it from 30 June to 24 July 2016, again with tickets completely sold out. However, the Malay comfort woman was just one character of the many in the play, which featured light musical performances followed by heavy dramatic stories. She did

---

[33] Wee and Lee, *Two Plays by Kuo Pao Kun*, p. 91.
[34] Wee and Lee, *Two Plays by Kuo Pao Kun*, p. 91.
[35] Wee and Lee, *Two Plays by Kuo Pao Kun*, p. 101.
[36] See Dylan Tan in *The Business Times*, 4 September 2015; Helmi Yusoff in *The Business Times*, 14 May 2016; and Akshita Nanda in *The Straits Times*, 23 January 2017.
[37] *The Business Times*, 4 September 2015.

not have the prominence of Hayatie in *Hayat Hayatie* or 'The Girl' who was the comfort woman in *The Spirits Play*.

The Malay comfort woman in *Hotel Singapore* is very different from the comfort woman in *Hayat Hayatie*. In fact, she is actually a mistress rather than a comfort woman. Scene Four of *Hotel Singapore* deals with the decade of the 1940s and is set in 1945. Japanese Captain Matsuda (played by Moo Siew Keh in 2015) has to tell his lover Sharifah (played by Sharda Harrison) that the end of the war will bring their relationship to an end. Both are broken-hearted by the prospect of parting. The story ends there and is followed by many stories of unrelated characters. The story of Sharifah resurfaces in Scene Eight in the year 1985. Japanese businessman Natsuo is in Singapore and uses the occasion to try to find his long-lost mother from a photograph of her taken during the war. An elderly Sharifah, who has concealed her past from her family, is finally reunited with Natsuo (also played by Moo Siew Keh), who is actually her long-lost son. Both are heartbroken when they finally meet after being separated for many years.[38]

Comfort Women on Singapore Television

The comfort women of Singapore were also represented in the 1990s and early 2000s in other avenues of Singapore popular culture. After the December 1991 international controversy, there were early depictions of the comfort women in Singapore television dramas. In March 1994, Singapore Chinese-language television began filming its first production with comfort women as major characters. It was a telemovie called *Li Jie Fusheng*, also known by its English name *Veil of Darkness*. The telemovie was about two comfort women in Singapore and starred two popular Singapore Chinese television actresses of the time, Chen Xiu Huan and Hong Zhao Rong as Jingzi and Miko respectively. They had been paired together in previous dramas. The plot, reportedly based on a true story, revolves around two women from Taiwan who are tricked into coming to Singapore, where they are beaten and tortured into offering sexual services for the Japanese soldiers. The character Jingzi is of mixed Japanese and Taiwanese ancestry. When Jingzi starts working as a comfort woman, she does not feel like living anymore. However, a young Taiwanese soldier serving in the Japanese military encourages her to go on by writing sweet letters to her. He dislikes the military and was forcibly recruited into the army. He and

---

[38] See the assessment of the premiere in 2015 by Singapore playwright and director Ng Yi-Sheng in his blog: https://www.sifa.sg/archive-blog/fhotel.

Jingzi fall in love. Miko falls in love with Taro, a Japanese soldier. However, after the war, she discovers that Taro is really her nephew. They both tragically kill themselves from the shame of this discovery.[39] Jingzi and her Taiwanese soldier are separated only to meet many years later when they have both grown old and grey.[40] The plot and its twists are very typical of Singapore Chinese television melodramas.

When *Veil of Darkness* was broadcast on Chinese television in Singapore on 2 July 1994, Yuan Ren Kang, the producer, explained that the purpose of the story was 'not to take up the grievances of the comfort women, but to show some touching love stories in the background of this significant era in the hope that members of the audience can understand past history and cherish what they have now and face the challenges of the future'.[41] Jiang Long, senior executive for drama operations in Singapore Chinese-language television (*Xinshi* or New Vision), described how the idea came to him to make the telemovie about comfort women in Singapore. When he first came to work in Singapore from China, he found many cemeteries with Japanese names on the tombs, which led him to figure that there were many stories related to the comfort women in Singapore.[42] At first, he wanted to do a whole television drama series on the comfort women. However, he found that the long-form TV series was not suitable as there was not enough historical material to draw upon to create a long multi-episode story. Thus, he settled on a television movie. While the television ratings of *Veil of Darkness* were not high, the movie was well regarded in the television industry of Singapore.[43] When the Chinese-language production company of Singapore television was invited to screen its work at the 1995 Sichuan International TV Festival, Jiang suggested *Veil of Darkness* 'because it had a certain sense of localness and was representative' of Singapore.[44]

The first depiction of a comfort woman in a Singapore English-language television drama production only occurred in 28 September 2001, in an episode of the 20-part war drama *A War Diary* called 'A Flower That Will Never Bloom'. In this episode, the main comfort woman character was played by Fiona Xie, then an up-and-coming Singaporean actress who would win 'Best Newcomer' at Singapore's 2001 television awards. She played a 15-year-

---

[39] *Lianhe Wanbao*, 9 March 1994.
[40] *Shin Min Daily News*, 1 September 1995.
[41] *Lianhe Wanbao*, 2 July 1994. See also *The Straits Times*, 30 June 1994.
[42] *Shin Min Daily News*, 1 September 1995.
[43] *Shin Min Daily News*, 1 September 1995.
[44] *Shin Min Daily News*, 1 September 1995.

old girl called Rita Lim, who soon after the fall of Singapore, in late February 1942, was forcibly taken away from her Chinese Peranakan family by Japanese soldiers when walking in the street with her mother, and made a comfort woman in a comfort station.[45] Upon being brought to the comfort station in a shophouse, Rita discovers that her friend Tsau Ting has also been forced to became a comfort woman. With them is a Korean comfort woman, Kim Joo. The comfort station appears to have local Chinese and Korean women with a local Chinese female manager, who beats the comfort women and does what the Japanese military demands in sending girls to be raped by the Japanese soldiers. On Rita's first day, the soldiers want her because she is the 'new girl' and the manager forcibly gives Rita to them. To help her cope, Tsau Ting tells Rita to 'pretend you are in a movie, acting in it. But this movie is going to end very soon.' Tsau Ting recalls Kim Joo's advice to her: 'The trick she told me is to imagine your body is dead and the soldier is just raping your dead body.'

Interestingly, Rita and the other comfort women were shown wearing uniforms—knee-length dresses in a dark blue and grey tartan plaid pattern. The television series' depiction of the comfort women drew upon the memories of its advisor, Lee Kip Lee, the younger brother of Lee Kip Lin. Lee Kip Lee had written about his encounters with the comfort stations at Katong and Cairnhill Road in his diary and memoir of his boyhood during the Japanese Occupation.[46] Chan Swee Kung was also listed as a historical consultant to the production, although the rape and presence of local women as comfort women in the drama seems to be at variance with his 1992 assertion supporting Lee Kuan Yew's 1992 statement that local Singapore women were not comfort women (see the discussion in Chapter 1).

The story of Rita's life as a comfort woman explores many facets of the historical experience with a degree of dramatic licence. She is abducted off the street and taken to a comfort station by Mako, a Japanese *kempeitai*, or military policeman, who visits regularly so that she can serve him. Tragedy is a recurring part of her life as a comfort woman. When Rita's friend Tsau Ting finds that she is pregnant, rather than have the baby, she kills herself and the baby with a kitchen knife in front of Rita. The Korean comfort woman Kim Joo starts to look after Rita. After the death of Tsau Ting, Rita remembers what Tsau Ting told her and she becomes more defiant towards the soldiers and her female

---

[45] See *8 Days*, no. 572, 20 September 2001, p. 106; and *8 Days*, no. 573, 27 September, 2001, p. 90.
[46] Lee Kip Lee, interviewed by Kevin Blackburn, 1 December 2004. See Lee Kip Lee, *Amber Sands: A Boyhood Memoir* (Singapore: Federal Publications, 1995).

manager. Tsau Ting had ironically told Rita: 'Why let them win? I have my whole life ahead of me. If I kill myself, I lose.' Later a dramatic plot twist occurs. Rita is rescued from the comfort station and taken to her family by a young Japanese *kempeitai* officer, who unbeknown to her and her family, was born in the prewar period to her mother and her Japanese lover.

Rita is just one character in the Lim family, which the series traces. *A War Diary* contained many stories of the tragic fates of the members of the family at the hands of the Japanese. A son is sent away to be shot by the Japanese, while another is imprisoned and tortured. A daughter-in-law is raped by a Japanese soldier. The wife of their neighbour commits suicide after seeing the head of her husband on a table in the street with other heads of men executed by the Japanese for stealing. The series ends with the Japanese surrender in August 1945. At the end of the series, there are descriptions of what happened to each character in the Lim family. For Rita, her postwar fate is described tragically: 'Rita never overcame the emotional scars of the war. Unable to develop a lasting relationship with anyone, she took her life in March 1946. She was 19 years old.' *A War Diary*, with a number of well-known and talented Singaporean actors, such as Tan Kheng Hua and Tay Ping Hui, in its early episodes during August and September 2001 rated well. The drama series was soon moved from Wednesday night to the prime-time slot of Friday at 7.30 pm. The early episodes were even broadcast again in a special long episode for viewers who had missed them but had become engrossed in the series by the later episodes.[47]

The 1990s and early 2000s were the heydays for war dramas on Singapore television with a number apart from *A War Diary*, such as the Chinese-language *The Price of Peace* (1997) and *In Pursuit of Peace* (2001). Surprisingly, these two series did not feature the local abducted comfort women as major characters. However, sexual enslavement of Singapore women was portrayed in *In Pursuit of Peace*. Apple Hong, a Singapore-based Malaysian actress, played a prostitute, who at the start of the occupation is wearing a Chinese cheongsam serving both Chinese and Japanese customers at a Chinese brothel. However, by the end of the war, she and other prostitutes are shown wearing Japanese kimonos, sexually enslaved by a Chinese male manager and serving only customers from the Japanese military.

With the passing of the major 50th anniversary commemorations of the war, these major drama series dealing specifically with the war have also passed, and along with them depictions of the comfort women on Singapore television. Perhaps this is best illustrated by the fate of a television documentary

---

[47] *Today*, 12 September 2001.

on the comfort women proposed in May 2002. In the Singapore Broadcasting Authority's national scriptwriting competition, one of the notable Merit award-winning entries for docu-drama was *The Nameless Women of Syonan*. This was the story of Malay comfort women in Singapore written by 30-year-old Mashizan Masjum, who had worked on documentaries in Singapore television. He spent a month researching the topic and two weeks writing the proposed script. When discussing his script on the Malay comfort women of Singapore, he described the dilemmas of trying to bring to light a history that the local comfort women of Singapore did not want known: 'I find their story interesting. They exist among us but we do not know their names and faces. Everything is a secret. They prefer for themselves to be unrecognised. But, if they are not revealed, the younger generation will not know about the history.'[48] Mashizan Masjum had a decade-long career in Singapore television making documentaries before he went on to make his name in the international fashion industry, but he did not turn his script into a documentary with comfort women fronting the camera and telling the audience about their lives.

The Comfort Stations of Singapore as 'Dark Heritage'

At the same time as popular culture in Singapore was representing the comfort women, there were attempts to integrate the comfort women into notions of Singapore heritage as the locations of the comfort stations started to become better known through the efforts of Japanese historian Hayashi Hirofumi. They have become little-known sites of 'dark heritage' in the Singapore landscape. In his first published study, Hayashi identified six comfort stations in Singapore, most of which were also well represented in the memories found in Singapore's own *Japanese Occupation in Singapore 1942–1945* project of the Oral History Centre at the National Archives of Singapore.[49] These six Singapore comfort stations that he had identified in the early 1990s were: Cairnhill Road, Tanjong Katong Road, 27 Bukit Pasoh Road, the Seletar (Sembawang) naval base, Pulau Blakang Mati (Sentosa), and Pulau Bukom. As his research continued, Hayashi found more comfort stations in Singapore.

In 1995, Hayashi, working with *The Straits Times* journalist Phan Ming Yen, identified the exact location of another significant comfort station at the Jalan Jurong Kechil shophouses in the upper Bukit Timah area. Hayashi

---

[48] *Berita Harian*, 3 May 2002.
[49] Hayashi Hirofumi, 'Shingaporu no Nihongun Ianjo' [Comfort Stations of the Japanese Army in Singapore], *Senso Sekinin Kenkyu* [Studies in War Responsibility] 4 (1994): 34–43.

had found a document from a Japanese unit in the area that indicated how the comfort station was to be used by its soldiers. The document was one of the captured Japanese files translated by the Allied Translator and Interpreter Section, ATIS. This April 1942 document was part of the miscellaneous records of the 15th Independent Engineer Regiment, which was involved in the 1942 Malayan Campaign to capture Singapore.[50] The comfort station was called Chibune and had a restaurant next to it known as Hinomoto. Chibune and Hinomoto opened on 27 April 1942.[51] Hayashi told Phan: 'This is the first document that contains specific information on how a comfort station operated in Malaya. This is the first official document which specifies where the comfort house is. There have been some other documents on Japanese comfort houses in Malaya but they are very brief.'[52] Phan's investigative journalism established that the comfort women who had worked at the location, according to local eyewitnesses, were Korean and Indonesian women.[53]

The April 1942 document from the miscellaneous records of the 15th Independent Engineer Regiment outlined not just the exact location of where the Jalan Jurong Kechil comfort station was found for the Japanese soldiers barracked nearby, but also a schedule for its operation and charges. In the document, the comfort station was referred to euphemistically as a 'relaxation house'. According to the document, the comfort station's charges were similar to those of other comfort stations in Singapore and other parts of the Japanese-occupied Asia-Pacific. Ordinary soldiers were charged only 1 yen, while the sergeants and other Non-Commissioned Officers (NCOs) had to pay 1.5 yen. There was no cost listed for officers, which suggests officers went elsewhere, most likely to the many inexpensive *ryotei*. At some other comfort stations in Singapore, the officers would arrive in the evening and could spend the whole night with the comfort women. The comfort station was clearly designated for the three *butai*, or military units, located in the area. The April 1942 document listed their allotted days to use the comfort station, as well as the operating hours for the different days of the week. The document thus appears to have been meant for circulation amongst the soldiers of these three units. The

---

[50] Miscellaneous records of the Southern Expeditionary Force (Tomi 8125 Butai) in Malaya and the Philippines, Allied Translator and Interpreter Section, ATIS, AWM 55 5/1 (Australian War Memorial, Canberra).
[51] Hayashi Hirofumi, *Shingaporu Kakyo Shukusei: Nihongun wa Shingaporu de nani o shitanoka* [The Purge of the Singapore Chinese: What the Japanese Military Did in Singapore] (Tokyo: Kobunken, 2007), p. 182.
[52] *The Straits Times*, 19 August 1995.
[53] *The Straits Times*, 19 August 1995.

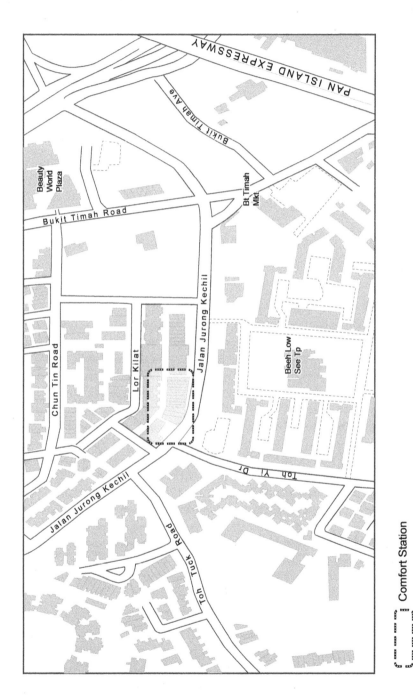

Map 7.1 Jalan Jurong Kechil Comfort Station

comfort women at Jalan Jurong Kechil seem to have worked all days of the week, except the one day of the week when they were to be medically examined for venereal disease.

Table 7.1: Operation of the Comfort Station at Jalan Jurong Kechil, Singapore

(i)	Days allotted to BUTAI [unit] which will make use of the relaxation house:		
	Takaya Butai	Sunday, Monday, Tuesday	
	Yokoyama Butai	Thursday, Friday	
	Western Corridor Butai	Saturday	
	Wednesday will be medical examination day		
(ii)	Charges and hours of use of house:		
	Privates	YEN 1	1200–1730 hrs
	NCOs	YEN 1.5	1200–2100 hrs

Source: Miscellaneous records of the Southern Expeditionary Force (Tomi 8125 Butai) in Malaya and the Philippines (ATIS, Australian War Memorial).

Dr Cheong Pak Yean was the owner of one of the Jalan Jurong Kechil shophouses. When in 1995 he discovered through the work of Hayashi and Phan that his house had been a comfort station, he expressed his view that the buildings were heritage, albeit 'dark heritage', from the war: 'It is part of our historical heritage and we have to know that such things happened during the war.'[54] Cheong had a long connection with the row of shophouses. They were built by his father, Cheong E. Peng, in 1936. The family owned the whole row until after the war when all but the one shophouse that contained his medical clinic were sold off by his family. Cheong's mother Goon Choi Thye had told him that during the war the Japanese military had taken over the row of shophouses and turned them into what she described as a brothel.

Cheong began a campaign to obtain government heritage recognition for the row of shophouses along Jalan Jurong Kechil.[55] In August 2000, he submitted documentation of the comfort station to the Preservation of Monuments Board in an attempt to get the Board to conserve the shophouses.[56] Again in 2002, Cheong gave feedback to an Urban Redevelopment Authority committee looking into the conservation of buildings in the Anak Bukit area. He produced a submission that detailed the history of the shophouses going

---

[54] *The Straits Times*, 19 August 1995.
[55] Cheong Pak Yean, interviewed by Kevin Blackburn, 25 January 2019.
[56] Cheong Pak Yean to Lily Tan, Chairperson, Research and Publicity Committee, Preservation of Monuments Board, Singapore, 1 August 2000, in the private papers of Cheong Pak Yean, Cheong Medical Clinic, 76 Jalan Jurong Kechil Singapore.

back to their construction by his father. It also contained Hayashi's claim that the documents he had found in 1995 were 'the first documents that contain specific information on how a comfort station operated in Malaya'.[57] In his submission Cheong declared that the shophouses were well-documented heritage with significant historical importance, concluding:

> Therefore the shop-houses conserved stand as the only physical structure that prove that running brothels was an integral part of the war-time Imperial Japanese Army's operations.[58]

In November 2002, the Urban Redevelopment Authority acceded to Cheong's request to conserve the Jalan Jurong Kechil shophouses in order to prevent any redevelopment of them. The decision to conserve was taken upon the recommendations made by Lily Kong, Professor in Geography at the National University of Singapore and head of the Urban Redevelopment Authority's Subject Group for Urban Villages and Southern Ridges and Hillside Villages, which was looking at the Anak Bukit area. Kong acknowledged Cheong's detailed research of the shophouses. She told the Singapore press how crucial Cheong's evidence about the existence of the comfort station had been: 'It's very easy to say, "Let's conserve this and that place because of the rich history." But does anyone know what exactly the history is? Now at least we have the research material to back up our case.'[59]

After 2002, the shophouses clearly became examples of what has been called 'difficult' or 'dark heritage', which is usually associated with places of human suffering, often where human rights abuses have occurred.[60] Singapore—thanks to Cheong's tenacity and belief in the value of local heritage—had become the first country to conserve a comfort station because it had been a comfort station. China would not do so until the 2010s. Former comfort stations had been conserved in Singapore, but not because they had been comfort stations.

---

[57] Cheong Pak Yean to Co-Chairpersons, Madam Halimah Yacob, Advisor, Mr James Chew Subject Group, Stakeholders' Dialogue Session, Identity Plan: Anak Bukit Area Urban Redevelopment Authority Singapore, 25 September 2002, in the private papers of Cheong Pak Yean, Cheong Medical Clinic, 76 Jalan Jurong Kechil Singapore.
[58] Cheong Pak Yean to Co-Chairpersons, Madam Halimah Yacob, Advisor, Mr James Chew Subject Group, Stakeholders' Dialogue Session, Identity Plan: Anak Bukit Area Urban Redevelopment Authority Singapore, 25 September 2002, in the private papers of Cheong Pak Yean, Cheong Medical Clinic, 76 Jalan Jurong Kechil Singapore.
[59] *The Straits Times*, 30 November 2002.
[60] See, for example, William Logan and Keir Reeves, eds, *Places of Pain and Shame: Dealing with Difficult Heritage* (London: Routledge, 2009).

The terrace houses along Cairnhill Road that had been a comfort station were conserved for their architectural significance and value, and were marked telling visitors so. The Chin Kang Huay Kuan Chinese clan association premises at 27 Bukit Pasoh Road in Chinatown was the site of many important meetings supporting China in its struggle against Japan, and it was conserved and marked accordingly. There were no markers put up indicating the 'dark heritage' of any of the former comfort stations, including the Jalan Jurong Kechil shophouses. Yet, there was public recognition of what had happened. Realising the significance of the conservation of the Jalan Jurong Kechil shophouses, *The Straits Times*, when reporting on the story, used the headline on the front page of its Singapore news section: 'Comfort houses to be conserved'.[61] Despite this well-publicised first conservation of a known comfort station from the war, still none of the former local comfort women of Singapore came forward to describe their memories.

A Comfort Woman Statue for Singapore from South Korea?

While the comfort women in Singapore maintained their silence, the comfort women of South Korea who had worked in Singapore under the Japanese military were not inclined to do so. Kim Bok-dong and the South Korean women's rights advocacy group, the Korean Council for the Women Drafted for Military Sexual Slavery by Japan, became increasingly interested in acknowledging the large number of Korean comfort women in Singapore during the Japanese Occupation that the research work of Hayashi had highlighted. Throughout 2012, Ahn Seon-mi, team leader of the International Cooperation Team of the Council, began to make plans to erect in Singapore a memorial to the women who had worked in Singapore as comfort women. The memorial was to be just like the first statue of a young Korean girl sitting on a chair that had been erected by Korean women's rights activists outside the Japanese Embassy in Seoul in December 2011 and which had become a focus of mass protests and demonstrations.

On 22 January 2013, Korean Council activist Doseul Jeong told the media in Seoul: 'A second girl statue will be erected in Singapore, probably in March, after consultations with authorities there.'[62] She added that 'the statue will be built in a place where Japanese troops used to run a brothel'.[63] Ahn Seon-

---

[61] *The Straits Times*, 30 November 2002.
[62] *Bangkok Post* (online version), 23 January 2013.
[63] *Bangkok Post* (online version), 23 January 2013.

mi also told the media that 'Kim Bok Dong regards the experience as one of her most difficult times, and hopes that the statue is erected before she dies.'[64] Singapore was to be the first Asian country other than South Korea to see the comfort woman statue.[65] Another member of the Korean Council elaborated that these statues were part of what it called the Butterfly Project. One of the project's aims was to 'erect comfort women memorials throughout Asia, where Japanese military brothels existed during the Pacific War', in places such as China, Malaysia, and Indonesia.[66] The transnational history of the comfort women appeared to be creating a transnational heritage.

Members of the Korean Council for the Women Drafted for Military Sexual Slavery by Japan planned to come to Singapore from 31 January to 3 February 2013 to visit the comfort stations of Singapore and to assess where and how to erect a comfort woman statue, in consultation with Singapore officials whom they hoped would be receptive to the idea. Hayashi arranged for Ahn and the women of the Korean Council to be shown around the comfort stations as possible sites for the statue by one of his research associates, Yosuke Watanabe. He was a PhD student in the Japanese Studies Department at the National University of Singapore studying the memory of the Japanese Occupation in Singapore.[67]

As their February 2013 visit to the comfort stations of Singapore drew nearer, the Korean Council, according to Ahn, did not contact the National Heritage Board under the Singapore Ministry of Culture, Community and Youth directly, but 'tried to set up a meeting with the Singapore Embassy in Seoul'.[68] The Singapore Embassy chose not to meet them. By 2013 it was well known that the erection of the comfort woman statue in Seoul and proposals for these statues to be erected elsewhere had created animosities between Japanese and Koreans, which had escalated into diplomatic incidents.[69] Observing these events and other controversies over Japan's wartime atrocities, the Singapore government had consistently expressed its reluctance to diplomatically involve

---

[64] *The Straits Times*, 1 February 2013.
[65] *Korea Times*, 23 January 2013.
[66] *Kyunghyang Shinmun* (online version), 23 January 2013.
[67] Yosuke Watanabe, interviewed by Kevin Blackburn, 26 August 2014.
[68] *The Straits Times*, 1 February 2013.
[69] Mary M. McCarthy and Linda C. Hasunuma, 'Coalition Building and Mobilization: Case Studies of the Comfort Women Memorials in the United States', *Politics, Groups, and Identities* 6, no. 3 (2018): 411–34. See also Rin Ushiyama, '"Comfort Women Must Fall"? Japanese Governmental Responses to "Comfort Women" Statues around the World', *Memory Studies* 14, no. 6 (2021): 1255–71.

Singapore in what were called the 'history wars' of Northeast Asia. It regarded as foreign interference any attempts to bring these divisive debates into Singapore civil society. For example, in August 2015, Singapore Foreign Minister K. Shanmugam publicly rebuked the Singapore World War II History Research Association, which he said was close to the Chinese Embassy, for what he saw as the group attempting to take China's side against Japan in the 'history wars' when marking the 70th anniversary of the end of the war.[70]

On 30 January 2013, the plans of both Kim Bok-dong and the Korean Council for the Women Drafted for Military Sexual Slavery by Japan to erect a comfort woman statue in Singapore were stopped by the Singapore Ministry of Culture, Community and Youth when it announced that 'it would not allow such a statue to be erected in Singapore'.[71] This Ministry was the parent organisation of the National Heritage Board of Singapore, which oversaw such matters. No reason was given for the refusal, but the action by the Ministry was in accord with government policy of not involving Singapore in the 'history wars' of Northeast Asia. The Korean Council members immediately cancelled their plans to come to Singapore and do a comfort station tour guided by Yosuke Watanabe. He turned up at the arranged meeting place in Singapore only to discover that none of the Korean Council members had informed him that the first comfort women heritage trail that he had planned for them would not take place.[72]

A Comfort Women Heritage Trail of Singapore

Watanabe's research identifying the comfort stations of Singapore and preparing a guided tour of them was not wasted. He was able to add the Jalan Jurong Kechil and the Bukit Pasoh Road comfort station sites to a Japanese-language guidebook that he published in 2016.[73] Many Japanese residents in Singapore and visitors to the island have used Watanabe's guidebook to Singapore, and sales of the book have been in the thousands. The comfort women issue has

---

[70] See in particular *The Straits Times*, 28 August 2015. Also see Kevin Blackburn and Ryoko Nakano, 'Memory of the Japanese Occupation and Nation-Building in Southeast Asia', in *Exhibiting the Fall of Singapore: Close Readings of a Global Event*, ed. Daniel Schumacher and Stephanie Yeo (Singapore: National Museum of Singapore, 2018), pp. 26–45.
[71] *The Straits Times*, 1 February 2013.
[72] Yosuke Watanabe, interviewed by Kevin Blackburn, 26 August 2014.
[73] Nobuyoshi Takashima and Yosuke Watanabe, *Shingaporu (ryoko gaido ni nai Ajia o aruku)* [Singapore: Tours of Asia not found in your usual tourist guidebook] (Tokyo: Nashinoki-sha, 2016).

been particularly contentious in Japan and has garnered much publicity. It is not surprising that Japanese visitors to Singapore, whether they embrace right-wing nationalist views that see the comfort women as paid prostitutes or so-called 'leftist' views that see them as sex slaves, have an interest in seeing for themselves the locations of these comfort stations. Japanese visitors to Singapore sometimes fondly describe his guidebook as 'the leftist Japanese guidebook to Singapore', as it tends to focus more than other Japanese guidebooks on visiting 'dark heritage' sites that are associated with Japanese atrocities and cruelty during the Japanese Occupation of Singapore.[74] Other Japanese-language guidebooks have long whitewashed Japanese military brutality during the war in the interest of not offending more conservative readers and visitors.

However, it was not just Japanese visitors to Singapore who were interested to see the 'dark heritage' trail of the Japanese military's comfort stations. South Korean visitors wanted to see the comfort stations where Korean women had worked. This Korean interest increased after the publication of *Ilbongun Wianso Gwanliin-ui Ilgi* [Diary of a Japanese Military Brothel Manager] in 2013 and the widespread controversy and publicity that it ignited in South Korea and Japan. This diary (discussed in Chapter 3) was popular and well read in both countries. South Korean visitors were especially interested in the office and residence of the Korean comfort station manager, Number 88 Cairnhill Road, which was mentioned many times in the published diary.[75]

Another factor behind the interest of Korean visitors was the high profile of one of the last surviving Korean comfort women who had worked in Singapore. In South Korea during the 2010s, Kim Bok-dong became increasingly prominent as she told the media of her experiences as a comfort woman, and one of the places she spoke about was Singapore. One of the original Korean comfort women from early 1992 who spoke out, Kim's profile increased as many of the comfort women passed away gradually. She remained in good health and was very articulate, granting interviews regularly right up to her death in January 2019. Towards the end of her life, she was visited by South Korean President Moon Jae-in, who acknowledged Kim's contribution by writing on his own Facebook page after visiting her that she brought 'light to the hidden history' and gave others 'courage to face the truth'.[76] Moon Jae-in even paid homage to Kim when visiting her wake, bowing on the floor before

---

[74] Ritsuko Saito, interviewed by Kevin Blackburn, 30 January 2019.
[75] Field notes from research fieldwork at Cairnhill Road on 13 July 2017 of eight Korean historians led by Lee Sin-cheol of Sungkyunkwan University, Seoul.
[76] *South China Morning Post*, 28 January 2019.

her body. Her funeral ended with a large procession through the streets of Seoul. A few months later, a documentary about her life, *My Name is Kim Bok Dong* was released, which further increased interest in her life.

Yet, Korean visitors wanting to walk in the footsteps of Kim Bok-dong in Singapore may never really know where she had worked and lived. Kim seems to have arrived in Singapore late in the war after having being sent to other locations in China, Hong Kong, Indonesia, and Malaysia. In interviews, when asked to describe the location in Singapore where she worked, Kim was unsure.[77]

In July 2017, perhaps what was the first comfort station guided tour of Singapore was conducted for eight visiting South Korean historians and women's rights activists to the most accessible comfort station sites. Of course, Korean activists had been visiting and documenting the comfort stations of Singapore since the 1990s when the testimony of Korean comfort women who had worked at Singapore comfort stations began emerging, but there had never been any locally arranged guided tour for this 'dark heritage'. Not surprisingly, Number 88 Cairnhill Road was of considerable interest to the visiting South Koreans because of it figuring so prominently in *Ilbongun Wianso Gwanliin-ui Ilgi* [Diary of a Japanese Military Brothel Manager].[78] This first comfort station guided tour was conducted by Kevin Blackburn and it drew upon the tour put together in 2013 by Yosuke Watanabe for the aborted visit of the Korean Council for the Women Drafted for Military Sexual Slavery by Japan. It started with a visit to the Bukit Pasoh Road comfort station, then proceeded to the site of the Blakang Mati comfort station at Sentosa, where it is possible to see, but not visit, Pulau Bukom. The tour then continued with the Jalan Jurong Kechil shophouses. After a Korean lunch and a visit to the nearby Memories at Old Ford Factory museum of the Japanese Occupation, the tour continued to Tanjong Katong Road before ending at the Cairnhill Road terrace houses.[79]

During the July 2017 comfort station guided tour of Singapore, the interest of the South Korean visitors was clearly on Korean comfort women who had worked in Singapore. Comfort women of other nationalities did not elicit the same interest. This reflects the focus in 2013 when the Korean Council for the Women Drafted for Military Sexual Slavery by Japan sought to commemorate

---

[77] Field notes from research field work at Cairnhill Road on 13 July 2017 of eight Korean historians led by Lee Sin-cheol of Sungkyunkwan University, Seoul.

[78] Field notes from research field work at Cairnhill Road on 13 July 2017 of eight Korean historians led by Lee Sin-cheol of Sungkyunkwan University, Seoul.

[79] Field notes from research fieldwork at Cairnhill Road on 13 July 2017 of eight Korean historians led by Lee Sin-cheol of Sungkyunkwan University, Seoul.

Korean comfort women in Singapore with the statue of a Korean woman and gave little recognition of other women in Singapore from various ethnic groups and nationalities who were also comfort women.[80] However since 2013, comfort woman statues erected in various Asian locations have reflected the role of local comfort women, with statues of local women as well as the Korean women sometimes side by side.

Perhaps what was most surprising for the South Korean visitors was that not one of the comfort stations was marked with a notice or sign. They were impressed that many of the buildings have been conserved by the Urban Redevelopment Authority because of their age and architectural attributes, and are marked so, but they were puzzled that there was no indication that they had served as comfort stations, despite much wartime heritage being abundantly marked and given copious signage in Singapore.[81]

The July 2017 Korean visitors to the 'dark heritage' of the buildings of the former comfort stations and the Memories at Old Ford Factory museum of the Japanese Occupation were surprised by the complete lack of local Singapore comfort women in local narratives of the Japanese Occupation and their absence as survivors giving testimony, as is common in South Korea. In Singapore, as in South Korea during the 2010s, the number of comfort women and other women involved in the Japanese military's wartime sex industry still present in the community with their stories was dwindling. In Singapore, these women would occasionally be uncovered when history teachers initiated large oral history projects in schools, where students were required to carry out oral history interviews with their grandparents. One such project was conducted at St Andrew's Secondary School in 2014, which saw around 200 schoolboys interviewing their grandparents, mainly about the Japanese Occupation. When the teacher in charge of the project, Denise Fernandez, was interviewed on the nightly news television programme called *Singapore Tonight* in late November 2014, among the first of her comments about the school project was the remark: 'We had one young boy whose grandaunt was actually a comfort woman.'[82] However, while this former comfort woman was found, she did not

---

[80] Field notes from research fieldwork at Cairnhill Road on 13 July 2017 of eight Korean historians led by Lee Sin-cheol of Sungkyunkwan University, Seoul.
[81] Field notes from research fieldwork at Cairnhill Road on 13 July 2017 of eight Korean historians led by Lee Sin-cheol of Sungkyunkwan University, Seoul.
[82] *Singapore Tonight*, Channel News Asia, 28 November 2014.

want to give an interview about her experiences for the project, which included a selection of interviews for a website.[83]

In conclusion, despite the increasing presence of the comfort women in the culture and heritage of Singapore, the dwindling number of women in Singapore who worked in the Japanese military's sex industry have still chosen to remain silent. This silence of the local Singapore comfort women has puzzled South Korean visitors to the former comfort stations of Singapore. In Singapore, the development of the comfort women issue has followed that of South Korea and elsewhere by transitioning from an emphasis on human rights in the early 1990s to a focus on representation in culture and heritage in the twenty-first century. Perhaps this confirms what previous chapters have suggested: The window of opportunity for the local Singapore comfort women to speak out and give their testimonies about their experiences was only open very briefly in the 1990s.

---

[83] See some of the interviews from the project at: https://www.schoolbag.sg/story/my-grandparents-my-history.

Conclusion

The evidence brought to light from the history and memory of the comfort women in Singapore suggests some answers to the ongoing debates about the comfort women in Japan, South Korea, and China. These debates centre around three key questions. Were the comfort women forcibly recruited by the Japanese military? Did the Japanese military control the comfort women or were they working in privately managed brothels separate from the military? Were they sex slaves or working as paid prostitutes? These three questions, particularly the last, have received greater attention due to the 2021 controversy over Harvard Law Professor Mark Ramseyer's claims that the comfort women were only paid prostitutes working on contracts, who also knew the conditions of their work before they agreed to these contracts.[1] Ramseyer's claims echo the opinions of Japanese right-wing nationalists, who have long been denying the existence of the comfort women, seeing them as an affront to their nationalistic pride in Japan's history. It is worthwhile bringing the experiences and memories of the comfort women in Singapore into these debates. When these three much debated questions over the comfort women are applied to the investigation of what happened to the comfort women of Singapore, the answers help reveal why local Singapore comfort women have remained silent.

The first of these questions concerns how the comfort women were recruited. In the 1990s, Japanese conservative historians and right-wing nationalists began to attack the notion that had been put forward by many of the comfort women—that they had been forcibly recruited or abducted by the Japanese military.[2] They pointed to inconsistencies in the women's testimonies and the uncorroborated nature of such oral history. While there was documentary evidence for the system of comfort stations, they argued there were no official documents that reported women being abducted by the Japanese military, as the comfort women claimed in their oral history accounts. Some comfort

---

[1] J. Mark Ramseyer, 'Contracting for Sex in the Pacific War', *International Review of Law and Economics* 65 (March 2021), 105971, doi:10.1016/j.irle.2020.105971. See also Concerned Scholars, 'Responses by Concerned Scholars to the Problematic Scholarship of J. Mark Ramseyer', https://sites.google.com/view/concernedhistorians/home?fbclid.

[2] See Hata Ikuhiko, *Comfort Women and Sex in the Battle Zone*, trans. Jason Michael Jordan (Lantham, Maryland: Rowman & Littlefield, 2018), pp. 272–6, 359.

women also gave contradictory accounts. A comfort woman who claimed she had been taken by force later said that she had agreed to the work to earn money. Sociologist Yoshiko Nozaki has argued that the right-wing nationalists exploit these inconsistencies—which are not uncommon in oral history accounts—in order to sow doubts about an issue that they are already ideologically opposed to anyhow.[3] At times, right-wing nationalists go so far as to completely dismiss the testimony of the comfort women. Using a very limited range of documentary evidence, they then insist that all the comfort women were paid prostitutes who chose to provide sexual services.[4]

Evidence from the history and memory of the women working in the sex industry of the Japanese military in Singapore suggests that there was a variety of experiences of sexual enslavement. This would not be surprising. While the experiences of women working in the sex industry serving the Japanese military in Singapore were similar to those elsewhere, the women were very diverse in origins. The diversity of comfort women in Singapore was perhaps unrivalled. The local women of Singapore involved in the sex industry serving the Japanese military included Chinese, Malay, Indian, and Eurasian women. From outside Singapore came large numbers of Koreans, who appear to be the majority of the women working at comfort stations in Singapore. Japanese women were also present, particularly in the *ryotei*. Women from Taiwan and China were also among the comfort women of Singapore. There were a few captured European women. Indonesians were brought to Singapore to serve as comfort women and work along with Koreans at the Tanjong Katong Road comfort station, while at the comfort stations of Katong and Pulau Bukom, there were only Indonesian women. Local Singapore women were also forced to serve the Japanese military outside Singapore at comfort stations in Java, Malaysia, and Thailand, in addition to being scattered across local locations, such as Bukit Pasoh Road, Kallang, Jalan Kayu, and Tanjong Pagar. It is little wonder that men serving in the Japanese military record in their reminiscences, diaries, and memoirs how they saw Singapore as an island for their sexual pleasure, well away from the horrors of the battlefront, with its comfort stations, numerous *ryotei*, and many women of different races and nationalities offering sexual services.[5]

---

[3] Yoshiko Nozaki, 'The "Comfort Women" Controversy: History and Testimony', *The Asia-Pacific Journal: Japan Focus* 3, no. 7 (6 July 2005): 6–7.
[4] See, for example, Archie Miyamoto, *Wartime Military Records on Comfort Women* (Amazon Japan, 2017).
[5] See Chapter 10, 'Nanpo sensen no ian-sho' [Comfort Stations of the Southern Front], in Kim Il-myon, *Tenno Guntai to Chosenjin Ianfu* [The Emperor's Armed Forces and the Korean Comfort Women] (Tokyo: Sanichi Shobo, 1992), originally published in 1976, pp. 190–4.

Examining these diverse groups of women working in the Japanese military's sex industry in Singapore reveals diverse, yet similar, ways in which they were recruited. There is considerable oral history evidence that supports the contention that a significant number of Korean women in Singapore were tricked into becoming comfort women on the pretext of working in restaurants and factories, or being educated as nurses. These women certainly include at least Kim Bok-dong and the Korean women at the Pulau Blakang Mati (Sentosa) comfort station. Similarly, women brought from Indonesia appear to have been tricked into coming to Singapore to work as comfort women, believing the Japanese officials in Java who told them that they would be educated as nurses. As for the Japanese women, they had varying degrees of awareness of the roles they were to perform in the military's sex industry once they arrived in Singapore.

For local women, there is substantial evidence that soon after the fall of Singapore, they were rounded up and forced into the Japanese military's sex industry. Jing-Jing Lee's fictional account of local comfort women who were young virgins abducted soon after the fall of Singapore has its basis in historical fact. But it only reflects part of the truth. Large numbers of prostitutes in Chinatown were also forcibly recruited by the Japanese military. Other women were procured and trafficked amid worsening living conditions. The existence of this diversity in terms of how local Singapore women became involved in prostitution under Japanese rule perhaps helps explain the long postwar silence about their experiences. For many Singapore women, entering prostitution during the Japanese Occupation was not as black-and-white as being virgins who were forcibly recruited.

The second question covers the contested debate over the extent to which the Japanese military was involved in the setting up, organising, and running of the comfort stations. Conservative Japanese historians and right-wing nationalists have contended that the Japanese military had no involvement in the operation of the comfort stations.[6] They argue that the comfort stations were managed by private operators who had no connection with the Japanese military, and that these private operators, who were mainly Korean, recruited the comfort women through their own procurement networks.[7] However, Yoshimi Yoshiaki and other researchers have delineated three types of comfort stations that had

---

[6] Tomomi Yamaguchi, 'The "History Wars" and the "Comfort Woman" Issue: The Significance of *Nippon Kaigi* in the Revisionist Movement in Contemporary Japan', in *The Transnational Redress Movement for the Victims of Japanese Military Sexual Slavery*, ed. Pyong Gap Min, Thomas R. Chung, and Sejung Sage Yim (Berlin: De Gruyter, 2020), pp. 237–43.
[7] Hata, *Comfort Women and Sex in the Battle Zone*, pp. 295–300, 359.

some type of involvement from the Japanese military throughout the Japanese Empire. The first were comfort stations directly run by the military. The second type of comfort stations were formally run by private operators but were effectively under the control of the military and exclusively used by its soldiers, officers, and civilian employees. The third type were run by private operators, but priority was given to the Japanese military. Then there were simply brothels run by private operators. The second category of comfort stations were the most common, with these privately operated comfort stations using the military's buildings and being run according to military rules and regulations.[8]

What does the situation in Singapore suggest? The evidence again reveals a diverse rather than uniform experience. Comfort stations that employed mainly Korean women were managed by private Korean operators, such as Park, manager of the Cairnhill Road comfort station. Park in *Ilbongun Wianso Gwanliin-ui Ilgi* [Diary of a Japanese Military Brothel Manager] makes it clear that he was not a member of the Japanese military himself. He describes how in Singapore there was a union or association of comfort station managers that had an elected president, who during his time in Singapore appears to have been Japanese. In his diary, Park also mentions a Japanese military officer who was in charge overall of the comfort stations of Singapore. From reading the diary of Park, it seems that while he ran his comfort station privately, he worked closely with the Japanese military. Park described how he and other private operators returned regularly to Korea to recruit more women for the Singapore comfort stations.

Most comfort stations in Singapore appear to have had strong links to the Japanese military. The isolated comfort stations on the islands around Singapore seem to have been organised and run by the Japanese navy. The Seletar (Sembawang) naval base comfort station was at the South Gate of the naval base. The *ryotei* were not run directly by the military but by private operators from Japan who had connections in the Japanese military in order to set up these establishments. However, such was the number of these restaurants that offered sexual services in Singapore that there were entrepreneurial local businessmen who set up similar restaurants and prostituted local women for members of the Japanese military with the money to spend on sexual services.

---

[8] Yoshimi Yoshiaki, 'Historical Understandings of the "Military Comfort Women" Issue', in *War Victimization and Japan: International Public Hearing Report*, ed. Executive Committee, International Public Hearing Concerning Postwar Compensation of Japan (Tokyo: Toho Shuppan, 1993), p. 84; and Gay J. McDougall, 'United Nations Commision on Human Rights report', in *Comfort Women Speak: Testimony by Sex Slaves of the Japanese Military*, ed. Sangmie Choi Schellstede (New York: Holmes & Meier Publishers, 2000), p. 138.

The trafficking of local women to these places of prostitution by local brokers and procurers suggests significant local involvement in prostitution both within and outside the Japanese military's sex industry. This local trafficking of women into the sex industry likely would have contributed to Singapore women not wanting to speak out about their experiences as their traffickers were in their very own community. A reluctance to blame local traffickers can be seen in the testimony of Korean comfort woman 'Doo', who was trafficked as a teenage runaway working in restaurants and a cotton mill in Seoul. She replied to an advertisement by a Korean recruiter and broker in the spring of 1943. He promised her a better-paid job doing laundry, nursing, and cleaning for soldiers in Singapore. She was asked about her feelings towards her recruiter by an interviewer in the *Can You Hear Us?* oral history project of the Commission on Verification and Support for the Victims of Forced Mobilization under Japanese Colonialism in Korea. The interviewer asked: 'Don't you hate Koreans because it was a Korean who took you away?' She replied bluntly:

> Right. But it was the Japanese men who made him do that. Korean people were forced to do all kinds of things for Japan. Blame is on the Japanese bastards. Why point fingers at Korean people? It was because of the Japanese bastards, even though a Korean took me with him.[9]

The third question concerns the debate over whether the comfort women were sex slaves or paid prostitutes—what the Japanese right-wing nationalists call *kosho*.[10] This question is closely tied to the first question about how the comfort women were recruited. There were comfort women in Singapore who were paid, but from many oral history accounts, there is considerable evidence that it was not unusual for the women to receive very little money, or none at all, because of the 'debts' that they had to pay off to their brokers and managers. These 'debts' often included the cost of their passages to Singapore, their clothes, their food, and any other expenses that were incurred by the brokers who sold them, or by their managers at the comfort stations.

---

[9] Ji-hyeon Yoon, ed., *Can You Hear Us? The Untold Narratives of Comfort Women: Oral Narrations of Japanese Military Comfort Women* (Seoul: In-hwan Park, Kindle Edition, 2014), p. 174.

[10] Chunghee Sarah Soh, 'From Imperial Gifts to Sex Slaves: Theorizing Symbolic Representations of the "Comfort Women"', *Social Science Japan Journal* 3, no. 1 (April 2000): 60. See also Chunghee Sarah Soh, 'Prostitutes versus Sex Slaves: The Politics of Representing the "Comfort Women"', in *Legacies of the Comfort Women of World War II*, ed. Margaret D. Stetz and Bonnie B.C. Oh (New York: M.E. Sharpe, 2001), pp. 69–100.

However, the diary of Park, the manager of the Cairnhill Road comfort station, does suggest that there were some comfort women who were able to save from whatever they were paid and have Park remit the money back to Korea. This variation could be explained by the differences in managers. Although the comfort women system was an inherently exploitative form of sexual enslavement, the lives of the comfort women as individuals would have depended considerably upon the character of the manager of their comfort station. Many managers, such as Yi Sunok's *Obasan*, who was also in Singapore, would appear to have been more unscrupulous than Park. From the oral history testimonies of the comfort women who worked at comfort stations in Singapore, as well as eyewitnesses who talked to them at the comfort stations, such as Sukaimi bin Ibrahim at Pulau Bukom and Takashi Fujiwara alias Takashi Nagase at Pulau Blakang Mati (Sentosa), the women certainly experienced conditions of work that were akin to enslavement. They were beaten if they refused to have sex with the soldiers. Their lives were also highly regulated and controlled by their managers. While the diary of Park indicates that some women could return home, the oral history testimony indicates that the women themselves did not feel free to do so and felt imprisoned by a system of sexual slavery. Park's diary and some of the oral history accounts from the women themselves do indicate that on occasions, some comfort women could exercise a surprising degree of agency for women in their difficult position. Nonetheless, his diary also demonstrates how Park controlled their lives as they were forced to sexually serve as many as 30–50 men a day to make profits for him.

In Singapore, perhaps the most telling indication of how working conditions in the Japanese military's sex industry resembled sexual enslavement comes from the testimony of Ho Kwai Min, the Chinatown 'high-class' prostitute who accepted a life of prostitution as a business just like any other, and who was able to save and accumulate assets and property from working in her profession. Ho seems to have been well aware of what working directly for the Japanese was like from observing the comfort stations around Singapore, particularly at Bukit Pasoh Road, near where she worked.

Perhaps, Ho's actions as a woman of considerable resourcefulness are the answer to the question of whether women involved in the Japanese military's sex industry were sexual slaves. Ho's answer was yes. Thus, she chose to remain working privately. The degree of sexual enslavement that Ho evaded was probably unavoidable for other local women who did not have her experience in the 'high-class' sector of the sex industry before the war. They would have hardly had the resourcefulness to negotiate their conditions and circumstances as Ho appears to have done.

Ho was able to prevent the local pimps and brokers of Chinatown from trafficking her to work for the Japanese under worse conditions than what she experienced working privately. In Singapore, long-established practices of trafficking women into prostitution before the war, as described by historian James Francis Warren, were used to traffic women into prostitution for the Japanese military.[11] The continuing persistence of this process of trafficking women into prostitution after the war has been further documented by anthropologist Lai Ah Eng.[12] The degree of sexual enslavement associated with this process may also have been a contributing factor to the silence of many Singapore women who were drawn into prostitution during the Japanese Occupation.

However, what appears to have been the strongest factors contributing to the silence of the Singapore women involved in the Japanese military's sex industry were their experiences after the war, which were similar—but not the same—as those of the women of Korea, Japan, China, and other societies in Asia. In early postwar Singapore, there was a considerable number of women who had been former comfort women or were involved in the Japanese military's wartime sex industry. Also, local Singapore comfort women were being sent back from overseas comfort stations. One boat from Java brought 15 local Singapore comfort women in March 1946. Others returned from Malaysia and Thailand. Some comfort women sent to Singapore stayed and became Singapore women. Members of the Malay community had historically migrated from Indonesia to Singapore, so Indonesian comfort women became part of this historical pattern of migration. Thirty Indonesian women from the Tanjong Katong Road and Katong comfort stations decided to stay, mainly settling down at the nearby Malay village of Amber Road. Indonesian women who had worked at the Pulau Bukom comfort station during the war also settled in Singapore at the Malay village of Pasir Panjang.

In the early postwar period, many former local comfort women from the Japanese Occupation, fearing being shunned and rejected as 'impure' if they returned to their families and local neighbourhoods, continued earning a living in prostitution. The proliferation of prostitution during the Japanese Occupation was evident when the British came back in 1945. The large number of streetwalkers prompted a backlash against these women that led to them

---

[11] James Francis Warren, *Ah Ku and Karayuki-san: Prostitution in Singapore 1870–1940*, 2nd edition (Singapore: Singapore University Press, 2003), pp. 77–81.
[12] Lai Ah Eng, *Peasants, Proletarians, and Prostitutes: A Preliminary Investigation into the Work of Chinese Women in Colonial Malaya* (Singapore: Institute of Southeast Asian Studies, 1986).

being stigmatised as 'fallen' women and ostracised as 'a stain of the womanhood' of Singapore by both the colonial administration and community leaders. The colonial state acted and rounded up the girls who were under 18 years of age and placed them in a Girls' Training School, at which they were taught vocational and homemaking skills. In 1947, there were 30–35 young women at the school who had worked in the sex industry of the Japanese Occupation. In 1948, 103 such women were rounded up and 50 placed in the school. Their lives followed what had happened in prewar colonial Singapore to girls under 18 who were taken out of prostitution by the colonial state and placed in a home. These women were trained for working as maids or in home-making skills so they could be married to Chinese working-class men who found it less expensive to marry such local women than pay for a wife from China.

Having experienced considerable public disapproval and scorn soon after the war, these women would have had every incentive to keep silent even when the comfort women issue arose in 1992 and journalists sought them out. Lee Kuan Yew's 1992 statement implying that there were no local comfort women and that Singapore women remained 'chaste' would have further discouraged them from speaking out as other comfort women in other Asian societies voiced their experiences in order to seek justice and obtain compensation from Japan. The absence of support from the Singapore government and the feminist movement for Singapore women who had worked in the Japanese military's sex industry most likely gave these women reason to continue to remain silent even though the early 1990s was the best time for them to come forward, as it was when the international controversy encouraged women in other Asian countries to seek justice and compensation. Coming forward to tell their stories in the early 1990s held out the prospect of satisfying any enduring desire for justice and obtaining compensation, especially after Japan set up the Asian Women's Fund in 1995 to compensate the comfort women of Asian countries. By the 2000s, prospects for justice and compensation had faded. The Asian Women's Fund was wound up in 2007.[13]

Hani Mustafa, a journalist of *Berita Harian*, offers an explanation of why she was unable to persuade local Singapore comfort women to come forward to tell their stories in the 1990s and had to seek out Malaysian comfort women instead. She argues that Malaysian comfort women were living in poverty and compensation would have made a difference in their lives, whereas many Singapore women who were financially better off had little to gain but everything to lose by making public the stories they had kept private since their

---

[13] Hata, *Comfort Women and Sex in the Battle Zone*, pp. 249–70.

ostracisation soon after the war.[14] William Bradley Horton has described this same situation when researching the comfort women in Indonesia. He observed that often the act of telling their stories after years of silence undermined the comfort women's social status, which they had spent years building up.[15] Other oral historians interviewing comfort women, such as Nakahara Michiko in Malaysia, Qiu Peipei, Su Zhiliang, and Chen Lifei in China, and Maki Kimura in Japan, have similarly observed how the act of telling publicly their story has led to disapproval from their families and communities.[16] This was confirmed in the Singapore context by the experience of Ho Kwai Min, who revealed her past in a Singapore television documentary on prewar Cantonese prostitutes in November 1992, and was subsequently shunned by some members of the public and even people in her social circle.[17]

Yet, despite the silence of local Singapore comfort women, they have found representation in Singapore's heritage and culture. The most powerful representation has been in the play *Hayat Hayatie*, which is a strong critique of the society that has silenced them. There has also been the state-sponsored conservation of the Jalan Jurong Kechil comfort station. In the 2000s, the comfort women of Singapore have come to be seen as part of the 'dark heritage' of Singapore, with Korean and Japanese visitors increasingly interested in visiting former comfort stations. Still, there are limits to that representation, which is evidenced by the flat rejection by Singapore heritage authorities of the Korean comfort women's proposal to erect a statue at a former comfort station to the comfort women who worked in Singapore. By rejecting the comfort woman statue, the Singapore government saw its actions as preventing the contentious 'history wars' of Northeast Asia being brought into Singapore's controlled civil society.

---

[14] Hani Mustafa, interviewed by Kevin Blackburn, 4 December 2019.
[15] William Bradley Horton, 'Pramoedya and the Comfort Women of Buru: A Textual Analysis of *Perawan Remaja dalam Cengkeraman Militer* (Teenage Virgins in the Grasp of the Military)', *Journal of Asia-Pacific Studies* (Waseda University), no. 14 (March 2010): 79.
[16] Nakahara Michiko, 'Comfort Women in Malaysia', *Critical Asian Studies* 33, no. 4 (2001): 581–9; Qiu Peipei, with Su Zhiliang and Chen Lifei, *Chinese Comfort Women: Testimonies from Imperial Japan's Sex Slaves* (Oxford: Oxford University Press, 2014); and Maki Kimura, *Unfolding the 'Comfort Women' Debates: Modernity, Violence, Women's Voices* (London: Routledge, 2016), pp.193–215.
[17] Ho Kwai Min, interviewed by Tan Beng Luan, 24 December 1992, accession number 001393, reel 5 (National Archives of Singapore).

Nonetheless, remembering the comfort women of Singapore has produced a transnational heritage because of the diversity of the nationalities and ethnicities of the women who were sexually enslaved on the island by the Japanese military. Representing the comfort women of Singapore in popular culture means not just dealing with the painful memories of significant numbers of Korean, Japanese, and Indonesian women brought to Singapore, as well as smaller numbers of women brought from other places, such as China and Taiwan. It also means coming to terms with the traumatic experiences of the local Singapore women of the different ethnic communities—Chinese, Malays, Indians, and Eurasians. It is not surprising therefore that local Singapore television dramas and plays have reflected this transnational history and the diversity of the women who were sexually enslaved by the Japanese military in Singapore.

It remains very likely that local Singapore women who worked in the Japanese military's sex industry will maintain their silence that they have kept since the end of the war and will take to their graves their private experiences. In Singapore, as in South Korea, all but a very small handful of these women have died. But, every now and then for at least a few years more, mass oral history projects, such as that conducted by teachers and history students at St Andrew's Secondary School in 2014, may perhaps uncover one of them who has lived into her nineties. Yet, these ageing women will continue to decline to give their testimony for fear of undermining the very social status that they have fought so hard and so long to maintain in their families and communities by keeping silent. As scholars researching the lives of the comfort women, we incur ethical obligations to respect their wishes and let it be so. Still, local Singapore women may not be the exception in remaining silent. Researchers on comfort women in other Asian countries have noticed that most comfort women preferred not to come forward to give their testimonies in public for fear of the stigma of doing so.[18] Many women have been reluctant to tell their stories of sexual enslavement. Across Asia, the brave women who have come forward have been a small fraction of the women who were sexually enslaved.

---

[18] Nakahara, 'Comfort Women in Malaysia', pp. 581–9; Qiu, with Su and Chen, *Chinese Comfort Women*, pp. 158–9; and Kimura, *Unfolding the 'Comfort Women' Debates*, pp. 193–215.

Bibliography

Archival Sources

National Archives of Singapore
British Military Administration files
Colonial Secretary's Office
Social Welfare Department files
Speeches

Oral History Centre, National Archives of Singapore
Japanese Occupation in Singapore 1942–1945 oral history collection. See the catalogue: Oral History Department, *Syonan: Singapore under the Japanese: A Catalogue of Oral History Interviews* (Singapore: Oral History Department, 1986)
Communities of Singapore oral history collection. See the catalogue: Oral History Centre, *Communities of Singapore: A Catalogue of Oral History Interviews*, 4 Parts (Singapore: Oral History Centre, 1989–96)
Women Through the Years oral history collection.

National Institute of Education, Nanyang Technological University, Singapore
Oral History Collection

The National Archives, United Kingdom
CO 273 Straits Settlements Original Correspondence files
WO 203/5032 Malaya's Political Climate

The Imperial War Museum, United Kingdom
Comfort Women from Penang recovered at the Andaman Islands material

Arkib Negara Malaysia (The National Archives of Malaysia), Kuala Lumpur
British Military Administration files
Malayan Union files

The Women's Active Museum on War and Peace (WAM), Tokyo
Documents on comfort women in Southeast Asia lodged from the research work of Hayashi Hirofumi

Resources documenting the Singapore comfort stations have recently been made available online: https://wam-peace.org/ianjo/area/area-sg/

Nishino Rumiko, Kim Puja, and the Women's Active Museum on War and Peace, eds. *Shogen mirai e no kioku: Ajia 'ianfu' shogen-shu* [Testimonies for the Future: The Asian 'Comfort Women' Testimonies Collection], 2 Vols. Tokyo: Akashi Shoten, 2006 and 2010.

National Diet Library, Japan
Allied Translator and Interpreter Section (ATIS) files, including the translated intercepted messages and captured documents

National Archives of Japan and the Archives of the National Institute for Defense Studies, Japan
Marei Gunseikanbu [Military Administration of Malaya], Regulations of Military Administration, Series 3, 11 November 1943
War diaries of the units of the 5th Division of the Japanese Imperial Army

National Archives and Record Administration, USA
Allied Translator and Interpreter Section (ATIS) files
Office of Strategic Services Interrogation Reports

Australian War Memorial
Allied Translator and Interpreter Section (ATIS) Interrogation Reports

Newspapers, Magazines, and Other Media

Bangkok Post (online version)
Berita Harian
Berita Minggu
The Business Times (Singapore)
Channel News Asia
Comrade
8 Days
Indian Daily Mail (Singapore)
Japan Times
Jiji Press English News Service
Korea Times
Kyunghyang Shinmun (online version)
Lianhe Wanbao
Lianhe Zaobao
The New Paper
Shin Min Daily News

Sin Chew Jit Poh
Singapore Free Press
South China Morning Post
The Straits Times
Sunday Times (Singapore)
Sunday Tribune (Singapore)
Syonan Shimbun
Syonan Sinbun
Syonan Times
Today

Interviews, Private Papers, and Personal Correspondence Sources

Cheong Pak Yean, private papers
Chin, Ann, private papers.
Hani Mustafa, interview
Kim Bok-dong, interview on *Asian Boss* in October 2018
Lee Kip Lee, interview
Lee Sin-cheol and Lee Sang-dong, interview and correspondence
Ng Yi-Sheng, blog
Phan Ming Yen, interview
Saito Ritsuko, interview
Singapore school oral history, https://www.schoolbag.sg/story/my-grandparents-my-history
Watanabe Yosuke, interview
Wee, Ann, interview
Wong, Mark, correspondence and discussion

Books, Documentaries, and Journal Articles

A. Samad Said. *The Lazy River*. Trans. Harry Aveling. Kuala Lumpur: Heinemann Asia, 1981.
_____. *Salina*. Trans. Hawa Abdullah. Kuala Lumpur: Dewan Bahasa and Pustaka, 1991.
Abdul Rahman Yusof. 'Ideology in *Salina* or in Defence of a Marginalised Masterpiece', in *Critical Perspectives on Literature and Culture in the New World Order*, ed. Noritah Omar, Washima Che Dan, Jason Sanjeev Ganesan, and Rosli Talif, pp. 197–209. Newcastle upon Tyne: Cambridge Scholars Publishing, 2010.
Ahn, Yonson. *Whose Comfort?: Body, Sexuality and Identities of Korean "Comfort Women" and Japanese Soldiers during WWII*. Singapore: World Scientific, 2020.

Bayly, Christopher, and Tim Harper. *Forgotten Armies: Britain's Asian Empire and War with Japan*. London: Penguin, 2005.

———. *Forgotten Wars: The End of Britain's Asian Empire*. London: Penguin, 2008.

Beginnings, The First Report of the Singapore Department of Social Welfare. June to December, 1946. Singapore: Government Printer, 1947.

Between Empires. VHS. Singapore: Singapore Broadcasting Corporation, 1992.

Blackburn, Kevin. 'The Comfort Women of Malaysia and Singapore as Transnational History and Memory'. *Women's History Review* (forthcoming).

Blackburn, Kevin and Karl Hack. *War Memory and the Making of Modern Malaysia and Singapore*. Singapore: NUS Press, 2012.

Blackburn, Kevin and Ryoko Nakano. 'Memory of the Japanese Occupation and Nation-Building in Southeast Asia', in *Exhibiting the Fall of Singapore: Close Readings of a Global Event*, ed. Daniel Schumacher and Stephanie Yeo, pp. 26–45. Singapore: National Museum of Singapore, 2018.

Brownmiller, Susan. *Against Our Will: Men, Women, and Rape*. New York: Simon and Schuster, 1975.

Chan, Fook Pong, Eddie. *Chinatown Unspoken: The Untold Story of War, Vice and Glory in One of Singapore's Most Notorious Districts*. Singapore: Candid Creation Publishing, 2020.

Chan, Jasmine S. 'Prostitution and Stigmatization: Perspectives on Deviance'. Academic exercise, National University of Singapore, 1987.

Chin Kee Onn. *Malaya Upside Down*, 3rd ed. Singapore: Federal Publication, 1976 (orig. pub. 1946).

Choe Kil-song. *Chosen shusshin no choba hito ga mita ianfu no shinjitsu — bunka jinrui gakusha ga yomitoku 'ian-sho nikki'* [The truth of the comfort women as seen by a manager from Korea: A cultural anthropologist interprets the 'comfort station diary']. Tokyo: Hatoshuppan, 2017.

Concerned Scholars. 'Responses by Concerned Scholars to the Problematic Scholarship of J. Mark Ramseyer', https://sites.google.com/view/concernedhistorians/home?fbclid=.

Dolgopol, Ustinia and Snehal Paranjape. *Comfort Women: An Unfinished Ordeal: Report of a Mission*. Geneva: International Commission of Jurists, 1994.

Fu Peilin. 'Yi gu "pipa zai" yue xiao yan yi ai renjian juan bisheng jixu 29 wan yuan gei san jigou' [The late "Pi Pa Girl", Yue Xiao Yan, donating her life savings of $290,000 to three organisations], Channel 8 online news, 4 May 2021, https://www.8world.com/news/singapore/article/tuesday-report-streets-of-memory-s2-e1-keong-saik-road-1466601.

Fusayama Takao. *Nankai no Akebono* [South Seas Dawn]. Tokyo: Sobunsha, 1983.

Gluck, Carol. 'Operations of Memory: "Comfort Women" and the World', in *Ruptured Histories: War, Memory, and the Post-Cold War in Asia*, ed. Sheila Miyoshi Jager and Rana Mitter, pp. 47–77. Cambridge, Massachusetts: Harvard University Press, 2007.

Goh Sin Tub. *The Nan-Mei-Su Girls of Emerald Hill*. Singapore: Heinemann Asia, 1989.

Hara Fujio. *Malayan Chinese and China: Conversion in Identity Consciousness, 1945–1947*. Singapore: Singapore University Press, 2003.

Hata Ikuhiko. *Comfort Women and Sex in the Battle Zone*. Trans. Jason Michael Jordan. Lantham, Maryland: Rowman & Littlefield, 2018.

Hayashi Hirofumi. 'Mare hanto no Nihongun Ianjo' [Comfort Stations of the Japanese Army in the Malay Peninsula], *Sekai* [The World], March 1993, pp. 272–9.

_____. 'Shingaporu no Nihongun Ianjo' [Comfort Stations of the Japanese Army in Singapore]. *Senso Sekinin Kenkyu* [Studies in War Responsibility] 4 (1994): 34–43.

_____. 'Japanese Comfort Women in Southeast Asia'. *Japan Forum* 10, no. 2 (1998): 211–9.

_____. *Shingaporu Kukyo Shukuseii Nihongun wa Shingaporu de nani o shitanoka* [The Purge of the Singapore Chinese: What the Japanese Military Did in Singapore]. Tokyo: Kobunken, 2007.

Henry, Nicola. *War and Rape: Law, Memory and Justice*. London: Routledge, 2011.

Henson, Maria Rosa. *Comfort Woman: A Filipina's Story of Prostitution and Slavery under the Japanese*. Lanham, Maryland: Rowman & Littlefield, 1999.

Hicks, George. *The Comfort Women: Sex Slaves of the Japanese Imperial Forces*. Sydney: Allen & Unwin, 1995.

Hong Jin Tang. 'Ri Kou Yu Ge Minzu' [The Japanese Army and the Ethnic Groups], in *Malayan Chinese Resistance to Japan 1937–1945 — Selected Source Materials*, ed. Shu Yun-Ts'iao and Chua Ser-Koon, comp. Chuang Hui-Tsuan, pp. 462–3. Singapore: Cultural and Historical Publishing House, 1984.

Horton, William Bradley. 'Pramoedya and the Comfort Women of Buru: A Textual Analysis of *Perawan Remaja dalam Cengkeraman Militer* (Teenage Virgins in the Grasp of the Military)'. *Journal of Asia-Pacific Studies* no. 14 (March 2010): 71–88.

_____. 'Comfort Women', in *The Encyclopedia of Indonesia in the Pacific War*, ed. Peter Post, William H. Frederick, Iris Heidebrink, and Shigeru Sato, pp. 184–96. Leiden: Brill, 2010.

Howard, Keith, ed. *True Stories of Korean Comfort Women*. London: Cassell, 1995.

Huff, Gregg and Shinobu Majima, eds. *World War II in Singapore: The Chosabu Reports on Syonan*. Singapore: NUS Press, 2018.

Johnston, William. *Geisha, Harlot, Strangler, Star: A Woman, Sex, and Morality in Modern Japan*. New York: Columbia University Press, 2005.

Josei no tame no Ajia Heiwa Kokumin Kikin [Asian Women's Fund], ed. *Seifu chosa: 'jugun ianfu' kankei shiryo shusei* [Government Investigation: A Collection of Documents on the 'Military Comfort Women'], 5 vols. Tokyo: Ryukei Shosha, 1997–98.

Kamata Hisako. 'Chikamatsu no Okami: Imai Koshizu' [Chikamatsu's Proprietress: Imai Koshizu], *Minamijujisei* [Southern Cross]. Singapore: Japanese Association of Singapore, 1978, pp. 552–4. (Magazine of the Japanese Association of Singapore compiled into a single volume in 1978 by the Japanese Association of Singapore.)

Kawata Fumiko. *Indoneshia no 'Ianfu'* [The Comfort Women of Indonesia]. Tokyo: Akashi Shoten, 1997.

Kho Ee Moi. *The Construction of Femininity in a Postcolonial State: Girls' Education in Singapore*. New York: Cambria Press, 2013.

_____. 'Economic Pragmatism and the "Schooling" of Girls in Singapore'. *HSSE Online* 4, no. 2 (2015): 62–77.

Kim Il-myon. *Tenno Guntai to Chosenjin Ianfu* [The Emperor's Armed Forces and the Korean Comfort Women]. Tokyo: Sanichi Shobo, 1992 (orig. pub. 1976).

Kim Puja. 'The Failure of the Asian Women's Fund: The Japanese Government's Legal Responsibility and the Colonial Legacy', in *Denying the Comfort Women: The Japanese State's Assault on the Historical Truth*, ed. Nishino Rumiko, Kim Puja, and Onozawa Akane, pp. 93–113. London: Routledge, 2018.

_____. 'The Comfort Women Redress Movement in Japan: Reflections on the Past 28 Years', in *The Transnational Redress Movement for the Victims of Japanese Military Sexual Slavery*, ed. Pyong Gap Min, Thomas R. Chung, and Sejung Sage Yim, pp. 43–70. Berlin: De Gruyter, 2020.

Kimura, Maki. *Unfolding the 'Comfort Women' Debates: Modernity, Violence, Women's Voices*. London: Routledge, 2016.

Klein, Ronald E. *The Other Empire: Literary Views of Japan from the Philippines, Singapore, and Malaysia*. Diliman, Quezon City: University of the Philippines, 2008.

Koh Choo Chi. 'Implementing Government Policy for the Protection of Women and Girls in Singapore 1948–66: Recollections of a Social Worker', in *Women and Chinese Patriarchy: Submission, Servitude and Escape*, ed. Maria Jaschok and Suzanne Miers, pp. 122–40. Hong Kong: Hong Kong University Press, 1994.

Kratoska, Paul H. *The Japanese Occupation of Malaya, 1941–1945*. Sydney: Allen & Unwin, 1998.

Lai Ah Eng. *Peasants, Proletarians, and Prostitutes: A Preliminary Investigation into the Work of Chinese Women in Colonial Malaya*. Singapore: Institute of Southeast Asian Studies, 1986.

_____. 'The Women I Met', in *The Makers and Keepers of Singapore History*, ed. Loh Kah Seng and Liew Kai Khiun, pp. 221–31. Singapore: Ethos, 2010.

Lee Eng Kew. *Riben Shou: Taiping Ri Ju San Nian Ba Ge Yue* [In Japanese Hands: The Japanese Occupation at Taiping for Three Years and Eight Months]. Petaling Jaya, Selangor, Malaysia: SIRD, 2006.

Lee, Jing-Jing. *How We Disappeared*. London: One World, 2019.

Lee Kip Lee. *Amber Sands: A Boyhood Memoir*. Singapore: Federal Publications, 1995.

Lee Kiu (Li Qiu). 'Yige Ma Gong Dangyuan de Huiyilu' [Memoirs of a Malayan Communist]. *Journal of the South Seas Society* 55 (December 2000): 83–112.

Lee Kuan Yew. 'Lee Kuan Yew On Marriage, Education, and Fertility in Singapore'. *Population and Development Review* 13, no. 1 (1987): 179–85.

_____. *The Singapore Story: Memoirs of Lee Kuan Yew*. Singapore: Singapore Press Holdings, 1998.

Lee, Terence. 'The Politics of Civil Society in Singapore'. *Asian Studies Review* 26, no. 1 (2002): 97–117.

———. 'Gestural Politics: Civil Society in "New" Singapore'. *Sojourn: Journal of Social Issues in Southeast Asia* 20, no. 2 (2005): 132–54.

Liu Kang. *Chop Suey: A Selection from a Host of Gruesome Events that Occurred in Malaya During the Japanese Occupation*. Singapore: Global Arts & Crafts, 1991 (orig. pub. 1946).

Logan, William and Keir Reeves, eds. *Places of Pain and Shame: Dealing with Difficult Heritage*. London: Routledge, 2009.

Low, N.I. and H.M. Cheng. *This Singapore (Our City of Dreadful Night)*. Singapore: City Book Store, 1947.

Lyons, Lenore. 'Internalised Boundaries: AWARE's Place in Singapore's Emerging Civil Society', in *Paths Not Taken: Political Pluralism in Post-war Singapore*, ed. Michael D. Barr and Carl A. Trocki, pp. 248–63. Singapore: NUS Press, 2008.

———. *A State of Ambivalence: The Feminist Movement in Singapore*. Leiden: Brill, 2010.

Masuda Sayo. *Autobiography of a Geisha*. Trans. G.G. Rowley. New York: Columbia University Press, 2003.

Mat Zin Mat Kib. 'Persatuan Bekas Buruh Paksa dan Keluarga Buruh Jalan Keretapi Maut Siam-Burma 1942–46 Persekutuan Tanah Melayu 1958–1973: Satu Tinjauan Sejarah Perkembangannya' [The All Malaya Association of Forced Labourers and Families of Forced Labourers of the Burma-Siam Death Railway, 1958–1973: A Survey of its Development]. BA thesis, School of Humanities, Universiti Sains Malaysia, 1988.

———. *Persatuan Buruh Keretapi Maut Siam-Burma* [The Association of Labourers on the Burma-Siam Death Railway]. Kuala Lumpur: UPENA, 2005.

Mauzy, Diane K. and R.S. Milne. *Singapore Politics Under the People's Action Party*. London: Routledge, 2002.

McCarthy, Mary M. and Linda C. Hasunuma. 'Coalition Building and Mobilization: Case Studies of the Comfort Women Memorials in the United States'. *Politics, Groups, and Identities* 6, no. 3 (2018): 411–34.

McGregor, Katharine. 'Transnational and Japanese Activism on Behalf of Indonesian and Dutch Victims of Enforced Military Prostitution During World War II'. *Asia-Pacific Journal: Japan Focus* 14, issue 16, no. 7 (2016): 1–22.

Milner, Anthony. *The Malays*. Oxford: Wiley-Blackwell, 2011.

Min, Pyong Gap. *Korean "Comfort Women": Military Brothels, Brutality, and the Redress Movement*. New Brunswick: Rutgers University Press, 2021.

Miyamoto, Archie. *Wartime Military Records on Comfort Women*. Amazon Japan, 2017.

Mohd Zariat Abdul Rani. 'Salina: The Story of a "Noble" Prostitute'. *Malay Literature* 22, no. 2 (2009): 133–51.

Muzaini, Hamzah and Brenda S.A. Yeoh. *Contested Memoryscapes: The Politics of Second World War Commemoration in Singapore*. Farnham, Surrey: Ashgate, 2016.

Nakahara Michiko. 'Comfort Women in Malaysia'. *Critical Asian Studies* 33, no. 4 (2001): 581–9.

Naoi Masatake. *Sen Tamashi: Shingaporu Koryaku-sen Parao-jima Boei-sen* [Battle Spirit: The Fall of Singapore, The Defensive Battle of Palau Island]. Tokyo: Tosen Publishing, 1973.

National Archives of Singapore. *The Japanese Occupation 1942–1945*. Singapore: Times Editions, 1996.

Norma, Caroline. *The Japanese Comfort Women and Sexual Slavery During the China and Pacific Wars*. London: Bloomsbury, 2016.

Nozaki, Yoshiko. 'The "Comfort Women" Controversy: History and Testimony'. *The Asia-Pacific Journal: Japan Focus* 3, issue 7 (6 July 2005): 1–16.

Oehlers, F.A.C. *'Jock', That's How it Goes: Autobiography of a Singapore Eurasian*. Singapore: Select, 2008.

Ong Jin Hui. 'Singapore', in *Prostitution: An International Handbook on Trends, Problems, and Policies*, ed. Nanette J. Davis, pp. 243–72. Westport, Connecticut: Greenwood Press, 1993.

Ooi Yu-lin. *Pieces of Jade and Gold: An Anecdotal History of the Singapore Chinese Girls' School, 1899–1999*. Singapore: Singapore Chinese Girls' School, 1999.

Oon, Clarissa. 'Shameful histories'. *Mekong Review*, Issue 5 (April 2019), https://mekongreview.com/shameful-histories/.

Othman Wok. 'Working with Death', in *The Bamboo Fortress: True War Stories*, ed. H. Sindhu, pp. 165–84. Singapore: Native Publications, 1991.

Park [name deliberately obscured to protect identity]. *Ilbongun Wianso Gwanliin-ui Ilgi* [Diary of a Japanese Military Brothel Manager]. Trans. Ahn Byung-jik. Seoul: Isup, 2013. There is a Japanese version by Hori Kazuo, of Kyoto University and Kimura Kan, of Kobe University, who also provided English-language excerpts: https://drive.google.com/file/d/1xUn-IWuIoWDMqgByTDeo61Cm4z5GMfLh/view.

Peterson, William. *Theater and the Politics of Culture in Contemporary Singapore*. Middletown, Connecticut: Wesleyan University Press, 2001.

Pramoedya Ananta Toer. *Perawan Remaja dalam Cengkeraman Militer* [Young Virgins in the Military's Grip]. Jakarta: KPG, Kepustakaan Populer Gramedia, 2015 (orig. pub. in 2001).

Purcell, Victor. *The Chinese in Malaya*. Kuala Lumpur: Oxford University Press, 1967 (orig. pub. 1948).

Qiu Peipei, with Su Zhiliang and Chen Lifei. *Chinese Comfort Women: Testimonies from Imperial Japan's Sex Slaves*. Oxford: Oxford University Press, 2014.

Quah Bee Lian, Connie. 'Prostitution in Singapore Society'. MSc., National University of Singapore, 1991.

Ramseyer, J. Mark. 'Contracting for Sex in the Pacific War'. *International Review of Law and Economics* 65 (March 2021), 105971, doi:10.1016/j.irle.2020.105971.

Report of the Social Welfare Department 1950. Singapore: Colony of Singapore, 1951.

Report of the Social Welfare Department 1951. Singapore: Colony of Singapore, 1952.

Reynolds, E. Bruce. 'History, Memory, Compensation, and Reconciliation: The Abuse of Labor along the Thailand-Burma Railway', in *Asian Labor in the Wartime Japanese Empire*, ed. Paul H. Kratoska, pp. 326–47. Singapore: NUS Press, 2006.

Sahlan Mohd. Saman. *A Comparative Study of the Malaysian and the Philippines War Novels*. Bangi, Malaysia: Penerbit Universiti Kebangsaan Malaysia, 1984.

Sandhu, Kernial Singh. *Indians in Malaya: Some Aspects of their Immigration and Settlement (1786–1957)*. Cambridge: Cambridge University Press, 1996.

Schellstede, Sangmie Choi, ed. *Comfort Women Speak: Testimony by Sex Slaves of the Japanese Military*. New York: Holmes & Meier Publishers, 2000.

Shamala Kandiah. 'Women in a Patriarchy: The Singapore Case'. Academic exercise, National University of Singapore, 1986.

Shimizu Hiroshi and Hirakawa Hitoshi. *Japan and Singapore in the World Economy: Japan's Economic Advance into Singapore*. London: Routledge, 1999.

Shingaporu Shiseikai [Singapore Municipal Association]. *Shonan Tokubetsu-shi Shi: Senji-chu no Shingaporu* [Syonan Special Municipality History: Singapore During the War]. Tokyo: Nihon Shingaporu Kyokai [The Japan-Singapore Association], 1986.

Shinozaki, Mamoru. *My Wartime Experiences in Singapore: Institute of Southeast Asian Studies, Singapore Oral History Programme Series No. 3 August 1973*. Singapore: Institute of Southeast Asian Studies, 1973.

_____. *Syonan: My Story: The Japanese Occupation of Singapore*. Singapore: Asia Pacific Press, 1975.

_____. *Shingaporu Senryo Hiroku: Senso to Sono Ningenzo* [A Secret Memoir of the Occupation of Singapore: The War and the Human Image]. Tokyo: Hara Shobo, 1976.

Sinha, Lalita. *The Other Salina: A. Samad Said's Masterpiece in Translation*. Penang: Penerbit Universiti Sains Malaysia, 2006.

Social Welfare Singapore 1947: The Third Annual Report of the Department of Social Welfare. Singapore: Colony of Singapore, 1948.

Social Welfare 1948: The Fourth Annual Report of the Department of Social Welfare. Singapore: Colony of Singapore, 1949.

Soh, C. Sarah. 'Japan's National/Asian Women's Fund for "Comfort Women"'. *Pacific Affairs* 76, no. 2 (2003): 209–33.

_____. *The Comfort Women: Sexual Violence and Postcolonial Memory in Korea and Japan*. Chicago: University of Chicago Press, 2008.

Soh, Chunghee Sarah. 'The Korean "Comfort Women": Movement for Redress'. *Asian Survey* 36, no. 12 (1996): 1226–40.

_____. 'From Imperial Gifts to Sex Slaves: Theorizing Symbolic Representations of the "Comfort Women"'. *Social Science Japan Journal* 3, no. 1 (April 2000): 59–76.

_____. 'Prostitutes versus Sex Slaves: The Politics of Representing the "Comfort Women"', in *Legacies of the Comfort Women of World War II*, ed. Margaret D. Stetz and Bonnie B.C. Oh, pp. 69–87. New York: M.E. Sharpe, 2001.

Spender, Dale. *Man Made Language*. London: Routledge and Kegan Paul, 1980.

Suzuki Shogo. 'The Competition to Attain Justice for Past Wrongs: The "Comfort Women" Issue in Taiwan'. *Pacific Affairs* 84, no. 2 (2011): 223–44.

Suzuki Yuko, Yon'e Yamashita, and Tonomura Masaru, eds. *Nihongun 'Ianfu' Kankei Shiryo Shusei* [A Collection of Materials on the Japanese Army's 'Comfort Women'], 2 vols. Tokyo: Akashi Shoten, 2006.

Tai, Eika. *Comfort Women Activism: Critical Voices From the Perpetrator State.* Hong Kong: University of Hong Kong Press, 2021.

Takashima Nobuyoshi and Watanabe Yosuke. *Shingaporu (ryoko gaido ni nai Ajia o aruku)* [Singapore: Tours of Asia not found in your usual tourist guidebook]. Tokyo: Nashinoki-sha, 2016.

Tanaka Yuki. *Japan's Comfort Women: Sexual Slavery and Prostitution during World War II and the US Occupation.* London: Routledge, 2002.

Tuesday Report: Behind the Red Lantern. Singapore Broadcasting Corporation and National Archives of Singapore.

Ushiyama Rin. '"Comfort Women Must Fall"? Japanese Governmental Responses to "Comfort Women" Statues around the World'. *Memory Studies* 14, no. 6 (2021): 1255–71.

Vickers, Edward. 'Commemorating "Comfort Women" Beyond Korea: The Chinese Case', in *Remembering Asia's World War Two*, ed. Mark Frost, Daniel Schumacher, and Edward Vickers, pp. 174–207. London: Routledge, 2019.

Warren, James Francis. *Ah Ku and Karayuki-san: Prostitution in Singapore 1870–1940*, 2nd ed. Singapore: Singapore University Press, 2003.

Wee, Ann. *A Tiger Remembers: The Way We Were in Singapore.* Singapore: NUS Press, 2017.

Wee, C.J.W.-L. and Lee Chee Keng, eds. *Two Plays by Kuo Pao Kun: Descendants of the Eunuch Admiral and The Spirits Play.* Singapore: SNP International, 2003.

Wong, Diana. 'Memory Suppression and Memory Production: The Japanese Occupation of Singapore', in *Perilous Memories: The Asia-Pacific War(s)*, ed. T. Fujitani, Geoffrey M. White, and Lisa Yoneyama, pp. 218–38. Durham: Duke University Press, 2001.

Xie Song Shan. *Xue Hai* [Sea of Blood]. Singapore: Nanyang Baoshe, 1950.

Xie Yong Guang. *Rijun Weian Fu Neimu* [Inside the Comfort Women Issue]. Hong Kong: Mingpao Publishing, 1993.

Yamaguchi Tomomi. 'The "History Wars" and the "Comfort Woman" Issue: The Significance of *Nippon Kaigi* in the Revisionist Movement in Contemporary Japan', in *The Transnational Redress Movement for the Victims of Japanese Military Sexual Slavery*, ed. Pyong Gap Min, Thomas R. Chung, and Sejung Sage Yim, pp. 237–43. Berlin: De Gruyter, 2020.

Yoon Ji-hyeon, ed. *Can You Hear Us? The Untold Narratives of Comfort Women: Oral Narrations of Japanese Military Comfort Women.* Seoul: In-hwan Park, Kindle Edition, 2014.

Yoshimi Yoshiaki, ed. *Jugun Ianfu Shiryoshu* [Collection of Comfort Women Materials]. Tokyo: Otsuki Shoten, 1992.

Yoshimi Yoshiaki. 'Historical Understandings of the "Military Comfort Women" Issue', in *War Victimization and Japan: International Public Hearing Report*, ed. Executive Committee, International Public Hearing Concerning Postwar Compensation of Japan, pp. 81–93. Tokyo: Toho Shuppan, 1993.

———. *Comfort Women: Sexual Slavery in the Japanese Military during World War II*. Trans. Suzanne O'Brien. New York: Columbia University Press, 2000.

Yoshimi Yoshiaki and Hayashi Hirofumi, eds. *Nihongun Ianfu: Kyodo Kenkyu* [Japanese Military Comfort Women: Joint Research]. Tokyo: Otsuki Shoten, 1995.

Zhou Xuji. 'Xinjiapo Jungang Gongren Diyu Shenghuo Huiyilu' [The Hellish Life of Singapore Military Port Workers: A Memoir], in *Malayan Chinese Resistance to Japan 1937–1945—Selected Source Materials*, ed. Shu Yun-Ts'iao and Chua Ser-Koon, comp. Chuang Hui-Tsuan, pp. 485–6. Singapore: Cultural and Historical Publishing House, 1984.

Index

10 Teck Lim Road, Singapore, 58
15th Independent Engineer Regiment, 166
25th Army, 31
27 Bukit Pasoh Road, Singapore, *see* Bukit Pasoh Road, Singapore
88 Cairnhill Road, *see* Cairnhill Road, Singapore

abduction, *see* recruitment and enslavement
advertisements for comfort women, 43–5
Ah Hua, 33
Ahn, Yonson, 13, 37, 39
Ahn Byung-jik, 71–2
Ahn Seon-mi, 170–1
Air View Hotel, Singapore, 58
Akshita Nanda, 156
Alfian Sa'at, 160–1
Allied Headquarters, 110–11
'Amenities in the Japanese Armed Forces', 76
Ang Guang Hiang, 35
'APO 689 Prisoner of War Interrogation Report No. 49', 85
Asahi Club, Singapore, 44
Asahi Shimbun, 18, 99
Asakusa, Japan, 52
Asian Art Festival, 159
Asian women, 'roar of', 2–3, 28
Asian Women's Fund, 149–50, 184
Association of Women for Action and Research (AWARE), 140–1

Bae Tok Gan, 61
Bak (comfort station manager), *see Diary of a Japanese Military Brothel Manager*
Bendi Weian Fu [Local Comfort Women], 28
Berita Harian, 156
see also Hani Mustafa
Between Empires, 32–3
Blackburn, Kevin, 174
Britain, 109, 120–1
see also Singapore Advisory Council to the British Military Administration
Broken Birds, 157
Broome, R.N., 120, 126
brothels, *see* comfort stations; sex work
'Bubu', 158
Bukit Pasoh Road, Singapore
conservation of, 170
demographics of, 26, 46–7
maps and guides to, 59, 172
Singaporean attitudes to, 26, 149
Burma (Myanmar), 74, 84, 143–4
Burma-Thailand Railway Association, 145
Busan, South Korea, 83–6
Butterfly Project, 171–2

Cairnhill Road, Singapore
conservation of, 170
demographics of, 16–17, 24–6
life inside, 64–5, 77, 79
map, 15

Singaporean attitudes to, 13–14, 16–26, 38, 92, 113
  see also Diary of a Japanese Military Brothel Manager
Can You Hear Us?, 66–7, 74
  see also 'Coo'; 'Doo'
Cantonese sex workers and comfort women, 47–8, 147
  see also Ho Kwai Min
Chan Swee Kung, 20–1, 163
chastity, *see* gender ideology
Cheah Fook Ying, Charlie, 38
Chee Keng Soon, 24
Chen Su Lan, 54–5, 117–20, 124
Cheng, H.M., 42, 47, 116–17
Cheong family, 168–9
Chew, Ernest, 136
Chew Chin Hin, 81
Chibune and Hinomoto, 165–70, 172
Chikamatsu, Singapore, 52–3
childbirth, 68–9, 139
Chin, Mr, 43
Chin Kang Huay Kuan Chinese clan association, *see* Bukit Pasoh Road, Singapore
Chin Kee Onn, 152
China, 65–6, 86
Chinatown, Singapore
  comfort women in, 42–3, 46–7,
    see also Bukit Pasoh Road, Singapore
  sex work in, 20–1, 42–3, 79,
    see also Ho Kwai Min
Chinese comfort women in Malaysia, 6–7
Chinese comfort women in Singapore
  media coverage of, 27, 145–6
  rape outside stations, 33
  recruitment and enslavement, 42–4, 56–7, 86
  in ryotei, 54
  trafficked to Malaysia, 47–8
  A War Diary, 162–4

Chinese media, 28, 43–4, 164
  see also Jiaodian [Focus] program; *Lianhe Wanbao*; *Lianhe Zaobao*; *Veil of Darkness*
Chinese sex workers, 47–8, 147
  see also Ho Kwai Min
Chong, Robert, 92, 94, 96, 100
Chong Song-myong, 83–4
Chop Suey, 113–14
Chuang Hui-Tsuan, 29
civilians, violence against, 42, 60–1, 70, 181
  see also rape
clothing, 91, 97, 146–7
comfort stations
  administration and finances, 69–70, 73–6, 79, 180–2
  conservation of, 165–70
  customer procedure, 97
  demographics of, 178
  establishment of, 39–40, 46, 179
  layout and appearance, 96–8
  of Malaysia, 4–7
  maps and guides to, 8–9, 165–6, 172, 174–5
  number of, 80
  ryotei compared to, 49
  terminology, 1
  see also Bukit Pasoh Road; Cairnhill Road; comfort women; Emerald Hill; Kallang; Katong comfort stations; Newton Road; Onan Road; Pulau Bukom; Railway Station Road; ryotei; Seletar (Sembawang) base; Sentosa; Sinmazi
comfort women
  terminology, 1
  see also Chinese comfort women; clothing; comfort stations; Filipina comfort women; health; Indonesian comfort women; Korean comfort women; Malay

comfort women; Malaysian comfort women; post-war life; recruitment and enslavement; Singapore, comfort women in; social dynamics; Taiwanese comfort women
Comfort Women Speak, 84–5
Commission on Verification and Support for the Victims of Forced Mobilization under Japanese Colonialism in Korea, 66
compensation, 7, 27
   Asian Women's Fund, 149–50, 184
   Filipina women seek, 150
   Korean women seek, 2–3, 17, 116, 150
   local Singaporean women and, 143, 150, 184
   Malaysian women seek, 142, 145, 150
   Taiwanese women seek, 150
conservation of comfort stations, 165–70
contraception, 68
'Coo' (former comfort woman), 67–9, 86–7, 89, 91
Corner, E.J.H., 101

Dalifah Shahril, 155
dancing shows, 91
Diary of a Japanese Military Brothel Manager, 71–6, 84, 173–4
disease, *see* health
'Doo' (former comfort woman), 66–8, 87, 92, 181
drug use, 67–8

economics, 55–6
education, 103–6, 138–9
   see also Girls' Training School
Emerald Hill, Singapore, 20–1, 38
English-language press, 136–9
   see also *The Straits Times*

enslavement process, *see* recruitment and enslavement
escapes and rescues, 40–1, 70–1, 74
   see also post-war life
'Ex-Japanese Prostitutes in British Singapore', 120

feminism, *see* gender ideology
Feng Bi Hui, 148
Fernandez, Denise, 175–6
Filipina comfort women, 27, 150
'A Flower That Will Never Bloom', 162–4
Foo, Rosalind, 123–4
food insecurity, 55–6
forced labour, 102–3
   see also comfort women
Fort Canning, Singapore, 157
Fourth Comfort Corps, 84–6
   see also Diary of a Japanese Military Brothel Manager
Fu Yao Hua, 145–7
Fujiwara, 70, 99
Fukumizu Rikimatsu, 45
Fusayama Takao, 45

Gay Wan Leong, 94, 96
geisha, 28, 49–50, 54
   see also Japanese comfort women in Singapore; Japanese sex workers; ryotei
gender ideology
   feminist approaches to comfort women, 2–3, 7–8, 62, 139–40, 142–3, 155–6
   objectification of women and trivialisation of rape, 19–20, 22–4, 37–9, 65, 79, 96, 100, 159–60
   purity culture's effect on comfort women, 7, 13, 25–6, 29, 109–22, 133–4, 137–43, 145–6, 150–2, 175–6, 183–6

purity culture's effect on sex workers, 109–22, 133–4, 148–9, 151–2
women's role in Singaporean society, 139–40
see also Ahn, Yonson; Association of Women for Action and Research; Chan Swee Kung; Lee Kuan Yew; 'rehabilitation' of local comfort women; Singapore Advisory Council to the British Military Administration; Soh, C. Sarah
Girls' Training School, 125–32, 184
Goei, Glen, 160
Goh Sin Tub, 20–2, 26
Goh Yu Yap, 40
'Goo' (former comfort woman), 74

Hamada Jitaro, 44
Han Cho-soo, 114–15
Haname, 70
Hani Mustafa, 142–5, 150, 153–4, 184
Harami Keiji, 57
Hata Ikuhiko, 83
Hayashi Hirofumi, 171
  on administrative nature of records, 62
  chronicling of comfort stations, 1, 4–6, 8–10, 80, 136, 165–6, 169
  defines comfort women, 31
  on Malaysian comfort women, 28
  on post-war lives of comfort women, 114–15
  on recruitment and enslavement, 31, 39, 43, 45
Hayat Hayatie, 154–6
health, 99
  see also drug use; hospital work; sexually transmitted infections; violence against civilians
Heng, Ivan, 160
Heng Chiang Ki, 38
Hinomoto and Chibune, 165–70, 172

Hirakawa Hitoshi, 43, 53, 83
Ho Kwai Min
  death, 148
  early life, 57–8
  marriage and retirement, 61
  philanthropy, 148
  sex work, 57–8, 60–2, 147–8, 182–3
  stigma surrounding, 147–9
  violent experiences, 58, 60, 62
Ho Teck Fan, 46, 149
Hone, H.R., 120, 123
Hong Jin Tang, 29, 44–5
Horne, D.R., 55
Horton, William Bradley, 104–6, 137, 150
hospital work
  post-war, 114–15
  recruitment using promise of, 84–5, 100–3, 105–6
Hotel Singapore, 160–1
Hougang, Singapore, 34, 37
How We Disappeared, 3
Huo Yue Wei, 145–7

ianfu, *see* comfort women
ianjo, *see* comfort stations
Ichifuji-ro, Burma, 74
Ilbongun Wianso Gwanliin-ui Ilgi, *see Diary of a Japanese Military Brothel Manager*
Imai Koshizu, 52–3
Imperial Japanese Navy, *see* naval bases
In Pursuit of Peace, 164
Indonesia, 102–3, 107–8
Indonesian comfort women in Buru Island, 137, 150
Indonesian comfort women in Singapore
  comparing with Korean experiences, 104–8
  post-war life, 110–13
  recruitment and enslavement, 100–8
  station demographics, 100–2, 108

infections, *see* sexually transmitted infections
International Commission of Jurists, 83
isolation, *see* social dynamics

Jalan Besar, Singapore, 34, 119
Jalan Jurong Kechil Comfort Station, 165–70, 172
Jalleh, Ken, 55–6
Japan, role of women in, 138
Japanese Army of Korea, 86
Japanese Army Propaganda Unit, 43
Japanese comfort women in Singapore
    background and demographics, 91
    at Bukit Pasoh Road, 46–7
    conditions for, 89
    depictions of, 157–60
    social dynamics, 89, 91
    in Tanjong Katong Road, 96
    see also geisha
Japanese government, 28, 170–2
    see also compensation; Shinozaki, Mamoru
Japanese military
    degree of control, 180
    officers' treatment of comfort women, 61
    organisation and training, 19–20
    rape by, *see* rape
    see also 25th Army; *Between Empires*; comfort stations; Fourth Comfort Corps; Japanese Army of Korea; National Institute for Defense Studies; naval bases; Southern Army; violence against civilians
Japanese Occupation in Singapore 1942–1945, 22–3, 62, 165
Japanese sex workers, 43, 94
    see also geisha
Japanese visitors to Singapore, 172–3
Java, Indonesia, 47, 100–1, 107–8, 150

Jeong, Doseul, 170
Jiang Long, 162
Jiaodian [Focus] program, 27
Jiji Press, 72
job opportunities, *see* hospital work
Joo Chiat Road, Singapore, 94–6
journalism, *see* media interest in comfort women
Jugun Ianfu, 86
Jumaiyah bte Masbin, 47

Kallang, Singapore, 45
Kamata Hisako, 52
Kampong Lorong Engku Aman, Singapore, 34
Kansai Zaikai seminar, 17
karayuki-san, *see* Japanese comfort women in Singapore; Japanese sex workers
Karayuki-san, the Making of a Prostitute, 157
Katong comfort stations
    attempted repatriation of women from, 110–11
    conditions at, 100–1
    demographics of, 100–1
    establishment of, 94, 96
    map of, 93, 95
    recruitment of women for, 100–2
    see also Tanjong Katong Road
Kelolaan Hanim Mohd Saleh, 156
Khairi Razaai, 154–6
Kho Ee Moi, 139
Kikusui Club, *see* Cairnhill Road, Singapore
killings, civilian, 42
Kim Bok-dong
    death and legacy, 173–4
    post-war life, 115–16, 170–3
    time in comfort station, 66
Kim Il-myon, 1
Kim Sang-hi, 65–6

Kimura, Maki, 150–1
Kimura Kan, 72
Kiong Beng Swee, 46
Klein, Ronald D., 21
Koh Kim Hiang, 34
Kong, Lily, 169
Kono Statement, 152
Korea, pre-war trafficking, 106–8
Korean comfort women, 2, 13, 16–17, 26, 150–1
Korean comfort women in Singapore
 at Cairnhill Road, 16–17, 24–6, *see also Diary of a Japanese Military Brothel Manager*
 comparing with Indonesian experiences, 104–8
 conditions for, 80–1, 89
 depictions of, 170–2
 hierarchy, 180
 legacy, 173–5
 post-war life, 113–16, 140
 recruitment and enslavement, 83–8, 108
 social dynamics, 89, 91
 station demographics, 26, 65, 80–1, 83–4, 86, 91–2, 100, 106, 108
 see also 'Coo'; 'Doo'; Kim Bok-dong; Kim Sang-hi; Sentosa; Tanjong Katong Road; *A War Diary*; Yi Sunok
Korean Council for the Women Drafted for Military Sexual Slavery by Japan, 69, 116, 170–2
Kuala Lumpur, 6
Kuo Pao Kun, 157–60
Kuomintang, 6
Kuroda Shigenori, 52
Kwan Weng Kin, 18
kyodo benjo, term, 19–20

Lai Ah Eng, 62
law, military, 40

Le Blond, Raoul, 137
Lee, Jing-Jing, 3
Lee Beng Kway, 37
Lee Kip Lee, 163
Lee Kip Lin, 23, 94, 100
Lee Kiu, 122–6, 129
Lee Kuan Yew
 1992 comfort women statement, 14, 16–20, 25–9, 143
 on gender roles, 137–40
 on Tanjong Katong Road, 92
Leow Shuan Fong, 47–8
Li Jie Fusheng, 161–2
Lianhe Wanbao, 25–7
Lianhe Zaobao, 27–9, 145–7
Lim Ah Hua, 36
Lim Chu Kang, Singapore, 36
Lim Ming Joon, 37, 56–7
Lim Seng (alias Lim Tow Tuan), 37
Lim Soo Gan, 40–2
List of Absences, 114–15
Liu Kang, 113–14
local comfort women, *see* Singapore, comfort women in
Loh Poh Ying, 33
Loke, Granny, 35
Low, N.I., 42, 47, 116–17
Luo Mei, 35
Lyons, Lenore, 141

Malay comfort women in Singapore, 160–1
 at Cairnhill Road, 16
 The Nameless Women of Syonan, 165
 recruitment and enslavement, 33, 35
 trafficking to Malaysia, 47
 see also Hayat Hayatie
Malay community in Singapore, 111–12
Malay media, 142–5
 see also Berita Harian
Malaya Upside Down, 152
Malayan Campaign, 166

Malaysian Chinese Association (MCA), 7, 142
Malaysian comfort stations, 4–7, 39
Malaysian comfort women
    post-war life, 7–8, 28, 150
    recruitment and enslavement, 47–8
    see also Malay comfort women in Singapore
Manila, Philippines, 76
marriage, 33
Maruhana, Japan, 52
masculinist perspective, see gender ideology
Mashizan Masjum, 165
Mauzy, Diane K., 141
McKerron, P.A.B., 124
media interest in comfort women, 136–9, 142–5
    see also Berita Harian; Chinese media; The Straits Times
medical field, see hospital work
men, role of, see gender ideology
Miki, Lieutenant, 77
Milne, R.S., 141
Min Pyong Gap, 2
Moon Jae-in, 173
Murayama, Tomiichi, 149
murder of civilians, 42
My Name is Kim Bok Dong, 174
Myanmar, 74, 84, 143–5

Nagase, Takashi (alias Fujiwara Takashi), 76–7, 79
Nair, V.K.G., 120–2
Nakagawa Hana, 52
Nakahara Michiko, 7–8
Nakayama, Mitsuyoshi, 99
The Nameless Women of Syonan, 165
Nan Hwa Girls' School, Singapore, 49–51
The Nan-Mei-Su Girls of Emerald Hill, 21–2
Naoi Masatake, 16

National Archives and Records Administration (US), 114
National Archives of Malaysia, 6
National Archives of Singapore, 22–3
National Day Rally Speech, 138
National Institute for Defense Studies (Japan), 6, 114
National University of Singapore, 138, 140
naval bases, 46, 77–8, 88–90
New Democratic Youth Party, 122
The New Paper, 25–6
Newton Road, 81
Nha Trang, Vietnam, 99
Norma, Caroline, 106–7
Nozaki, Yoshiko, 178
nursing work, see hospital work
Nyonya Hidayat, 110

Odate Shigeo, 51
Oehlers, Farleigh Arthur Charles, 81
officers, 61
    see also ryotei
Oh Choo Neo, Patricia (alias Mrs Chia Kin Teng), 33
'Ojisan', 54
Old Club, Taiping, 48
Omar Ahmad, 144–5
Onan Road, 80–1
Ong Chit Chung, 136, 143
Ong Keng Sen, 156–8
Ong Soo Mui, 39
opium, 67–8
Oral History Centre, 57–8, 60–1, 148–9
    see also *Japanese Occupation in Singapore 1942–1945*
oral history's importance, 62–3
Oshiga, Keiji, 89
Othman Wok, 92, 101, 111–12

Paglar, Eric Charles Pemberton, 80

Index

Pak Ok-nyon, 84–5
Park (comfort station manager), see *Diary of a Japanese Military Brothel Manager*
Pasir Panjang, Malaysia, 112, 128
patriarchy, see gender ideology
People's Action Party, 143
Perawan Remaja dalam Cengkeraman Militer [Young Virgins in the Military's Grip], 103–4
Persatuan Bekas dan Warisan Buruh Paksa Malaya, 145
Perumal, Sundarajulu Lakshmana, 46
Phan Ming Yen, 136, 139, 165
Philippines, 27, 150
Pipa Meng [Pipa Dream], 147–9
Poh Leung Kuk home, Singapore, 123–4, 128
post-war life
    for Indonesian comfort women, 110–13
    journeys home, 183
    for Korean comfort women, 113–16
    for local comfort women, 109–10, 116–17, 133–4, see also 'rehabilitation' of local comfort women; Singapore Advisory Council to the British Military Administration
    see also compensation; gender ideology
poverty, 55–6
Pramoedya Ananta Toer, 103–4
pregnancies, 68–9, 139
press, see media interest in comfort women
prosecution of rapists, 40
prostitution, see sex work
Pulau Blakang Mati, Singapore, 77–8
Pulau Bukom, Singapore, 102, 112
Purcell, Victor, 122, 124
purity, see gender ideology

Rabaul, New Guinea, 85
racial violence, 42

Raffles Hotel, Singapore, 44
Railway Station Road, Taiping, 48
Ramly, Norsiah, 154
Ramos, Fidel, 27
Ramseyer, Mark, 75
Rangoon, Burma, 84
rape, 31–3, 35–9
    decline outside comfort stations, 39–40
    military sanctioning of, 39–40
    see also comfort stations
recruitment and enslavement
    in 1944, 75
    abduction, 33–5
    local involvement, 42, 181
    military sanctioning of, 177–9
    using deceit, 43–5, 67–8, 84–8, 100–3, 105–6, 179, 181
Red Cross, 110
'rehabilitation' of local comfort women, 109–10, 123–5
    see also Girls' Training School
rescues and escapes, see escapes and rescues
Research Association on the Women Drafted for Military Sexual Slavery by Japan, 69
restaurants, 106, 117–18, 166
    see also ryotei
Rijun Weian Fu Neimu [Inside the Comfort Women Issue], 28
romusha, 102–3
ryotei
    administration, 56–7, 180
    atmosphere, 50
    comfort stations compared, 49
    demographics of, 4, 6, 49–50, 53–7, 94
    karayuki-san in, 43
    in Katong, 94
    leading to post-war prostitution, 117–18
    recruitment and enslavement, 21–2, 54–6

Singapore Chinese Girls' School, 14
see also Chikamatsu; Tsuruya; Yamato
  Butai

Sadiah Mat, 143–5, 153–4
Salimah bte Ehksan, 33
Santoso, Maria Ulfah, 110
Sasaki Masao, 109
Sato Ryuichi, 89
schooling, 103–6, 138–9
  see also Girls' Training School
Selangor, 6
Seletar (Sembawang) base, 46, 88–90
Sendenbu, 103
Sentosa, Singapore, 77–8
sex work
  association with other jobs, 54, 105–6
  belief comfort women were
    prostitutes, 20–6, 113–14,
    177–8, 181–3
  comfort women becoming
    prostitutes, 109–10, 117–22,
    183–4
  forced, see comfort women
  income from, 79
  pressures behind, 54–7, 183
  purity culture's effect on, 109–22,
    133–4, 148–9, 151–2
  recruitment of prostitutes to comfort
    stations and ryotei, 29, 45
  regulation of, 119–20
  see also Cantonese sex workers and
    comfort women; Japanese sex
    workers; 'rehabilitation' of local
    comfort women; Singapore
    Advisory Council to the British
    Military Administration;
    Tamagawa
sexism, see gender ideology
sexual violence, see rape
sexually transmitted infections, 81, 99,
  120–1, 124, 128, 131–2

Shamala Kandiah, 139
Shanmugam, K., 172
Shimada, Yoshiko, 158
Shimizu Hiroshi, 43, 53, 83
Shin Kiraku, Singapore, 94
Shin Min Jit Poh, 47
Shinozaki, Mamoru, 6, 14, 49–51
Singapore, comfort women in
  1942 assaults and enslavement of
    local comfort women, 31–9
  defining local comfort women, 30–1
  escapes of local comfort women,
    40–1
  media interest in, 25, 164–6
  post-war prostitution of local
    comfort women, 117–21, 133–4,
    see also 'rehabilitation' of local
    comfort women; Singapore
    Advisory Council to the British
    Military Administration
  recruitment and enslavement of local
    comfort women, 37–8, 42–5,
    54–7, 181
  in *ryotei*, 54–7
  sexism silencing local comfort
    women, see gender ideology
  stations with local comfort women,
    45–7
  see also Chinese comfort women
    in Singapore; comfort stations;
    Indonesian comfort women in
    Singapore; Japanese comfort
    women in Singapore; Korean
    comfort women in Singapore;
    Malay comfort women in
    Singapore; rape; Taiwanese
    comfort women; *A War Diary*
Singapore, pre-war trafficking, 107–8
Singapore, sex workers in, see sex work
Singapore Advisory Council to the
  British Military Administration
  Chen Su Lan's statements, 55, 117–20
  Lee Kiu's statements, 122–6, 129

support for Chen Su Lan's policy, 121–5
  see also Girls' Training School
Singapore Chinese Girls' School, 14
Singapore Council of Women's Organisations, 139
Singapore Cricket Club, 51
Singapore Embassy, Korea, 171
Singapore Ministry of Culture, Community and Youth, 171–2
Singapore Social Welfare Council, 126–7
Singapore Tonight, 175
Singapore Women's Association, 139
Singapore Women's Federation, 129
Singapore World War II History Research Association, 172
Singaporean government, *see* conservation of comfort stations; Lee Kuan Yew; Oral History Centre; Singapore Advisory Council to the British Military Administration
Singaporean Malay community, 111–12
  see also Malay comfort women in Singapore
sing-song girls, 47
Sinmazi, Singapore, 66
social dynamics, 81–2, 89, 91, 116
  see also gender ideology
Social Welfare Department (Singapore), 111, 127–9, 131, 133
Soh, C. Sarah, 13, 19, 23, 79, 100
Sook Ching [cleansing of anti-Japanese Chinese], 42
South Korea, 66, 170, 173–5
Southeast Asian women, 'roar of', 2–3, 28
Southern Army, 86
Spender, Dale, 110, 112
The Spirits Play, 157–60
St Andrew's Secondary School, Singapore, 175–6
starvation, 55–6
stigma, *see* gender ideology

The Straits Times, 18, 20, 113, 156, 170
  see also Phan Ming Yen
study opportunities, 103–6, 138–9
  see also Girls' Training School
Sukaimi bin Ibrahim, 102, 112
Sukemura Iwao, 53
Syonan Jit Poh (*Syonan Daily News*), 43–4
Sze, Madam, 36

Tai Eika, 2
Taiping, Malaysia, 47–8
Taiwanese comfort women
  at Bukit Pasoh Road, 26, 46, 48
  journey to comfort stations, 84, 86
  post-war life, 27, 150
  Veil of Darkness, 161–2
Takahashi, Kazuo, 88
Takami Toyotaro, 53
Takase Toru, 51
Tamagawa, Singapore, 94
Tan, Susannah, 42
Tan Ah Seng, 32
Tan Beng Luan, 60–2, 148
Tan Guan Chuan, 37
Tan Hoe Song, 34
Tan Kek Tiam, 64–5
Tan Peck Siok, 33
Tan Sock Kern, 14, 23
Tan Tock Seng Hospital, Singapore, 81
Tanaka, Yuki, 40
Tanjong Katong Road
  clothing of women in, 97
  demographics of, 92, 96, 100–2
  equation with brothel, 96
  layout and appearance, 92, 96–9
  map, 93
  popularity of, 97, 99
  post-war, 110–11
  see also Fu Yao Hua
Teater Kami, Singapore, 154
Teck Lim Road, Singapore, 58

Teo Soon Koon, 26
Terauchi Hisaichi, 51
terminology, 1
Thailand, comfort women sent to, 47
Theatre Practice, 157–8
TheatreWorks, 157
This Singapore (*Our City of Dreadful Night*), 116–17
Time Capsule Museum, South Korea, 71
Tiong Bahru, Singapore, 38
Tokyo National Theatre, 159
Tsang, Susan, 156
Tsuruya, Singapore, 49–51
The Tuesday Report, 147–9

United Malays National Organisation (UMNO), 7, 142
United Nations, 127
Urban Redevelopment Authority (Singapore), 168–9

Vanderstraaten, Marcia, 160–1
Varma, M.S., 81
Vasu Krishnan, 88
Veil of Darkness, 161–2
venereal disease, 81, 99, 120–1, 124, 128, 131–2
Vickers, W.J., 124
Victoria Theatre, Singapore, 157–8
violence against civilians, 42, 60–1, 70, 181
   see also rape
virginity, *see* gender ideology

waitressing, *see* restaurants
Wang Li Feng, 148
A War Diary, 162–4

Warren, James Francis, 54–5
Watanabe, Yosuke, 171–2, 174
Wee, Ann, 129, 133
'Were there Singaporean Comfort Women?', 136
'When Petals Fall Like Snow—The World Of Kuo Pao Kun, Playwright', 159
Wild Rice theatre company, 160
women, role of, *see* gender ideology
Women and Girls' Protection Ordinance, 119–20
Women Through the Years, 61
Women's Active Museum on War and Peace, 8–10
'Women's Choices, Women's Lives', 140
Wong, Diana, 152
Woodford, Esme, 80
Workhorse Afloat, 156
World War II, *see* Allied Headquarters; Japanese military; post-war life

Xie Song Shan, 54, 56
Xie Yong Guang, 28
Xue Hai [Sea of Blood], 28, 54, 56

Yamato Butai, Singapore, 51–2
Yang Fan, 35
Yang Peh Fong, 129
Yi Sunok, 69–71, 87–8, 116
Yoshimi Yoshiaki, 19, 31, 45, 86, 99
Young Women's Christian Association (YWCA), 123–4
Yuan Ren Kang, 162
Yuasa, Ken, 99

Zhou Xuji, 88